NURTURING JOURNEYS FROM BOTH SIDES OF THE VEIL

BY
VIRGINIA OZUE SEIBERT

Copyright @2009
Virginia Ozue Seibert
ALL RIGHTS RESERVED
No portion of this publication may be reproduced, stored in any electronic system, or transmitted in any form or by any means, electronic, mechanical, photocopy, recording or otherwise, without written permission from the author. Brief quotations may be used in literary reviews.

Ozue and Granny's First Meeting Photo by Ginger
Granny's Back Porch Photo by Paola
Beyond the Veil Drawings by Mollee Huntsman
Creative Computer Enhancements by Cameron Berry

First Printing: November 2009 150 copies
FOR INFORMATION CONTACT:
Virginia Ozue Seibert
<u>virginiaseibert@yahoo.com</u>

First published by Dog Ear Publishing
4010 W. 86th Street, Ste H
Indianapolis, IN 46268
www.dogearpublishing.net

ISBN: 978-160844-329-1

This book is printed on acid-free paper.

Printed in the United States of America

DEDICATION

This collection is dedicated to you the reader, and to those who inspired these writings. They are gifts, plain and precious, to you to help you find appreciation, not only for the joys of life, but also, the sorrows.

Dear Jan,

I'm so very pleased to have met you tonight. Write, write, write. You have so much to share with others.

You are such a special woman. Believe it. Share it, because there are others who need to hear/read what you have to give.

God bless.

Virginia

ACKNOWLEDGEMENTS

For the love, guidance and gifts that I have received from my Heavenly Father, I can never give enough thanks. He has allowed obstacles in my life which have shown me an inner strength that I never knew was there, until I needed it the most. He has nurtured me with the love of family and friends along the way, as well as "strangers unaware". He has blessed me with joy and knowledge and the time and talents emerged from love to help me to return to Him one day. All of you who have aided me along my journey, I thank you. I hope that I have written something here to help you with yours.

To the special folks who shared their journeys with me and allowed me to share with you, I am indebted. I thank each and every one of you from the bottom of my heart.

To my children and grandchildren and my extended family (including the adoptees), please know that you bring light into my life. You have encouraged and supported me even when you wished I had moved in a different direction. I am blessed to have known you. Very special thanks to each of my posterity: Micah, LuCretia, Ozue, Mollee, Noah, and Jonah, and for the blessed inspiration and joy that you and my sweet grandchildren, Coree and Sidney, are to me. (And no, Susan, Ashley, and Sean, you are not "chopped liver". You, too, as partners to my kiddos have supported me, helped me learn, and encouraged me along the way. A special thanks to you Sean for your computer savvy. Thank you.) How fortunate I am to have been blessed with my family members now passed into Spirit who have guided me and still continue to lead me to enlightenment. Because of Molly Cory (my very own Fairy Godmother), Nellie and Leola, and Stonewall, Arthur, Emil, and Earl, along with a myriad of cousins, loving aunts and uncles, I am able to know that I am loved on both sides of the veil. I am truly privileged to be a part of this humorous, often mischievous, and always hard-working family indeed. Thank y'all for all your gifts of love and faith in me.

Micah, you were the first person to say, "My mom, the author!" Of course, we laughed then, but I never forgot it. Cretia, thanks for giving me your little PT Cruiser. It has carried me to many places while seeking the answers which inspired this book. Thank you both for reading my efforts and all your encouraging words through the years. .Noah, thank you for your collaboration (most especially on Seibert's Cafe), all your great ideas, the edits, the extra words, and helpful hints from one writer to another. Jonah, I appreciate you for being so positive (even when you're trying to give me computer help), and thank you for all the late night chats and readings with me. What a joy it was to have you share those special times with me! Mollee, what a trip to have you drawing the faces of people that I'm writing about from beyond the veil, before you've even heard their stories! Many thanks for the consults, confirmations, and validations, to say nothing of the drawings. It's been nice to have my own team. I love each of you the best. (My grandchildren, I love the very best!)

To my close friends, Lyn Jalving, Susan Covington, Barbara Weller, Neva Arrendondo, Jan Osborn, Pam Hinojos, Linette Champneys, Cindy LaGreca, and so many more of you (you know who you are) who have encouraged me to pursue my dreams, I thank you. You've been subjected to reading or hearing my first efforts, in addition to my incessant chatter. You deserve a gold star! For those of you who have opened your homes and hearts to me, the Jalvings (my earthship "other" home) in Lake Helen, Florida, the Clarkes of Louisiana; the Champneys of Arkansas; the Huntsmans of Arkansas; the Thomases and Berrys of Virginia, I owe you all a debt of gratitude for putting up with me, as well as putting me up. I'll be seeing you. You are all the best of the best.

There are simply no adequate words to express my thankfulness to my teachers and guides. Joan Piper and Dr. James Thomas, you have been fantastic teachers. As for you, Joan, you have shown me that the only limits I have are the ones that I inflict upon myself. You buoy me up and bring direction. Linda Sacha, my author friend extraordinaire, what an inspiring example you are! Cameron Berry, you have the patience of Job; thanks for all your computer wizardry! And, to those special folks with whom I've shared classes and growth, especially Lyn, Elisha, Nora and Kellie, thank you for being there on my trip.

Last, but not least, Thank you to my mother, Leola Lytle Seibert, who made my dreams come true.

TABLE OF CONTENTS

Introduction xiii

Prologue xv

FROM THIS SIDE OF THE VEIL ....(2-41)

SEIBERT'S CAFÉ (written 9 September 2009) 2-14

Arthur owned a café in LaGrange, Texas. He is a successful business man in a small German town in the Fifties, but life is never simple, is it?

OUR BLESSING (written 28 November 2001) 15-30

Our sweet baby was greatly desired. We took her home full of happiness and love. What happened along the way changed my outlook on life forever.

NO MORE SECRETS (written 7 February 2003).............31-41

Mother's hip was shattered. We gathered to be with her. She was a strong "Strong" lady who saw beauty everywhere. She waved, but was it "Hello" or "Goodbye?"

AND FROM THE OTHER SIDE OF THE VEIL ....(44-235)

RUTH AND MARGARET, Their Shared Journal of Secrets
(written 2 May 2009)...44-134

Two sisters from Ireland came to America. They share their secrets from 1836 forward; secrets, dark and shameful. Their lives were difficult at times, but they never lost sight of what kept them together.

Dedication..44		
Prologue...45		
Journal Entry I	Ruth..46-49
Journal Entry II	Margaret...50-52
Journal Entry III	The Journey 53-57
Journal Entry IV	Ellis Island..58-60
Journal Entry V	Settling In...61-66
Journal Entry VI	What Now?...67-73
Journal Entry VII	The Next Step...74-78
Journal Entry VIII	Now, To Work 79-84
Journal Entry IX	Venturing Out 85-87
Journal Entry X	The Showdown..88-90
Journal Entry XI	The Best Laid Plans 91-98
Journal Entry XII	Time To Move On 99-102
Journal Entry XIII	Our Time To Move......................................103-105
Journal Entry XIV	Margaret's Escape......................................106-112
Journal Entry XV	Our Grand Opening...................................113-118
Journal Entry XVI	CLOSED 119-122

Journal Entry XVII   The Ride 123-129

Journal Entry XVIII Coming Home 130-135

JOHN'S TESTIMONY (written 28 September 2009)......137-235

Prologue 138

Born a slave, John traveled life's journey to freedom. Through all his ups and downs, he tried his best to stay true to himself. Sometimes, he succeeded; sometimes, not. See his life's journey through his eyes. Ride the rails.

Chapter One	Fair is Fair	139-145
Chapter Two	Galveston	146-156
Chapter Three	Judge Not	157-160
Chapter Four	Christmas	161-165
Chapter Five	She Went One Way	166-173
Chapter Six	I Went The Other Way	174-181
Chapter Seven	A New Chapter	182-188
Chapter Eight	That Thicket's Thick	189-196
Chapter Nine	New Beginnings	197-207
Chapter Ten	A Want Deep Inside	208-213
Chapter Eleven	Do The Best You Can	214-225
Chapter Twelve	Life Happens	226-232
Chapter Thirteen	Mine Eyes Have Seen	233-235

INTRODUCTION

Whether you believe in Christ, the Gifts of the Holy Ghost, the Oneness, or Spirit, we are all traveling on a bumpy road in this life. Sometimes, we cannot see past the curve. Other times, we see mirages in the road bed. The most important thing to know is that we are always moving. Some roads are easily seen as nurturing. Some seem to be anything but nurturing. The point is that they are all how we see them, what we learn from them, and mainly, what we do with them, as we move farther down the road. They are indeed "Nurturing Journeys" if we appreciate what is to be learned, as we negotiate the terms of travel. Where and how we go here determines who we are when we leave life on this side of the veil and continue to travel to the other side. We take with us our personalities and our stories. Some of the paths in this book reflect the journeys on this earth plane; others, the memories and lessons as told by Spirits from the other side. People are just people on either side of the veil. See if you see yourself in any of their walks. I hope then that you will identify and reflect upon your own personal journeys, and share them with your loved ones. All of us have a path that is uniquely ours, but paths cross, and it is up to us individually what we chose to collect as souvenirs from those intersections. It is up each of us to choose to release the grip of the past, and move into the future.

PROLOGUE

Lots of people question whether or not these stories are fiction or non-fiction, and here is what I say to that, Yes. Seibert's Café is inspired by my Uncle Arthur's true story, but it is written intuitively. Basically, the facts are correct. Our Blessing is a true story, as is No More Secrets. It is important for you the reader to understand that my writing is based on my perceptions. The way I behold things is not necessarily the way even another member of my family might, but it's my perception and my memories.

As for Ruth and Margaret's shared secrets and John's Testimony, those are just what they say they are. These spirits shared with me. Molly Cory Strong, my great-grandmother, brought them to me, because she knew what they had to say was significant to them and others. I believe Ruth and Margaret are somehow linked to my family, and one day I have no doubt that how we are related will become apparent. Oddly enough, once you read No More Secrets and then John's Testimony, you will most likely discover the connection on your own. It wasn't until two days after John and I had completed his story that I became aware of why it was he shared his journey with me. There is no such thing as coincidence. We have family and loved ones on the other side who want to help us. All we have to do is be available with childlike curiosity and love, and they will come. I acted as their scribe. What a thrill to have received this information through the veil! It was exciting to sit down to the computer and never know exactly what was about to be revealed. At times, we would write one chapter; other times, two or three. We worked as long as they wanted, and then we would rest to let the dust settle so to speak. They had final approval on everything written. I realize that this may sound strange to many of you, but it is the truth. This most definitely is not an ordinary experience. They have taught me so much. My pact with them was to just write their story, and after that, if they wanted to allow it to be shared, then they would tell me. Ruth and Margaret agreed after the third Journal Entry. John held out until Chapter IX. It's just like on this side, it's all about trust and love. Think of sharing your most personal and intimate secrets with strangers, and you will have an idea of how they must have felt. A friend of mine told me months ago that these particular spirits are in some way aligned with my family and that they have carried these experiences, sorrows, and joys. In short, she said, "You are acting as their therapist and helping them get these experiences and lessons out in the open once and "for all." This is how they can completely share their life lessons and help others to heal. What a wonderful gift "for all"!

Is everything totally accurate? I'm not sure. Does it matter? It is their perception, as my perceptions in my stories from this side of the veil are mine. No research has been done before or after to corroborate what they shared with me. I am acting on faith with them, as they are with me, and that is a huge part of the trust between us. It is not about the minute details, on this side of the veil or the other that should be the focus, it is the journey.

FROM THIS SIDE OF THE VEIL

SEIBERT'S CAFÉ

I walked into the barber shop.

"Smitty, you old Schwein Hof, how ya doing?"

"Just fine, Arthur. How are you? Want me to get some of that scheitze off your neck?" Smitty mumbled not even looking up, as he continued to work on a teenage boy.

"Whew!" It's hotter in here than it is outside. All your fan is doing is making it swampy. You trying to make a man look for a new barber?

"You've been threatening that for years. You ain't going nowhere. Come on in; sit down, and if you're good, I'll give you a sucker."

"Smitty, I bet you get a lot of business doing those flat top haircuts, don't you?"

"Yep, sure do. Good for business, don't last too long, and all the goop that makes it stand straight up, that Butch Wax stuff, sells like hotcakes to these young boys. I can't keep enough of it."

"Think some of that goop would help my hair stand up?"

"Only, if you can get you some hair, Arthur!" We laughed. "Sit on down and rest yourself. I'll be with you in a jif."

Smitty paused as he was finishing with the boy's cut and shut the doors. The inside of the shop had cooled off now, and it was beginning to feel better to me.

A very pretty young mother came in with a little boy.

"Want a coke, Smitty? I'm buying."

"Don't mind if I do. You got a little time?"

Smitty popped the tops off our cokes.

He busied himself sweeping up the clippings. "How about we cut your hair and then I give you a hot towel treatment and a close shave?"

"Sure I'm the boss. They can get along without me at the cafe for a while longer." I replied.

"Sounds good to me," I agreed, as I plopped down into his chair. It was so comfortable there in the chair lying back with the hot towel wrapped around my face. I was so relaxed; I couldn't keep my eyes open.

"I'm gonna run over to the drug store. I'll be right back. "

I feel myself dozing off, and then the dreams begin to come and go. I am moving between mists and earth.

I am frying hamburgers on the café grill and talking to meine mutter who was sitting in the red booth nearest the kitchen. Just seeing her makes me smile. Sweat's dripping off my face. I wipe at it with the white towel draped around my neck. She smiles and says "Arthur, it's going to be good. Don't worry. It will all be good." Then, meine onkel, my mother's brother, walks into the restaurant. He smiles and waves. I smile back, and he says 'Bringen Sie Sich hier.' I leave the kitchen to go to him. I say 'Hi', and suddenly, they're both gone.

I hear screeching tires! I wake with a start!

I'm still at home in bed soaking in my own sweat! Fine! I've had enough of his! No more in this bed! I wish I could say no more sweating, but I've gotten used to that. I'm getting up. I am so tired. I just don't know how I'll get through this day without a nap. Oh well, I might as well eat and go get that haircut I dreamed about. I'm up for sure now. I fix myself a bowl of cereal and reflect on the dream.

My mother died five years ago. She was an old woman when she died, but in my dream, she was young like she was when I was a boy at home. She always loved me. She had a way of making me feel better about myself. She saw the loving side of me. I guess what I am trying to say is that I never had to worry about her "not" loving me, because she always saw what was good about me. She expected me to be good, and for her, I tried to be.

My uncle still looked exactly like he did the last time I saw him in life. Seeing him again like that reminded me of how close we really were. We had the same sense of humor, so our jokes were never wasted. He came to live with us when he got to the point that he couldn't care for himself any more. I remember giving him a bath right before he died. My, is that already eight years? What a nice memory. We made jokes and laughed the entire time. I was happy to be able to provide that service for him knowing his time was short. I knew he loved me, even though neither of us would ever have acknowledged such a thing! Instead, he'd give me that special look and say "Bring yourself here!" It was our secret code. I'd always go to him happily. I miss him. Not many men in my life understood me and how I think, but he did.

I'm a wealthy man, or I was, until this whole divorce thing. I will be again someday. For now, I have to split everything with my wife. She left me. It hardly seems right, but I'm tired of fighting. I just want this over. My guess about the dream is that they were reassuring me regarding my upcoming divorce, and that everything will "all be good" again. What a comfort!

All I want to do now is get a haircut.

LaGrange, Texas is hot in June. The way I see it, a little sweat is a small price to pay for living in this little town that I love so much. Besides, hot has never particularly bothered me, but today it is. It's sweltering. On top of that, I'm extremely tired this morning. Too much dreaming I guess. Sweat's pouring off my face, but isn't it always? Fat men sweat. I'm a fat, jolly man, or so I've heard myself described.

I like going to Smitty's Barber Shop. It's small enough to be cozy and large enough not to feel squashed-in when they're busy. Two red barbering chairs face long mirrors, and on the opposite wall are a variety of chairs for waiting. Best thing is that the shop is right on the town square which means that I can stop by and say hi anytime I need to hear an honest voice.

Today is Wednesday, so Smitty will probably be the only one there today. He's quite a character, though you'd never guess it just looking at him. He looks like an aging countrified mild mannered man. He has a beautiful head of white hair. His eyes are a pale blue; however there is nothing particularly remarkable about his looks. He's just a typical Southern barber. a good ole boy. He exemplifies his chosen profession! The truth is, he's a pistol. He is quick on the trigger and very witty. He has that dry kind of humor that you're never really expecting. Nobody, but nobody, ever gets over on Smitty. I like that about him. He's my kind of man. And yet, his wife of over fifty years still dresses him in the pocket littered square bottom shirts that she sews herself. He wears them too! He wouldn't dare not wear them. She's the only person that he doesn't talk back to! I get a kick out of him!

It shouldn't be too long a wait. After all these years, I still enjoy going to the barber shop, and the wait is sometimes the best part of the overall experience. A hair cut can take fifteen minutes or an hour, depending on whether Smitty likes you and feels like talking or not. Coming here reminds me of simpler days, better days. When I was a little boy, my father would sometimes take me to town with him. I'd get a sucker; he'd get a trim and catch up on all the stories and news. It's not called gossip in the confines of the barber shop. It's one of the few places that men can talk to each other and still be considered men, as long as we don't talk about feelings or other nonsense like that! The shop still smells of witch hazel, pomade, and cigar smoke. As a kid, it made me want to throw up, but as a grown man, it smells just right. I crave that atmosphere, when it's been too long. The smells, the sounds, the usual crowd, and the timeless décor create a refuge for men and boys, especially for me. We know exactly what awaits us there.

That step up and through the barber shop door seems a little taller today. I must be more tired than I thought. "Smitty, you old Schwein Hof, how ya doing?" I holler at my friend pretty much the same as I always do.

"Just fine, Arthur. How are you? Want me to get some of that scheitze off your neck?" Smitty mumbled not even looking up, as he continued to work on a teenage boy. He knows me too well.

"Whew!" It's hotter in here than it is outside. All your fan is doing is making it swampy. You trying to make a man look for a new barber?

"You've been threatening that for years. You ain't going nowhere. Come on in; sit down, and if you're good, I'll give you a sucker."

The front and back doors were open. to let a hint of a breeze blow through. However, even with the occasional draft and addition of a water cooled fan, the shop is barely tolerable, and certainly not comfortable. If it weren't for Smitty's friendly banter and genuine concern, this swampiness might make a man stay home, have his wife cut his hair, or at least, look for another barber. Smitty's right though, he knows I'll stick with him. The old buzzard!

"Smitty, I bet you get a lot of business doing those flat top haircuts, don't you?"

"Yep, sure do. Good for business, don't last too long, and all the goop that makes it stand straight up, that Butch Wax stuff, sells like hotcakes to these young boys. I can't keep enough of it. Focusing on the teen's hair, Smitty volunteered, "I tell you what. I don't particularly like these flat top cuts, but they put bread and butter on my table." He impishly continued, "What I do like is when I get to cut those duck tails off them hoodlums!" He laughed at himself. He'd told this joke a million times.

He was grooming the boy's hair now with a palm full of pink stuff. "Hey! I inquired, "Think some of that goop would help my hair stand up?"

"Only, if you can get you some hair, Arthur! We both give a deep belly laugh. "Sit on down and rest yourself. I'll be with you in a jif."

I can't help thinking, this is just too much like my dream. So, just to change things up a bit, I dropped into the empty barber chair next to where Smitty was working. As expected, he circled the shop closing the doors and came back to his young man who was almost done and decent enough to go into the world again. From my perch, I smiled as I stared past the assortment of waiting chairs eyes peeled for that pretty young thing who'd soon be bringing her little boy for his first hair cut.

It was still pretty warm in the shop. I couldn't help dozing. I drifted off into green.

I see Bluebonnets and Indian Paintbrushes dotting the sides of the road and the fields. The sun is bright. The air, cool. I am eight years old and walking home from school. It's a beautiful day, but I'm not happy. I'm angry, so angry. I hate school. I hear them running behind me. "Hey, you, Kraut kid!" "Hey, fat boy!" "Come back Sausage boy!" They are bigger and stronger than me. There are five of them following. I run. I cry. They chase me. They throw rocks and clods of dirt at me. I run, until my side hurts. I can hear them behind me. I get to the turn off where Mother is waiting. A dust cloud hangs behind me, but no boys.

I rouse. The fear and anger bring me back abruptly to the barber shop.

I'm panting loudly. as I wake. I'm slumped forward still sitting in the swivel chair. Perspiration is pouring off my body, as I face Smitty and the confused teenager. My face is red with anger! Smitty asks "You all right man?" I sheepishly look down.

"Just dreaming! I was running. I'm fine, really, I'm good."

The young man stared at me. He and Smitty shared a glance. I wasn't offended by their concern. Had it been anyone else in that chair, it would have been me and Smitty sharing that glance. As Smitty put the finishing touches on the boy, I leaned back to think.

This was just too real! It was a replay of my early days in school. I couldn't speak anything but German, when I first started school, and the language problems accompanied by my restlessness in a one-room schoolhouse made my life miserable. I had trouble paying attention. The teacher punished me for not being able to answer her questions. The boys from town picked on me. They called me stupid, among other things. They did mean things to me. By the time I was eleven, World War I began, and then, they really hated me...just because I was German. I think that may have been why I had to be bigger and meaner than anybody else when I was a kid. I was really hurt inside by their meanness, but I wouldn't ever let anybody know except my mother. I think I understand now why I have always been a bully. I overate, because I felt bad. I felt bad, because I was big and awkward. Then I tried to hurt everyone else, before they could hurt me. Mostly, I pretended nothing hurt me. As part of that vulnerability, I picked on those younger or smaller than me, or those not as smart. Being the aggressor kept the attention off me, but then I had to pretend that hurting other people didn't hurt me too. The only place that I wasn't in danger was when I arrived at the place where I knew my mother would keep me safe.

I know, lately, that my sensitivities have been more obvious. I don't like for people to see my feelings can be hurt, and I really hate knowing there is someone else out there who knows my secrets and darkest fears who doesn't love me anymore and will manipulate me with them if she can. This divorce mess has been hard.

This is my second divorce. No one else in my family has ever been divorced, so once again, I am the bad boy in my family. The other thing is my brother. He's the next to youngest, and he's been acting crazy lately. He comes to my house, and he tries to tell me how to run my life. I told him the other day that he isn't doing such a great job with his own wife and daughter himself. It's been one exhausting round after another of me telling him what is right, and him telling me how to run my life. How dare he try to bully me!

So, what does this dream mean to me? I understand that I've been hurt and scared. I see how my bullying others keeps me safe most of the time. It keeps people away. Now as I can see my younger brother is more like me than I ever thought, I am beginning to realize that being a bully isn't such a great defense. Instead, it seems to perpetuate anger and hurt. I've made so many mistakes.

Smitty set the teenager free. As he left, he held the door for a pretty young mother who came in with a little boy. She was practically dragging him. The youngster appears to be about three. He has long, very curly strawberry-blond hair. He's a cute little fart! He's stocky and has fat little apple red cheeks. He reminds me of someone I know. Who is it? Oh, yes, I know. He looks just like the Campbell Soup Kid. Cute kid.

"It'll be a wait to do the boy's hair." Smitty offered. "Mr. Seibert's ahead of you."

"No, no," I say. "Go ahead. Take care of him. He doesn't look too pleased to be here, and I've got plenty of time today. I'm so tired anyway. It won't hurt me to just sit here. I didn't sleep much last night. I just may catch myself another nap. This time I willed myself to think of something pleasant as I dozed, and before I knew it, my eyes closed.

Her little blond head bobbed back and forth, while she talked to me. Motioning the directions with her long tiny fingers, she announced authoritatively, "Go that way, Uncle Arthur. That way!" Ginger, age five, stood on the passenger side of my car. She's so sure that she knows something that I don't! I can't help smiling. I play dumb. "It's this way home; turn here." She's wearing my favorite dress made by her mother. Across the front of the skirt is a Robin pulling a worm from an apple. The embroidery reads "The early bird gets the worm."

I became aware of the little boy crying. "No, No! Not hair!" he yelped.

Had I'd been dreaming again? So abruptly now was I passing from one to another. It seemed as though real life was merely an interlude. What a strange day! I'm so tired. Soon enough, I'd should be at the café, or will I wake in my bed at home again like the last time I thought I was at Smitty's? The little boy in the shop was crying full force now. He pulled me from consciousness, or was it unconsciousness?

I could hear his mother and Smitty talking to him. I didn't even bother to open my eyes.

It makes me smile just thinking about Ginger. She has been my little girl, since the first time I saw her bald baby head. Never had any children of my own, but I feel like she is partly mine. This dream is one of my favorite memories of her guiding me home after she and I went to a wrestling match.

This time, when I fell asleep, I was smiling, and then, I wasn't.

Vater hit my bruder Emil. Emil protected his face with his hands. He was being beaten again. He peeked through his fingers at me pitifully. He begged me with his eyes to help him. I did nothing. I watched paralyzed.

I awoke again with sweat dripping from my face fully expecting to see my bedroom walls. My shirt was soaked all the way to my undershirt. Instead of my bedroom, however, the daylight was pouring through the plate glass window. I could see Smitty's signs in red and blue announcing "Little Boy Haircuts Half-Price on Wednesday". The red and white swirls on the pole outside confirmed that I was still in the chair at Smitty's. The shop was actually cold, or was it was me that was cold? That wasn't a dream! It was a nightmare! I am not going to think about it. Enough! I start to pull myself out of the chair.

"Want a coke Smitty? I'm buying."

"Don't mind if I do. Sit back down. Just a minute; I'll get it for you." Smitty dusted off the little boy's neck. He gave the kid a pat on the back saying "Now, you look like a big boy; no baby; no more!" With that he sent mother and "Big Boy" both out the door with smiles, a sucker, and a little boy's haircut.

Smitty popped the tops off our cokes. "If you're in no hurry, I think I'm gonna take a load off. I've got a corn that's killing me." He took a long swig of his coke.

"Sure. Sit down, rest a while." I replied. Besides, I didn't really want to move myself right now. I felt drained. I took a sip of coke and sat it on the counter.

He plopped down in his barber chair. It was quiet in the shop. The only sound was the cooler buzzing. We sat, as only good friends can, in silence. I didn't want to, but I couldn't help thinking of Emil.

Emil was older than I was. He was bigger, but truth is, he was a big boy with a little boy's brain, a dumme. I feel guilty and full of regrets for all the times that I could have helped Emil, and I didn't. So many times, I let him take the blame and take what should have been my beatings. I should have been kinder. I feel tears slipping down my cheeks. It's hard to think now of how I treated him. I can't even let myself think of the why. I am so sorry. I wish I would have told him that before he died. Still, retarded or not, Emil forgave me always. He wanted so much for me to like him. He tried his best to please me, no matter what pain I caused him.

I hear Smitty snoring. The light pouring through the storefront windows remind me that it will soon be lunch time. They need me there. My thoughts of Emil fade as I close my eyes and drift off. I am inside the café.

The bell on the front door jingles as an old man, filthy from the road, pushes his way inside. Then, seeing the quarter on the floor, he stoops to pick it up. He couldn't. He tries and tries. He looks to me for help.

The noise of Smitty extracting himself from his chair woke me. I feel an unspeakable sadness. Why? Oh, I know. It was the old man in the café. Another dream? Just what I need today is another dream. I must have eaten something that didn't agree with me last night!

Smitty grabbed his broom. He busied himself sweeping up the clippings. "How about we cut your hair, and then I give you a hot towel treatment and a close shave?"

"Sure, I'm the boss. They can get along without me at the cafe for a while longer," I replied. I guzzled down another swig of my coke. "Sounds good to me," I said, as I wedged myself into his chair.

Smitty began to cut my hair. I couldn't help thinking of the old man. I still felt the sadness in my gut. I was aware that he was in desperate need. He could see the prize, the quarter, but he couldn't get it, no matter how hard he tried. Odd, how that should make me feel so sad. Watching people in my café trying to pick up the embedded quarter always brought howls of laughter from me. It was a joke. The whole town played it. They brought their children and grandchildren; they brought their out-of-town guests to the café for that very reason. We all enjoyed watching kids and first time adult customers try to get the quarter. That's been going on as long as I've operated Seibert's Café. "If you can get it," I'd yell, "You can have it!"

Today, it wasn't funny. Today, it made me feel terrible. This man, unknown to me and obviously beaten down by life, broke my heart. I could feel his pain. I don't know why, but I don't want to think about it anymore. Smitty brushing off the back of my neck meant I wouldn't have to. (Maybe I'm having a nervous breakdown.)

The Osage Tonic smelled good on my hair, a little bit minty, not sweet. I like that. And, it was refreshing after all the sweating. I must be stinking by now. Hair cut completed, Smitty pulled a little fan from under the counter, and turned it right on me. "Took you long enough to notice I was sweating, you ole turd!"

Chuckling, he lathered my face with the soapy soft brush and skillfully wound the hot towel about my face and neck. "Oh, that feels so good," I moaned.

There was absolutely no way I could keep my eyes open after that. In the distance, I heard Smitty say, "I'm gonna run over to the drug store. Relax. I'll be right back."

I feel myself dozing off, and the dreams begin to come and go. Now I am moving between mists and earth.

I hear music. I don't know where it is coming from, but it's all around me. It's sweet. I know this song. I've heard it before. And then, it is very quiet. I feel the darkness closing in on me. I don't know this place. I'm curious and a little afraid.

The music swells, floating very softly at first and building. The darkness hovers.

I hear screeching tires! I wake with a start!

I feel good, rested at last and full of energy. It's about time. Guess I've finally had enough catnaps. Smitty isn't back yet. My shave has to wait. It's late. I need to go to the café now. The early lunch crowd will be coming in. All those boys from the bridge will be there waiting. They'll be mad at me for spending so much time trying to look pretty. Hmmm, now, because of me taking my time, they'll have to take their lunch back to work with them. I chuckle to myself. They'll just have to get over it.

I step outside the shop. What's this? I can smell the burned rubber from the tires. People are gathering down the block. I see Smitty a couple of doors down talking with the Sheriff. The Sheriff turns; he's walking this way in a hurry. Smitty's right behind him. I know Smitty; he's just like me. He doesn't like leaving his customers or more particularly, his friends in the lurch. Maybe there's something I can do to help. They look worried. No, no, I just don't have time. There's plenty of folks out there. I have to get to the café now. I can't wait despite the urge to stay and find out what's going on. I'll find out later what's going on. Smitty'll fill me in when he comes for lunch. I'll bribe him with an extra piece of chocolate pie.

I don't see the angry boys outside the café. Maybe they didn't get off for lunch at their usual time. That's good. I follow the pointing finger on the sign directing me to the kitchen at the back of the café. As I'm hurrying to the back, I catch a glimpse of a small boy hiding under a table. He's playing peek-a-boo and grinning at me. He makes me think of Emil, but in a happy way. His smile and Ginger's melt together as I heat up the grill.

The little boy scurries behind me into the kitchen as fast as his short legs carry him. I turn to tell him that he can't be in the kitchen. Before I can speak, he thrusts out his tiny hand to me. I smile and reach to shake his hand, but instead, he drops a shiny quarter into my hand. "For you," he insists. "You don't need to be sad anymore."

I am frying hamburgers on the café grill and talking to meine mutter who is sitting in the red booth nearest the kitchen. Just seeing her makes me smile. Sweat's dripping off my face. I wipe at it with the white towel draped around my neck. She smiles and says "Arthur, it's going to be good." Then, mein onkel walks into the restaurant. He smiles and waves. I smile back, and he says "Bringen Sie Sich hier." They stand side-by-side waiting for me. I leave the kitchen to go to them. Sweet music is in the air.

The "Closed" sign is on the door of the barber shop. Smitty sweeps the clippings from Arthur's hair into the dust pan. As he does, tears fall shamelessly. They say it was a heart attack. The Sheriff's gone. The gurney's gone. The only thing remaining now is what's left of Arthur's half-full coke bottle sweating on the counter.

OUR BLESSING

It was either stay home and drink, or go to the hospital and have an alcohol intravenous infusion in those days. I had two seven year olds, so it was better for me and them to remain at home. My body decided at four and a half months to begin preterm labor.

So much prayer had been offered for our baby that I believe Heavenly Father sent her to us on special request. My grandmother Nellie had passed away in July just a week after I had told her that I was pregnant. I was very close with Grandmomma. I missed her, but I knew somehow in my heart that Grandmomma was watching over me and my little baby.

Each of my children have been special gifts from God, but each different in their own way. I love each of them "the best". We laugh a lot about that, but it's the truth.

I'd been working as a kindergarten teacher for both special needs and so-called normal children when Bob and I married. I liked being a teacher, but when I learned I was pregnant, we decided that I should be a stay-at-home mother. I wanted to give Micah and Cretia as much attention as I could, before we had a new baby in our home. I was excited about being there, but was I sick! I couldn't keep anything down, and even though I was the right weight when I got pregnant, I dropped 12 pounds in 12 weeks. My doctor wanted to try one more thing before resorting to hospitalization. That turned out to be hypnosis.

We gathered with six other couples one evening in the doctor's office to be hypnotized. When it came our turn, the doctor told me to look inside of my brain and see an old-timey switchboard. "There are wires all over connected to the switchboard. They all have lights above them and switches below. You will see some of the lights are yellow; some, red; others, green. Each wire is in your control. Find the one connected to your right leg. What color is the light above the wire for your right leg?" he asked and then, he informed me that I could talk to him any time I chose. I told him that the light was red. "What does the red light mean?" I replied that my leg was tense. "As your husband rubs your leg, you will be able to see the light above the wire begin to change colors." I could see the light change to yellow. As my leg relaxed more, the light turned green. "You can allow your husband to help you relax any body parts in that manner, or you may turn the little switch beneath the light to whatever color you choose. Sometimes, it is important for parts to be tense instead of relaxed. Now, find the wire that is connected to your stomach. I looked through the criss-cross of wires, until I found the wire that controlled my stomach. "What color is the light?" I told him that it was bright red. "What does that mean to you?" I replied that my stomach was upset. "Turn the switch to the right and notice what happens." The light turned green. My stomach was no longer upset. With his instruction, I turned the switch to yellow. My stomach was all right, but still uneasy. When I turned it to red, I experienced debilitating nausea. We tried adjusting and turning the switch back and forth, until I was accustomed to the procedure. "There are wires attached to everything in your body, your head, and your belly. You can now turn a switch and control everything." Taking Bob's hand, he placed it on my belly, and he told Bob that at any time, he could gently place his hand on my belly, and it would totally relax. A nurse's hand could also do this; the doctor's hand could do the same, as could my own, but Bob would have that special touch for the rest of our lives. It was true.

The doctor further explained that labor pains were only called labor, because having a baby is hard work. "The pain comes" he said "if a person fights the work that the body must do to deliver the baby. When you feel a contraction begin in the future, and only when it is time for your baby to be delivered, see yourself lying on the beach. You will feel the warm ocean water washing up over your feet, up to your legs, and when that contraction peaks, the water will completely submerge your belly and lift and comfort the baby and you. As the contraction eases, the water will flow back into the ocean, until it is needed again."

It worked. I only threw up one more time during the entire pregnancy. We had gone on a rare date to the San Jacinto Inn and gorged on every kind of Gulf seafood available. I deserved to throw up. It only took once to learn that lesson!

I digress. I continued to baby sit for a sweet little boy that reminded me of Micah, when he was small. He was a shy little boy. When I had to go to bed, he was still with me. He was quiet and easily entertained. One month passed in bed; then two; then three; and by the time, the fourth month rolled around, I could prepare and cook a complete meal from the bed for my family. I'm not known as the "Crock Pot Queen" for nothing! When I hit the 36th week of gestation, I was allowed to get up. I could deliver anytime, so my doctor said. What a joke that was!

I went to church for two Sundays, yes two full weeks, before our baby was scheduled to be induced. That last Sunday, our bishop asked me if I would like a Mother's Blessing. I was relatively new to the church, but I was devoted to living the life that went with my newly found religion. We made plans for the Bishop to come to our home late Sunday evening.

As he anointed my head with oil and laid hands on my head with my husband, he began to speak about blessings. "You are about to receive one of the greatest of blessings of your life. This baby is already much loved and wanted by many, and with you, it will have a wonderful life knowing it is loved."

It was at that point, that he sighed deeply, and paused. When he began to speak again, it was with a more hushed tone. "You are not to be afraid. Someone who loves you very much has come to you, and wants me to tell you not to be afraid. This ancestor will be with you during your time of travail. You have been very close. You are not to be afraid. She loves you very much."

By the time I heard the words "You are not to be afraid," I had begun to snivel. When I heard the words "will be with you during your time of travail," my eyes were flooded, and when the Bishop said, "She loves you very much," I began to cry out loud. He sighed again, blessed me, and said "Amen." Me? I ran to the bathroom.

After composing myself, I returned to the living room to two men who were wondering what in the world was going on with me. Choking on tears and quite overwhelmed, I began to share with them that a couple of nights previous to this, I had a dream about Grandmomma that scared me so much that I'd told no one about it. She was wrapped in blood-stained white linen twisted around her body. She was lying on what appeared to be her ironing board in her kitchen. Then, she turned to look at me. As she did, the linens turned sparkling white. She looked me full in the face. I saw her once destroyed eye was restored. She was smiling, and I sensed she wanted to say something, but for some reason, she couldn't speak aloud to me. I awoke frightened and shaking. I didn't know what it meant.

There in my living room the night before my baby was born, the dream was explained to me.

I was so humbled. The Bishop said that my ancestor was trying to let me know that she would be there with me during my time of suffering, and that she is with the Lord now. That's why her garments were changed to a sparkling white. She wanted me to know that she is watching over me, while yet present with the Lord.

At five the next morning, we left for the hospital. I wore my favorite red and white checked maternity dress made for me by my mother. My long blond hair and make-up were perfect. I wanted to look my best to meet my child. The house was spotless. Everything was done, and I was ready to meet my baby at last.

We arrived at Southwest Memorial Hospital just before six. My doctor had reinforced the hypnosis with the ocean waves the week before on my regular visit. It was at that time that he had me see myself, as if I was looking at a television in the delivery room where I was about to deliver. There was a nurse at a blackboard in the room. As the baby was born, she wrote on the board that it was a girl born at noon. It was my doctor's theory that our bodies know all about us. Every cell has a memory and knowledge of its own. The doctor broke my water. The labor began.

The most difficult part of the labor experience was the back labor. Pressing hard on the tailbone helped with that, but it was over soon. The rest of the labor was a piece of cake. I used the ocean wave thing suggested in the hypnosis. It worked like a charm. I delivered a beautiful baby girl that weighed six pounds, six ounces. She was 20 inches long. She had curly reddish-blond hair, and she was born at 1:02 P.M. So, was I off with my noon delivery written on the blackboard? Not really, it was Daylight Savings time change! We sprang forward one hour! Funny how that worked! I was so happy. The adrenaline was flowing. My excitement kept me awake for almost two full days. My daughter was named after me first, and other strong women of my family. Her name had been picked for months. We are very big on family names. The plan was to call her "Little Nellie". Her full name, Ozue Marinell Huntsman. Ozue was born Monday, March 18, 1974. She was "Fair of Face".

A few people came to visit us in the hospital, but my mother wasn't one of them. She'd been in a car accident and was home with a chest injury. The day we left the hospital (five days after Ozue's birth), it was pouring rain, as it can only do in Houston, Texas. Ozue was dressed all in pink. She wore a sweet, old fashioned baby dress with booties a tiny sweater and bonnet. They were all made by her Granny. Wrapped tightly around her was a pink baby square with embroidery that I had made, as was the custom of our family. We covered her with a blanket to protect her from the rain, and away we went with Ozue Marinell to meet her Granny for the first time.

Now, you must understand that there is absolutely no one that I have ever met in my life that loves babies the way my mother does. The front door was standing open waiting for us. We dashed into the house. Bob gently placed our baby girl next to Granny on her bed. I have the sweetest picture of them together, as Granny began to undress her to look her over. She always inspected babies from top to bottom. She is so sweet with them.

We stayed a few hours with her, and in the course of the visit, Ozue had to be fed. Together, Ozue and I were learning about breast-feeding. I had never done it before, and neither had she. We had some awkward moments in the beginning, but by the day we arrived at Granny's, we were both doing much better. My mother

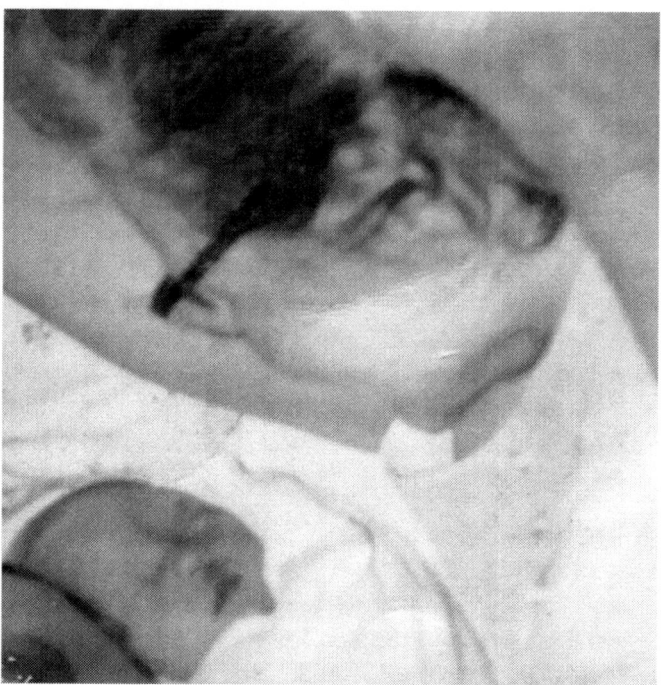

was fascinated with the breast-feeding aspects of our relationship. She got almost as close as Ozue did to me to watch her suckle. Such precious memories for us! Ozue held Granny's finger tightly. She looked from my face to Granny's and back again.

That afternoon, Bob, Ozue and I went home to our home. Micah and Cretia arrived from school. They were so excited to see her, touch her, and hold her. They watched closely as she nursed, and brought me diapers as needed. If she even acted like she might be beginning to squirm, one of the children cuddled her. The ultimate cuddler was Bob. He would lift her into his arms raised out in front of him and talk to her in their own special language. She would get so quiet and intently study his face. He was the only one who could place her in the nursery to sleep without her waking up.

The nursery itself was a large hallway walk-in closet from which Bob had removed the door. My friends and I had decorated her little room with baby decals and such. Her handmade baby squares made with such love were neatly stacked on the shelf above her baby bed. The mobile was in place on the rail of her bed. All of her baby dresses were ironed and hanging from a rod at the end of her bed. Above the dresses, booties to match her dresses (made by Granny of course) were lined up. The diaper stacker was full of tiny folded cloth diapers. Changing her outfits was so much fun.

Friday night was a good night. Ozue only woke twice to nurse. The next day was Saturday. My best friend, Susan, came with her three year old daughter to see us. While they were there, the time for feeding arrived. I unfastened my nursing bra, and began to let Ozue nurse. Susan's daughter screamed "No!" She cried. Poor little thing was convinced that I was going to be bitten. We had to show her that little babies have no teeth. It took a lot of talking to calm her down. It made for a sweet little story for Ozue's baby book.

On Sunday, Bob took Ozue and me to my mother's house to visit, while he and Micah and Cretia went to church. We spent the day with Granny. We had a wonderful time. Babies are such miracles. We just couldn't get enough of looking at her and touching her.

Monday, Micah and Cretia went to school. Bob went to work. Ozue and I were finally really alone for the first time. Ozue was bathed and dressed before nine in the morning. We ate and slept, slept and ate, and in between, I changed a few diapers. We talked. Of course, I did most of the talking. I remember distinctly thinking as I looked at her "This is the happiest I've ever been in my life." Even with all that activity, I managed to have dinner ready when everyone came home. That was easy compared to getting a bath. I took a quick dip while Bob held Ozue and visited with her. She was on a binge and eating almost every hour on the hour. Nobody had warned me about breast babies being binge eaters! Nothing like learning the hard way!

Tuesday, the little boy I babysat returned. The three of us had a pretty good day. The binge was over. Wednesday was about the same. On Thursday, however, in the early afternoon, the air conditioner stopped working. It was late March, but it can get very hot in Houston, and this was one of those days. Bob and Micah and Cretia opened all the windows. When I ran for a quick bath, Bob took Ozue to the window for a little cool air breeze. When I came back into the room, he said, "You know she looks a little yellow to me." She had been jaundiced in the hospital and under the ultraviolet lights to get her bilirubin count down. They had told us to watch her. "If you think she looks yellow, let's call the doctor?" He did. We were told to be there first thing in the morning,

The hotter it got in the house, the more miserable we all became. Ozue fretted off and on through the night, but she never cried. Next morning, we were out of the house very early to go to the doctor's office. Ozue vomited just as we reached the parking lot. "I'm glad we're here. I don't think breast-fed babies are supposed to throw up like that. Maybe the doctor will see her. She doesn't look good. Bob, look at her color."

We went right to the office. The nurse gave us a lab slip and told us to go to the lab in the complex to have Ozue's blood drawn. While we were still there in the pediatrician's office, Ozue began to nuzzle like she was hungry, so I sat down. She nursed staring right into my eyes with such concentration. She sucked a few times, rested, and then nursed a little more, but all the while, she searched my eyes with hers. I told the nurse that I wanted her doctor to see her when we were done at the lab. "Something is just not right," I said. She told us to come back.

Bob carried her to the lab. I went with them. The technician stuck her little heel. She cried out. Shortly after, as we were walking back to the doctor's office, we heard her little bowels move loudly. The nurse put us into an examining room, where Bob and I began to undress her together. I kept saying "Look at her. Look at her color. She doesn't look right."

Ozue was very still on the scales. "She's gained four and a half ounces," the nurse offered. "Put her on the table. The doctor will be right in."

Was he ever right in! The door barely closed, before he opened it stethoscope in hand. He listened to her tiny chest; he blanched white from head to toe; left the room; came running back in with another type of stethoscope and listened in her groin. He turned to us and said, "Wrap this little baby up, she's dead."

Simultaneously, Bob and I said, "That's not possible." It wasn't possible! It wasn't! I wrapped the blanket around her and sat in the chair holding her little body close to mine, my lips touching her head.

The doctor began firing questions at Bob and me. One question came right after another with barely time to answer. It felt like a movie. Someone was answering the questions, but who was it? It wasn't us. It didn't seem like it was anyway. Bob slipped out and called our bishop. I sat there holding her, rocking her. I could feel the heat of her slipping away. It's amazing how quickly her tiny body cooled. It didn't seem to matter how much more covering I wrapped around her sweet smelling baby body, it was never going to be enough to warm her again.

Someone came for the little boy I babysat. We'd brought him with us. Time passed. Bob came back and took Ozue from me. He held her. I called my friend Susan at work and told her bluntly "Ozue is dead". She gasped! Then she asked me what I wanted her to do. I asked her to call my brother and sister and get them to have my Aunt Jessie come to be with my mother. Mother was going to have a very hard time with this. She was waiting for us even now to come to her house to spend the rest of the day with her.

My mother! Oh, no! How am I going to tell her? How can I tell her?

I returned to the room. Bob gave me our precious girl to hold. We were waiting for the coroner. An autopsy has to be performed when there is a sudden death. As if her death wasn't enough, she was going to be taken by strangers and cut up! We were in shock. Both of us hardly knew what to say. We sat there. I rocked her and kissed her and rearranged her blanket dozens of times. Bob kissed her little face and held my hands holding Ozue.

Finally, a man came into the room with the doctor. He was very nice, but he was a stranger. We had to give our baby to him.

He and the doctor were going to unwrap her baby square and put her naked into a big white sheet. I couldn't bear the thought. "No, she has to have her blanket!" They let me wrap her snuggly, and then the man took her from me. He wrapped the white sheet around her. As he walked from the room, my heart went with her. He left with her. He left with my Ozue. He took me with him. I felt so lost and alone. The emptiness was overwhelming.

Guided by Bob and the baby's doctor, I was walked next door to my obstetrician's office. He gave me a shot to dry my breast milk up, and he also gave me a shot to calm me. I needed it to get through telling my mother. I couldn't fall apart with her. I had to be strong.

Bob and I drove in silence to my mother's home. The front door was open. I heard her coming to the door, as we walked up the steps to the house. My father was working in the yard, and he'd just been in the house telling her to stop worrying because we were so late. She looked at my arms. Then she looked at Bob's. Then she looked back to my face. "Where's my baby?"

I put my hands on her waist and replied, "She's gone Mom. She's gone to Heaven." She began sliding to the floor and me with her. Bob tried to catch us. His arms were around us, but it was my father who caught us all and held us up together in his arms. I never knew my father loved me until that tender moment. I will never forget the strength and gentleness of his arms, as he supported us there in the hallway.

We stayed with Mother as long as we could, but we had to go home for our other children. They would be arriving soon from school. When we got to our place, my dear friends LaDawn and Cookie were waiting. They had come for our laundry. What wonderfully special women! They left before the children came home. They couldn't bear to witness us telling them. They each had small children of their own, so our baby's passing was hitting them very hard.

Cretia and Micah came charging into the house, and before we could stop them they ran to the crib. "Where is she?" They called. We sat with them on the couch and tried to explain as best we could to two seven year olds that Ozue had gone to Heaven.

Very soon, people began arriving at the house. Friends with foresight brought sandwich stuff and banana nut bread, as I recall. I talked. I walked. I felt numb. I went through the motions. I wasn't sure I was there, until Susan arrived. The moment we saw each other, I fell completely apart. She and I went to the bedroom, where we cried and cried. My breasts were already bursting and heavy with milk made to feed my baby Ozue, but it would never touch her lips again. They hurt. I hurt. For the thousandth time, the phone rang. Someone called Bob to the phone. The pediatrician had pulled some strings. The autopsy was already completed. He told Bob that she was a baby who had contracted Rubella during gestation. During the autopsy, they discovered she had multiple heart defects. There were so many that they counter-acted each other and prevented detection, when she was examined after birth. They worked in concert, until apparently she gained the extra four and a half ounces. This little bit of extra weight required her heart to work harder. It was then that her little heart just sort of imploded. She was gone in an instant. She was ten days old. So brief a life, and yet, so very full of love! I had thought the dream about Grandmomma being with me in my time of travail meant labor. Little did I know that the real suffering was to follow the happiness of labor.

Late that night everyone left. The children went home with family members. The house was totally empty, as were we. Bob and I went to bed. We were in the same bed where we had slept with our little one just the night before. The last thing I remember that night before I shut my eyes was thinking that just yesterday I was the happiest I had ever been in my life, and today I was the saddest. We both fell asleep exhausted and devastated.

The next morning Bob and I went to Waltrip Funeral Home where we picked out a tiny casket that looked like a bassinet. It cost $125. Then, Bob took me to my mother's home. He went somewhere else. My mother, Aunt Jessie, and I went shopping for a dress in which to bury Ozue. My Aunt Jessie bought it. It was a long delicate white baby dress. My mother had crocheted a tiny white silky baby bonnet for Ozue before she was born. It was to be for her to wear when she was blessed. I had thought it so tiny that it would be too small for her, but it wasn't. I didn't want her to have to wear the bonnet, but because of the autopsy, she had to wear it. She had such beautiful hair, and now no one would be able to see her crowning glory.

Three of my church friends, Beth, LaDawn and Cookie agreed to dress her little body for the final time. I just couldn't bear the thought of any more hands of strangers touching her. LaDawn told me later that it was one of the most difficult, yet, rewarding things she ever did. She said that she was so upset and fearful that she had to have a special blessing to be able to be there. In my grief, it didn't occur to me what I was asking of them. They did as I asked. A few years later, one of my very dear friends asked me to do the same thing when her two year old boy died of complications from heart surgery. I did it with a willing heart, because I knew how much it meant to have that kindness done with love and care.

Friday night was the viewing. It was all happening so quickly, and yet, it seemed as if this part of my life would never end.

I walked. I talked. I cried. People tried to hug me never thinking of the excruciating pain that a hug brought to my swollen breasts and my broken heart. More food came to the house each day. Clean laundry was returned; dirty laundry taken out. A friend of Bob's collected all our undeveloped film since Ozue's birth. I didn't know quite what to think about that, but as it turned out, those pictures were so comforting. There we all were together in various poses at different times. We could share them with our family and friends. Many of them had never seen her alive. I recall those pictures circulating the night of the viewing. I remember too a man who was talking with my father and husband in the outer hall of the viewing room. He was making jokes and laughing. How odd I thought!

That last night before the funeral was the hardest for me. I sat at the dining table writing in my journal and contemplating what life would be like without my baby. I had stopped smoking years before she was born. I did it cold turkey, and never wanted one from the day I stopped, until that night! Whether it was the stress or the Devil trying to get in there, I don't know, but I wanted a cigarette more at two o'clock in the morning than I ever wanted one before or after. I didn't have one though. Instead I prayed for understanding and strength, and I was comforted.

Saturday morning at ten the funeral began. We had asked a good friend to tape the service for us. Everything was working prior to the beginning of the service. God in His wisdom rendered a blank tape at the end of the service. No explanation! It was working before the Service began, but nothing recorded. The Chapel was huge and filled with the most beautiful baby flowers. There were so many people that some had to remain outside in the hallway. The people from church took over completely. They made a program with praying hands on the front. Our home teacher who'd been through so much already with us gave the eulogy and cried. The music was magnificent. My friend, Jeanne who has a beautiful voice, rearranged the words of a children's song.

She is a Child of God, And He has sent her here, Has given her an earthly home With parents kind and dear, Lead me, Guide me, Walk beside me, Help me find the way. Teach me all that I must do, To live with her one day.

She is a Child of God, Rich blessings are in store. Help me to understand His ways, Before it grows too late. Lead me, Guide me, Walk beside me, Help me find the way. Teach me all that I must do To live with Him one day.

To tell the truth, this is pretty much all I remember of the service. The funeral was over. People filed past us to shake hands or hug (Oh, how that hurt!) The room was empty. Once more I looked into Ozue's little face. Bob and I put a tiny pink rosebud into her hand. Then, we were in my mother's Volkswagen on the way to Caldwell, Texas to the Masonic Cemetery. It was the same cemetery where I had played as a child. The same one where so many of my relatives were buried. There was a little open grave waiting. Our bishop and his family brought Ozue the hundred miles to Caldwell in the back of their station wagon. No hearse was required for such tiny cargo. Many of our friends and family drove those two hours with us.

At the gravesite, the tiny casket was opened once more, so that my Aunt 'Zue could see her namesake. My Ozue was buried in the plot meant for Aunt 'Zue and Uncle Edd, her husband. It was a solemn ceremony. The grave was consecrated. The casket closed. Of all the things I had been through, this was by far the most difficult. How empty I felt! How terribly lonely! Never would I see her or hold her again in this life, and she was going to be lowered into the ground. We were the last to leave, Bob and I.

We arrived at my Aunt 'Zue's home to find a crowd of relatives and friends. Her church family had provided food for everyone that came for the burial. We stayed a while, and then Bob and I slipped away back to the cemetery. We stood, arms around each other, looking at the mound of red dirt. A tiny steel marker on which was printed her name marked the spot. We ached with an indescribable pain. We left, and drove back to Houston.

Not knowing quite what to do with ourselves, since Micah and Cretia were still with family, we felt lost. Bob always roller skated for comfort. I wrote. So that is what we did. We went to a noisy roller rink. He skated, and I wrote.

I wrote, and I wrote for days it seemed. People have told me that they have saved the thank you notes and letters that I sent to them during that time, but I have no idea what I said in anything that people received. I cried. I didn't believe that I would ever stop. Bob withdrew. He was just trying to be strong. I didn't understand that. I thought he didn't miss her like I did. I was angry with him, until our bishop explained the difference in our grief. For three weeks, I stayed to myself writing, crying and sleeping. I just went through the motions of getting on with a normal life. I cooked and served meals for my family. I washed clothes, folded them and put them away. I tried to be there for my children, but I really didn't feel like I was anywhere at all.

Finally one day, after a particularly poignant answer to a prayer, I felt that I should go to see a shut-in that I had previously visited once a month. I needed to serve someone else and see if I wouldn't feel better. She was a gray haired lady in her fifties, a shut-in. Her husband had died the year before, but that morning I didn't know that. All I knew was how empty I felt. All I asked constantly in my racing mind was "Why? Why? Why?"

I went to see her. I was meant to see her. She ministered to me that day, not the other way round. In our conversation, she told me about her husband going to Dallas on a business trip. He called her that night, told her that he loved her, and said goodnight as he usually did. The next day she was expecting him to walk through the door at any moment, when a knock came. She went to the door. There stood two of his office coworkers. When he didn't leave his room as planned and didn't answer the door, the police were called. They broke in and found him dead from a heart attack.

She shared with me how crushed she was, and how she had wrestled with the same questions that I was asking. She continued. It used to be their morning ritual to get up and have breakfast around five alone. One particular morning, after he had been gone several months, she automatically put his plate on the table, and then collapsed sobbing, praying and asking the Lord "Why?" The reply she received was "Why not?" It was then that she understood that we could not see what might have been had he not died so suddenly, but God could, and he spared the both of them. It was at that moment that I began to heal.

Years later when my niece Stacilynn Corey lost her little boy Coleman at birth, I shared that story. My father bought family cemetery plots in the Masonic Cemetery in Caldwell for our family. When they dug Coleman's tiny grave, they also dug another for Ozue. The two are now side-by-side. Bob placed a marker for her grave that reads:

Ozue Marinell Huntsman, Little Nellie, March 18-28, 1974, "Our Blessing"

I believe that she was not only "Our Blessing," but she was and continues to be a "Blessing" for many others who have not thought about how swiftly loved ones can be gone from this Earth. If the doctors had discovered her heart defects, we would have never been able to bring Ozue home. We would have only been able to love her with great sadness from afar. What a blessing that she was with us, and we did not know of her problems. Our older children have shared with our younger children, and they all know her as a sister. What a blessing that Bob and I were together undressing her when she died. I could have been home alone with her giving her morning bath. What a blessing to know that there is one of my children who is already with her Father in Heaven, and she will be waiting. What a blessing that in all the years that have passed since that time that I have been given the understanding needed to comfort those who have lost their children.

"There will be a day when you will stop crying. It will come, and suddenly you will realize that you made it through the day. You will make it through the next day, the next month, the rest of your life, because 'She is a child of God,' and you will see her.

NO MORE SECRETS.....

"See those angels...It's so bright!" she said waving her right hand and looking towards the ceiling. Blue eyes searched mine for confirmation, as she swiveled her head towards me. We smiled at each other, and she said "They're so beautiful."

"Do you recognize anyone?" I asked.

"Just so many...there...see?" She repeated her waving movements. It was a gray Saturday afternoon in January in Houston, Texas. The light was barely seeping through the sheer curtains of the tall living room windows. The high ceilings and oak paneling didn't bring warmth to the large room, but the belongings did. There was the elephant collection on the small tiered table that had belonged to her parents; the cups and saucers arranged on the console television; and the flock of ceramic birds nesting on the top of the entertainment center. The entertainment center did double duty, so that her nebulizer and nursing supplies were close at hand. The ragged old carpet beneath her hospital bed was shaggy and gold and stained from the traffic of thirty years of children and pets. This room had served as the heart of the hundred year old house in Houston Heights for as long as I remembered. We spent our birthdays and holidays there making lots of noise, eating and sharing. The room, like this frail, old lady, was the hub of activity. In the past few years, the activity had moved to her bedroom. Now, the cycle of life had returned us all to the living room for dying. My eldest son and family members had moved the dining room table and chairs and the oak chest of drawers into other rooms, so that the necessary hospital equipment would not crowd the room. The old gas heater broke the chill in the room. What remained were the couch, love seat, and a few chairs for seating. The modern television and cordless phone integrated bizarrely with an antique Southern lady and her accumulations of ninety something years.

Running my fingers through her thick, white hair, I stared at her. Memories flooded my eyes. Silvery pools teeming with the activities and thoughts of past and present ebbed and flowed. I was incredibly sad, and yet even more incredibly, joyful that I was to be here with her for these defining moments. I could feel the creeping foam of death's surf rising. What a privilege to ride these waves by her side.

When the nurse arrived to take her vital signs that afternoon, she noticed that her patient was staring into space. She asked, "What are you seeing?"

The response came softly. "Don't you see them? Don't you see how bright they are? Look at all of them. How beautiful! Do you see them?"

"I wasn't looking in that direction, but I believe you saw them, and they're here." She sent a "knowing" look to me motioning to move to the other end of the room. "She's getting ready to go. From now on, she'll be partly in this world, and partly in the other."

On Sunday, Mother was chipper enough to have her morning coffee mixed with sweetened condensed milk, Eagle Brand to be specific. This is a family tradition passed from one Southern generation of the Strong women to the next. Just a few sips, she smiled and then, she choked, but she loved her morning brew. She never missed it. It was her favorite time of the day. Before the accident, she drank her coffee on the front porch or the back porch looking at her plants. Not now though. Not ever again.

I went to the grocery store and brought home several cans of the magical milk for her future morning coffees. I even bought a roll of Chocolate Chip Cookie Dough, just in case someone got ambitious in the kitchen. In addition, I brought Momma a double bouquet of cut flowers. They were Freesias with light pink and hot pink blossoms. We put them into her favorite cut glass crystal vase. I moved the arrangement a dozen times, until the flowers were right under the light on top of the television. From her position in bed, she could easily admire the blooms. Flowers were always special to her (home-grown, bought, or even stolen from the neighbors by little boys or girls to decorate her house)!

From Colorado, I brought a specially recorded tape cassette from my friend just for her. She had visited with us at Christmas 1996, and when we played some of the songs on the tape for her, she cried and was touched by them. This time, as Tennessee Ernie Ford and Cristy Gale sang to her, she was probably the only one in the house who didn't shed a tear or two. She enjoyed the music of her youth and recalled "My daddy used to play the fiddle on Sunday mornings for us when I was a girl. He played lots of songs. One of them was 'A Church in the Wildwood'." I sang along to most all the songs. She enjoyed that.

Her fragility was agonizing to see. Never a heavy woman, she had shriveled before our eyes over the past few years, until she was a tiny, tiny shadow of her former self. As I held her hand that Sunday afternoon, I was struck by the severe outline of her bony fingers. Each joint jutted rudely from the smaller finger bones, and visible to the naked eye was the whiteness of the tendons holding them together like rubber bands. My fingers moved upon hers. Once those fingers had been fleshed-out and strong. They had kneaded tons of bread dough; sewn a million stitches; planted thousands of plants; cleaned and cooked; made divinity and birthday cakes; painted and refinished the furniture and woodwork of this old house. They had bathed and attended with love the babies who came here. That would never happen again in this life! As if she knew my thoughts, she moved her fingers and grasped my hand tightly in hers. For the first time, I came to understand exactly what the term "death grip" means. It was as if she were with me and trying desperately to hold on to this side of life for a while longer. She held tightly to me and the memories.

"I'm not going to die today," she stated bluntly.

Stunned I replied, "So, you're not going to die today!"

"And," she said flippantly, "I probably won't die tomorrow either!"

"Okay, so do you know when it is you're planning to die?" I quizzed, and we laughed a little.

"It's a secret," she replied placing her right index finger over her pursed lips.

We both laughed aloud then at her antics. "So, will you tell me your secret when you're ready?

"Maybe," she grinned.

Later that day, I told her that anytime that she wanted to go that it was okay with me. "It's not that I want you to go, because I will always need you. You will always be with me, because I will tell everyone about my memories of you. You will be remembered as long as I live and even after." Taking my hand into her vise-like clutch, she looked deeply into my eyes.

"Seriously," she said, "I won't go while you're here. I don't want to hurt you that way."

Tears welled in my eyes. As the tears slipped down my cheeks, I whispered to her. "It would hurt more Momma, if I wasn't here. Whenever you are ready to go to Jesus, take your momma and daddy's hands, and let go of mine. I consider it an honor to be here with you when you let go of my hand and take theirs. I hope you will be there to take mine, when it's my time. Besides that, I can't imagine not being here with you. This is a blessing for me. How awful it would be if I was all the way in Colorado and not here with you." She smiled her sweetest smile. A tear slipped from her eye. She pulled my face to hers and kissed me on the cheek.

"Okay then."

Monday morning she had her coffee. There were fewer sips that day than the day before. It hurt her to swallow. There was no longer any point in trying to force her to eat or drink. As I moved to hold her hand for the first time that day, she pointed to the left side of the living room where a ceramic pitcher and bowl hung. She'd made it when I was a child. Swinging her hand in a sweeping arc, she smiled saying "Love, Pure love everywhere." Her eyes shone with that same kind of love.

I restarted the tape and with a trembling voice, I sang along,

"Love lifted me; Love lifted me; When nothing else could help, Love lifted me. I was sinking deep in sin, far from the distant shore…sinking deeply, there within, sinking to rise no more. Then, the Master of the Sea heard my despairing cry. From the waters lifted me; now safe am I. Love lifted me; Love lifted me. When nothing else could help, Love lifted me. Love lifted me; Love lifted me. When nothing else could help, Love Lifted Me."

It was a very quiet day. Momma moved deftly between this world and the next. The nurse came. She told us that it was hard to know when she would decide to go. "It could be tonight; it could be a week." We took turns sitting with her, talking to her, holding her hand. I sang to her.

Tuesday was an even quieter day. She rested more. In between her catnaps, she would point at the "babies in the bright light". She wanted us to see them so much, but probably not more than we wanted to see them! "I saw that little boy's foot. I tried to get it, but I couldn't reach him!" She smiled frequently as she gazed at what our eyes could not see. That afternoon her respirations slowed and became irregular. She had so little to eat or drink that there was practically no output to measure. The small amount that was there was very dark.

It was clear that her body was beginning to shut down. No more pills for her to gag down now! We only gave her liquid pain medications under her tongue. Family members, my son, and I were up and down most of the night with her. We thought that this might be her last. Each of us had our own special time sitting with her.

"Softly and tenderly, Jesus is calling. Calling for you and for me. See through the portals, He's waiting and watching...Watching for you and for me. Come Home. Come Home. Ye who are weary, Come Home."

Wednesday morning, she opened those lovely blue eyes and smiled brightly. "Where's our coffee?" She had fooled us all. Ha. She was perky and sassy, kidding with us. Once in the morning, she raised slightly on her elbow (which was quite a feat considering the condition of her pinned hip). "Harmie Is that you?" she asked. (Harmie is a cowboy cousin who passed many years prior. His daughter, as it happened, was on her way to visit that very afternoon.)

The day passed. Visitors (seen and unseen) came and went. The phone was ringing off the hook. There were phone calls from all over the country, grandchildren and friends. She was so prissy bossing us around and laughing. So many people loved her!

"I hear you are waiting for me to come there, Old Lady?" Mollee said when she called that night. "Are you wanting me to come?"

"Are you coming before or after?" she asked Mollee.

"After," she paused. "We talked about when I should come."

"Don't pay any attention to me," she replied. "I'm not all here."

Mollee continued. "Remember what you told me about being happy a few months ago?"

"Yes."

"I'm doing it."

"Good for you. Don't spend one more minute being unhappy."

"It's okay. I won't. I understand. So, when are you going?" Mollee queried.

"I'm just waiting for God to call me home."

"Okay then," Mollee took a deep breath. "Remember our deal. I love you. Bye…Bye."

Her Granny tightly shut her eyes. "Be sweet. I love you too."

Again, it was doubtful that she would make it through the night. But once again, she surprised us, and was "Fine" (as only she could be!) and sipping her loaded coffee on Thursday morning. It was even more noticeable that she was slipping more into the other world. Sometimes she reached out her hand. Occasionally, she spoke softly with her unseen visitors. "Aunt Mel?" she said. (That was her aunt, sister of her mother long ago passed). She spoke to us less frequently, but when she did that morning it was still with vigor, and her grasp remained firm. To me, in one of those moments when it was just the two of us in the room, she whispered "I think I'm ready to let go." Later that morning, she looked deeply into my eyes, as if to memorize my face and whispered "No more secrets…."

Not ten minutes later, she looked up at me, "What's the date?"

"It's January 23, Thursday," I told her.

"Well, that settles it. I'm not dying today or tomorrow! You can be sure of that! It's your daddy's birthday tomorrow, so tell all those people who keep calling to quit calling, and come on over here to see me!"

She rallied again, and that was the day of many visitors. She was present and attentive with them all. There were friends, children, nieces, nephews, cousins, grandchildren, and great grandchildren at her bedside. Once again, the living room was full of life and activity. By that evening, she was exhausted, but she continued to socialize and entertain. As the last of the company left, the chocolate chip cookie dough was placed in the oven. The house smelled wonderful.

How many times had I come home from school to smell that fragrant aroma! Unable to resist, she asked for and ate a chocolate chip cookie warm from the oven. It was the only solid food that she'd had in days. Wouldn't you know that this lady, who could barely swallow water, drooled over that cookie, as if it were her last.

It was late as we prepared her for sleep. I put the cassette tape on for her, and I entertained her by singing and dancing a jig to "Give Me That Old Time Religion". She giggled and grinned. I climbed into the hospital bed with her. Half my body was hanging over the side rails, but she was happy that I was there, and so was I. She'd been inviting people to get in the bed with her, but as it turned out, my niece Stacilynn Corey and I were the only ones who did. After all, her bed had been the family gathering bed forever. That's a family tradition of sorts too. So it seemed only natural to cuddle up with her there. It was a safe place; A loving place. We reminisced about her terrorizing the children by telling them the Devil was in the attic just to keep them out of her closet! We laughed about her four inch long green switches that she carried in her purse to keep kids in line. We laughed a lot. It was a sweet time.

When I clumsily fell (I mean climbed) out of the bed, she asked me to bring the vase of flowers to her. They were still fresh. I held the vase close to her. I held it and turned it round and round as she lovingly caressed each blossom. When she finished touching them, she smiled and closed her eyes. Her breathing was shallower now. Her output miniscule. Silence penetrated the night like an icy finger.

"Precious Moments, how they linger...how they linger in my mind..."

Early Friday morning, her caretaker and friend came to care for her. "Miss Leola, it is Paola" in a sing-song Spanish voice was her standard greeting. "Do you want some coffee now, Miss Leola?"

"Sure" was the barely audible whisper, but when the coffee came laced with Eagle Brand milk, she pursed her lips and kept her eyes closed. Paola couldn't contain herself. Probably for the very first time, she accepted the fact that the end was near. She sobbed for a while on the back porch, and then, Paola returned to bathe and attend to her Miss Leola's tiny body.

With the daily ablution concluded, Micah approached her bed. She knew somehow that he was there. She opened her eyes, put a hand to each side of his face, and spoke softly studying him. "I love you. You be a good boy." Those were the last words she spoke. She was still then. There were rare times, when her lips would move, but there was no sound for us to hear. Only her unseen guests could hear her.

Saturday came. She made it through Stonewall's birthday! She could go now. Still, she stayed with us, but not with us in the sense that she had been before. Her spirit seemed only to visit her body from time-to-time. We took turns sitting with her. We let her know how much we love her, and of course, there was me singing to her. I was sure she knew on some level it was me.

Mollee, my daughter, called late Saturday night from Colorado. She insisted that we put the phone to her Granny's ear. "Thank you," she said. "I got the sign, Old Lady!" On the phone with me, she explained that they had an arrangement. The deal was that Granny would give her a sign, when she was ready to go, if it was at all possible. At a kitchenware party Mollee attended that night, a woman was introduced to her as "Leola". Outside of the family, she was the first person my daughter had ever met with the same name as her Granny. As if that wasn't enough, as she talked with the woman, she learned that she had been born in Brenham,

Texas, but that she had spent every summer at her Auntie's house in Caldwell, Texas. She and her cousins had gone to Lytle's Grocery Store on a regular basis. Lytle's Grocery Store belonged to the "Old Lady's" momma and daddy. This Leola spoke of an old aunt by the name of Aider that her Auntie tended. Aider! That was "the Aider" that had been the nanny to Granny and her sisters, and then to Granny's own two oldest children. Granny had done it. Sign delivered and received!

Lytle and Mary Ann (my brother and his wife) were there Saturday evening with us. I was now giving Mother liquid morphine and other medications to keep her comfortable almost hourly. Her breathing was louder. It was quite disturbing at first, but after a while, the medications took care of the sounds. Once again, she panted quietly into the night with us wondering if she could possibly make it one more.

At one o'clock in the morning Sunday, the nurse who came to the house told us, "She could go in the next few minutes, or she could hang on another couple of days. It just depends on how her body shuts down, and when she is ready to let go. Has she seen everyone or talked to everyone that you think she would want to? Sometimes, people don't go, until all their business if finished."

She had to be kidding, right? But there was Momma still holding on when the sun came up! For a frail little lady with heart and respiratory problems, and a smashed hip and lots of little strokes, her pulse remained as strong and steady as her will.

I realized, as I paced the floor around her bed, how very much dying is like the birthing process. Each individual has their own time schedule. Each has their own way to make their journey. She was certainly holding true to her strong-willed personality! No one could ever push her into anything. She did it her own way. If she couldn't get anyone to help her, she would say "'I'll do it myself" said the Little Red Hen." And she did. She was dying just as she had lived. Grandchildren and great-grandchildren arrived. The house quickly filled. Cloudy skies and drizzling rain swallowed her old house. She had spent over sixty years within those walls taking care of others. There was always a place at her table and space on her floor for anyone who needed it. Today, we were gathered to take care of her, as she moved on. We were there to let her know that we loved her and were thankful to her for all her care and love.

Micah sat holding her hand. I counted her pulse and respirations. Her eyes opened. He said to me, "She's going now. She just let me know." I closed her eyelids. Lytle came to her and spoke quietly into her ear. Others came to her bedside to say their final goodbyes. She had said the week before "I am not going to say 'Goodbye' to anyone, because I am going to be right there watching over them." It was their goodbyes needing to be said, not hers.

For two more hours, she held on. Stacilynn Corey climbed up in the bed with her for a while. Micah and my niece held her hands. Her breathing slowed. First there was a minute between the breaths; then, a minute and a half; then, two; then, three. Still, she held on.

Three and a half minutes passed, and once again, she startled us by gasping another breath. Micah, Corey, and I were bewildered. It was a bit scary, when she would go without breathing for so long, and then she would suddenly gasp! It hit us all at the same time! We knew that she was probably getting a terrific kick out of scaring us! She had always enjoyed scaring us! We had to laugh. I have no doubt that she was laughing at us on the other side.

She was a strong "Strong" woman by heritage. It was the family name. She was a hard working, feisty, witty, and unpredictable woman. At ten minutes after three in the afternoon on January 26, 2003, she drew her last breath. At three fifteen, we knew she was really "Home". There in her old house, which will always be our "heartfelt home" surrounded by those she had loved and who still love her, my mother passed through the veil. Her body died, but not her spirit.

AND FROM THE OTHER SIDE OF THE VEIL

RUTH AND MARGARET

Their Shared Journal of Secrets

From 1836 forward……………………..

DEDICATION

For Ruth and Margaret

For allowing me to tell their secrets

And

For those who despair and forget that

Living is about hope, and most of all, Love

PROLOGUE

Down a darkened passageway, she saw a tiny young girl who appeared very frail and somewhat deformed. She was leaning against a shadowed wall, as if waiting for someone, and then, there was Margaret, a strapping young woman reaching out for her sister Ruth's tiny hand. She enclosed it in her strong one. Light seamed the bottom of the doorway. Trembling joined hands turned the crystal doorknob. The door was flung wide. Thousands of small pieces of paper covered with writing came raining through the doorway. Finally, their secrets were flying out into the world, and according to someone very wise, it is my job to share their story.

Even though no one might ever read their secrets, it is time for me to help them to be put onto paper. As I considered the task, I realized that many years ago, when I was working as a psychiatric nurse, I would tell my confused and distraught clients who were mired in the past that they must journal. Once on paper, it becomes real. They own it. They can then let it go.

What a privilege and honor it has been for me to act as their scribe.

Journal Entry I
Ruth

Ruth:

What was seen last week is the way I looked all my life, and there was nothing "pretty" about me. Anyway, not on the outside, but my Granny and Margaret told me that I was born beautiful inside.

Granny is my Da's mother. She came to help my mother the day my mother died. That happened to be the same day that I was born with a caul over my face. "Very special people who have very special gifts of sight and knowing are born with cauls" according to my Granny. My mother knew I was born and that I was special. Then, without even a whimper, she passed.

Not because I was big, but because of the squeezing as I was delivered, both of my shoulders were broken. As a result of these breaks, my shoulders never mended properly. They remained at odd angles to my body. Add to this, the fact that my body didn't use food the way other folks' bodies do, and I stayed small, always very small.

The doctor from a nearby village came soon after my birth at Granny's request. I cried a lot and didn't feed well. He told Granny, Da, and Margaret that my bones were crumbling, and that I would probably die soon, because of either the breaking bones or because I couldn't get what I needed to live from what I could eat. Everyone in my family was devastated when my mother died, but Da was the worse. My whole life I don't remember my Da ever looking me full in the face. At best, he ducked his head and looked sideways at me.

Margaret was seven years old; Granny was seventy, when I came into the world. They took care of me. Granny bartered for cow's milk in exchange for washing the cow owner's clothes. The Vicar begged parishioners for lamb's wool and cotton for padding to prevent more bone breaks. Together, Granny and Margaret padded my cot and anything that might cause me injury. She taught Margaret how to feed me and clean me and how to dress me, so as not to break my bones. My bones broke anyway no matter how much care they took; sometimes bad breaks; other times, tiny little splinter and chipping breaks. Large or small, they hurt terribly, especially when it was rainy or foggy. If you know Ireland, you know how often that is.

I was the size of a one year old (without any fat), when I was three, but I had a big heart. I knew what happiness and sadness were. They were my life. I was surrounded by Granny and Margaret's great love for me on one hand. That was happy. On the other hand, there was Da. Periodically, Da and his whiskey temper fits and ravings hurt me to my heart. He said terrible things about me. He called me names. That was sad.

"Da works hard. He's entitled to the drink" Granny would say in his defense. She took his side. He was her only son. She loved him like she did us. He ate one meal a day in the room below us. Granny started cooking it early in the morning, so that when he came home, it was ready and waiting for him. I have no memory of his face. Most of my early recollections of him were from the top of his head down. I could see him through the floor board cracks. His hair was thick and curly, and it was most always full of dirt. There was a redness (more than just the sun) to his neck and hands. His shoulders were wide; his hands, huge; his belly rounded more with each year. He seemed to be almost always angry. If my name was spoken at all, he referred to me as "The Freak!" I did my best not to think of him.

The loft room where I grew to the age of three was cozy. It had a window that looked down on the road. The sill was large enough for me to sit in my cocoon of padding and have a bird's eye view of life passing me by. Once or twice a year, when Da went to the city to "take care of his man business" per Granny, I got to go downstairs. Margaret and Granny would bundle me and carry me in a box. It was thrilling! If the weather was pretty, they would carry me outside. That was always a wonder! Oh! My how God loves us all to give us such a green, glorious place to live! Flowers of all kinds, purple heather, roses, all those sweet smells and the fragrant herbs in the garden were precious to a little girl who spent most of her days in the mustiness of cotton and wool and old wood dank from the mists. Even the smell of the dirt and manure was sweet to me. Those times were few. That made them all the more precious.

Granny insisted "No doctor is going to tell me to let my granddaughter die before her time!" And, she didn't. She taught my sister Margaret everything she needed to know about cooking and cleaning and taking care of a house and Da and me. Granny was good at sewing, and she taught Margaret how to make my dresses split open in the back for ties to accommodate for my misshapen body. (Nothing could ever be pulled over my head, because of my deformed shoulders.) She taught me how to sew too, as little as I was. I loved it, because she did. She read the Bible to us every day, and by the time I was three, I was reading too. What else did I have to do! There was nothing wrong with my mind, or eyes, or ears, or with my words either. I kept company with spirits. I saw spirits, heard them speak, and talked to them frequently in those long hours spent alone in the upstairs bedroom, while the housework was being done by sturdier hands. When I was two, I relayed a message to Granny, "Mother says to tell you she is waiting for you to come home. 'Hurry up and get ready.'"

Granny had us and herself ready two months after Christmas the following year. As ready as we'd ever be! In other words, we weren't ready. She passed away from a cough. She'd done everything she could to show love to Margaret and me. She always had time to pat me and kiss my cheeks. She had time to teach me to love reading and doing my numbers. I was her "good, smart girl". As she lay on her death bed, next to my cot, she told Margaret, "Always take care of Ruth, and Ruth will take care of you." She left us on a cold winter's day.

In the spring, we felt the weight of being alone with Da. If it hadn't have been for our garden and chickens, there would have been nothing to eat. Da could be gone for days, but if there wasn't a meal ready for him when he showed his face, there was an awful scene. Margaret cooked for him every day. Days when he ate, there was nothing left for us; days without him, we waited until the next day's food was prepared, before we dared to eat the day-old food. If the Vicar knew Da wasn't around, he would often share food prepared for him by the women of the congregation. Da hated the Vicar. He blamed him and God for mother dying and me living.

And so, Margaret cleaned, cooked, and washed clothes, so that we had milk. She took care of me and gardened, but no matter how much Margaret did, it was never enough for Da.

Journal Entry II
Margaret

Margaret:

No, it wasn't enough! Nothing ever was! I was ten and skinny, but I worked hard. I took plenty of beatings. Then, one night in early summer, Da came home drunk, but this time, he was singing at the top of his voice. Drunk wasn't so unusual, but singing was. He was happy for a change. I was happy, because he was. He demanded I sit at the table with him, while he ate. I remember thinking that maybe he would start being nicer to Ruth and me. Maybe he was getting over the pain and anger. I smiled. He smiled back. He said something funny. I don't remember what it was, but I threw back my head and laughed. This was the Da I knew from when Mother was alive.

He reached up with his big hand and touched my cheek. Then, he stroked my red hair. He smiled again. I smiled.

He moved his hand from my cheek to my neck; and then, to my chest. I had just begun to bud. He rubbed my chest, and said "You're turning into a fine little lady." I smiled. Da hadn't said anything nice to me in years...not since Mother died.

Abruptly, he left the table frowning. I didn't know what I had done wrong. One minute he was being nice to me; the next, he discarded me. I cleared the dishes and went upstairs. Ruth had seen everything from above, and she was as confused as I.

Two weeks passed. We returned to the same deafening silences, or drink-rages and brow beating. No more smiles. He was angry. Nothing I could do would change that it seemed. At the end of the fortnight, he came home late from the pub. He was singing again. There were no tears, no meanness.

"Come down Maggie girl. Come down and get your ole Da some food. Come down, me Sweetness!" Already in my nightgown, I came down the stairs. As soon as he looked at me, his eyes glazed over like a purring cat. I didn't know why, but I was afraid. I busied myself with his food.

"Do you love me Maggie girl?"

Of course, I do Da.

"You take care of me like a woman takes care of her man. You cook and clean and wash me clothes. What else can you do?"

I stared innocently back at him not knowing what he wanted me to say...not wanting to incur his wrath by answering incorrectly.

He slammed his fist on the table making the bowl jump; turned over his chair; and sullenly went to bed. I had upset him again. What was I to do? I bounded up the stairs to the loft. Sobbing into my pillow, I felt tiny fingers closing over my hand.

And so, our lives went on for a time with Da acting stranger and stranger.

One morning in early July, Da came home smiling from ear-to-ear. "Pack up, we leave for America in a fortnight."

"What? What about Ruth?"

"We'll be leaving that little freak at the orphanage in the city. Let somebody else take care of her."

Without thinking, I shouted back at him. "No! I'm not going without Ruth!"

He was stunned. (So, was I!) He stared at me for a long time. Then, he quietly said, "All right, Maggie girl, but you have to do everything for her if you want her to come."

Oh, I will Da. I will!

We sold what we could and gave away what we couldn't take with us. We set out walking. Da's belongings were in a bag, and Ruth's and mine were in a small trunk. I lined the insides of the trunk on one side with thick padding on one side to act as a bed for

Ruth. On the other side, I strapped Granny's Bible, her hankies, and our clothes. A kindly neighbor gave us an old pram she no longer needed, and even though Ruth was four now, she fit into it perfectly. Even with the padding, there was room to spare.

Ruth was excited! She was actually to be taken out of the house and travel down a road…a road to the city…to a new country…where everything would be different! She never stopped jabbering or asking questions.

I was excited too. It was a new beginning. Maybe Da would be happier. Maybe we could all be happier.

Journal Entry III
The Journey

Ruth:

It was a dream come true. I was out in the world. I could feel the sunshine on my face; the wind in my hair. Da still didn't look at me, but when we began to walk, he took the trunk that Margaret was dragging behind her, as she pushed me in the pram with one hand along the dusty road. He flung our trunk over his back just like it was a feather, and he marched on ahead of us. Arriving at the docks, my senses were overloaded. I felt dizzy. The aroma of the tangy fish soup and salt of the ocean tingled in my nose. The noises from the sailors and the market rose and fell just like the waves slapping against the ships. I couldn't see everything at once, and yet, I tried my best. My body ached from the jostling, but my mind was racing. I was worn out by the time Margaret maneuvered the pram into the ship's hold. It looked like a town in there. People were everywhere. Babies cried, young children ran and played. Men hauled in luggage and supplies, while women arranged belongings and claimed territories. There were many stacked beds in rows, tables and a stove in the center of the room. Scarred barrels of water stood on one side, and there were relief buckets scattered amidst the beds awaiting our needs. There was hay on the ancient wood flooring. I recall thinking "Why hay?" This strange place was our new home. I for one loved it!

Margaret:

Watching Ruth's face was the only thing that kept me going. I was so glad that Da took the trunk, because I was almost to the point of sitting on the side of the road and crying. Pushing the pram was difficult enough, but dragging the trunk behind me and not dumping Ruth was almost impossible. I winked at Ruth, and whispered, "See, Da is already acting different. We're going to be fine."

I wanted things to be fine so much. I had to believe it. I had to keep reminding myself and Ruth that things were going to be fine. Granny had told us so often that Da was a good man, a hardworking man, and that one day he would be loving again. We had faith in her and in what she told us, so we had faith in Da.

People stared at Ruth. Children made fun of her. Others made the sign of the cross and moved away. Women put their heads together and whispered. It didn't seem to bother Ruth. She was so caught up in all the excitement that she didn't seem to notice. It bothered me a lot. I wanted to fight, to scream, even to curse, but I didn't. I stayed proper. I kept my head down, moving carefully as I could to get us down into the hold of the big stinky ship. The rats seemed friendlier than the people! Ruth, on the other hand, laughed aloud, clapped her tiny hands, and greeted everyone that we passed. Did I feel shame? Not for us, but for those that ridiculed Ruth, I felt anger first. Watching Ruth's happiness, I (much later) felt a kind of pity for them and their ignorance.

Night fell, and our ship pulled away from the dock. From below, we could hear cheering and later singing from the sailors as they worked. It was a clear night and a full moon. Sails danced with the winds. The clouds kissed the sails. I kissed Ruth.

I believe God blessed us by making people move away from us (even if their reasons were theirs and not so nice). Because of their shunning, we had a place to stash the carriage and a big enough to place to open our trunk, so that Ruth had a safe place to sleep and sit. There was an older woman who slept on one side of us, and two younger women, in the bunks above us. Da found a bed across the hold with some of his friends, and they were already in their cups and playing cards.

I prepared our supper of bread and cheese, and after we had eaten, it was time to toilet. That old lady near us saw our struggles, and she held the pail still while I balanced with Ruth above it. She made us laugh, and that helped with having to hang over a bucket for the first time in public! The Lord provides, doesn't He? That night we slept peacefully. The waves lulled our worn out minds and bodies to blackness.

By noon the next day, the puking began. The ship pitched and rolled. There was no singing, very little talking, but lots of moaning. The sounds of gagging bombarded our ears. The stench was horrible. The ale and suppers from the night before stunk, as they were shared once more…this time with the buckets, until at last, the buckets overflowed.

Ruth:

And I understood exactly why hay was on the floor!

Margaret:

Three days passed before the storm and the puke stopped. The men threw the soiled hay overboard. The women and girls scalded the floors. Sailors threw fresh hay down, and the young children spread it out by kicking it.

Ruth:

It smelled wonderful. It was like the haystacks we had passed on the way to the ship…fresh and full of sunshine!

I wished I could have helped, but I learned long ago that I helped best by staying put. In the hours that passed, we played games, the old woman, Margaret and me. Sometimes the younger women would sit and talk. They told us stories of places they'd lived and where they were going in America. One of them was to be married upon her arrival, and the other was joining one of her brothers. The old woman and her husband had planned to go to America together. Their children had immigrated years earlier and had sent for them, but her husband died a few weeks prior to the sailing date. She was sad to be without him, but she was looking forward to seeing her children again and meeting her grandchildren for the first time.

The old woman and her kindnesses made Margaret and I long even more for Granny. How she would have loved to have been here with us for this adventure.

Margaret:

That hay spreading may have smelled wonderful to Ruth, but it was a nightmare! All the dust and grasses suspended in the air made it almost impossible to breathe. I put wet cloths over both our faces. Our eyes were another thing. Ruth thought everything was "wonderful". The rest of us choked and sputtered and whined.

Water was precious on the ship, so when we had rain, a few of us at a time were allowed to take clothes on deck and wash them with a strong soap provided for us. (We washed ourselves as best we could then as well.) Of course, unless the sun came out soon after, the freshly washed clothes soured below. I don't know which was worse, dirty or sour.

Ruth took advantage of the quieter, less active times to teach me to read better. I was never very good at reading, but I tried. I could write my name, and that was more than a lot of the people on the ship could do.

Ruth kept count of the days.

Ruth:

I heard people talking about how the journey could take eight weeks. At first that sounded great, but after three weeks passed, murmurings and arguments increased. Children who had played well together at the beginning were now fighting. Margaret and I kept to ourselves as much as we could. Da never came around. We didn't exist to him.

Margaret:

To Da, we didn't exist. I could see him when I walked about the quarters. He was either drinking or fighting or sidled up to this one particular woman. She had light colored hair, but it didn't look real, and she didn't look like a church-going woman. I pretended not to notice him at all.

Ruth:

Six weeks out, I could feel a swell of excitement beginning. There was more music and dancing. Spirits seemed to rise. People were friendlier to each other. They even stopped giving me the evil eye. I guess they knew our voyage was near an end, and all the close quarters would end soon as well. In any case, I noticed more smiling. Mother came in spirit often to be with me, and Granny did too. They told me that we were loved, and that we had what we needed to finish the journey. "You have everything you need. You have Margaret, and she has you."

Journal Entry IV
Ellis Island

Margaret:

Nell, one of the young women who slept above us, helped us with our trunk. Da was nowhere to be found. I was fearful that he had left us for good, but once we were in the long line waiting to give our information, he found us. He pushed his way into the line in front of us. We moved at a snail's pace towards the be-spectacled man who was dressed in a dark uniform. He wore a small pillbox kind of hat and sat on a very high stool with a big book on a stand in front of him. Da gave him our names and answered all his questions. Then, we were waved past him to be seen by the doctors and nurses. They thought for sure that Ruth and I had a lung disease, because we were so skinny. Ruth was a mystery to them. They asked me all sorts of questions about her. No questions for Da, because he wouldn't even stay around to go through customs with us. I explained about Ruth, and I told them that we hadn't had too much to eat on the ship. They passed us through to where Da was waiting, and we had our first decent meal in two months.

Ruth:

We were upstairs with the doctors and nurses. Talking amongst themselves, they examined us shaking their heads. Granny had told me not to fret, because they would let us enter, so I didn't concern myself. Margaret did that! She talked and talked to them. Me, I pushed the pram to the railing just outside the room. It was like a tiny narrow porch that looked down into the great room where the lines of people from all over the world stood waiting with everything they owned. As the knots of humanity reached the many uniformed men on stools, they were directed right or left. Right meant the doctors and nurses, and maybe a refusal to be admitted to America. Left meant freedom and a new start.

I was impressed to see the children waiting in line. They were either crying hysterically from hunger or tiredness, or they had blank, sad little faces with eyes that stared blankly. Probably, they were exhausted. It took a long while to get off the ships and through the lines. It was exciting, but draining.

At last we were released to go downstairs and to the left where Da was waiting for us. I have to say Margaret didn't think Da would be there, but he was. Margaret wasn't too happy with the way Da stayed away from us, while we were on the ship, but at least, he was there on the other side of the door. We went with him to the dining room, rather we followed him. Da sat by Margaret on one side. I was on the other end of the table in my pram. He refused to look at me, but I knew he knew I was there, and that satisfied me for the moment.

It was a heavenly meal! It was probably the best meal that I'd ever eaten in my whole life! There was warm bread and cold milk and cheese and even some fresh vegetables. Margaret and I each got an apple and an orange! What a land, this America!

We were on this island called Ellis. We could see the city of New York, as we came off the ship, but it seemed far away. Now that we were done in the building and the dining hall, we were herded like cattle onto a boat that would take us to the city itself. The boat was rocking. I was pitched upwards, and my arm hit the side of the railing. I could feel it break, but I felt the breeze from the bay on my face, and the ocean spray as it dampened my hair, my body, my clothes. I was so wrapped up in the moment that I felt no pain, just joy.

Margaret:

The first night in New York City was not the end of the journey. Da took us to a pub where I found a corner for Ruth's pram and me. I think the wife of the owner felt sorry for us, because she brought us something to eat and made the nasty men there stay away. Da acted like he was mad that she did that. After a while, he grabbed me by the arm and drug me to the kitchen telling me that if I wanted to eat and drink that I could "damn well" wash dishes to pay for it. The wife of the owner stroked my hair and wiped the tears from my face. She went to fetch Ruth to the kitchen.

"You're safer in here anyway Girlie."

And we were.

Ruth was hurting from the new break, but she hardly ever cried anymore. She just went somewhere in her head. I could tell she was gone, but that was okay.

There were rats in the kitchen and bugs, big ones. I hit them with a broom or pot when they came too close.

Da fell asleep at the table. The wife of the owner got into a fight with her husband, because he wanted to throw Ruth and me outside along with Da, but she begged him to let us all stay, because she said "those girls will be the ones to suffer, not him." I guess he felt a little sorry for us too, because he let us stay until morning. At dawn, however, he put us all out.

With Da in the lead, we went to the place where the little boat had delivered us from Ellis Island yesterday. It was cooler there in the street by the water. We could catch the breeze off the water. He told us to stay there. He left.

Ruth:

Margaret was upset that Da left us again, but I wasn't. Granny had come to me in the kitchen last night while Margaret slept. She said that Da would find a job and a place for us to live. I reassured Margaret of this, but she was still doubtful. Too many broken promises from Da to her had its effect.

Margaret was a smart one. She secreted some food for us from the kitchen. It was scraps that she'd scraped from the plates. We ate well that day. We saved a little just in case there was nothing later, but to us, it was another feast. There were no worms or weevils in it like on the ship.

The sun began to set. We could see the moon rising,. Glimmers of shine radiated from the water of the bay. How beautiful!

Journal Entry V
Settling In

Margaret:

Just as I was about to give up on him, Da strutted up grinning. He had a piece of paper in one hand, and money in the other! I couldn't believe my eyes.

"Maggie, me girl, give your Da a kiss! I have me a job on the docks loading cargo, and this is me pay for the first day in America! Now, let's us go find our home."

I kissed him and hugged him. I felt like doing a jig. I kissed Ruth. She was right. Granny was right. Things were going to be fine.

Da swooped up the luggage, and off he lumbered with me pushing Ruth behind him. Da was looking at the paper in his hand. He stopped from time-to-time asking people for directions. We crossed streets of shell. Then the streets had cobblestones, and later, they were just dirt. It wasn't easy to push the pram, but I couldn't stop. I was afraid of losing Da. A few times I thought we'd lost Da in the masses of people. There were so many people out, and it was dark. They were selling all kinds of things from carts in the streets, as well as in shops. To my amazement, Da actually stopped occasionally to wait for us to catch up to him. We wound around the streets, until Da at last stopped.

"This is it." We arrived at a building that looked like a haggard old lady, gray and worn. "This is home. Go inside to Number 4," he said glancing at his paper. With that, he turned and walked away.

I was afraid to leave the luggage in the street. It was all we had in the world, but I couldn't leave Ruth in the street to take our things inside either. I didn't know what to do. I was too tired to think at this point. I simply couldn't think anymore, so Ruth thought for us both.

Ruth:

"Push me a little Margaret. Drag the bag and trunk up in front of me. Now, do it again." Little by little, Margaret managed to get us into the building. The inside of the building was much worse than the outside. The rats didn't make any pretense of fear. They proudly patrolled the halls. They ran up and over our things, stopping on them to peer at me in my buggy. They had tiny black eyes and whiskers that wiggled. They were comical peering in at me, as if they were trying to figure me out. Margaret thought they might take a bite of me, but I didn't. By the smell of the place, they had much more appetizing fare than skinny little me.

Margaret:

I shoved the door to Number 4 with my hip. It was a filthy place. Bugs as big as my thumbs scattered. A big rat sat nibbling a part of the wall. What was I to do! How would I ever manage here!

Ruth:

Look, Margaret! There's a welcome party here for us, and you were worried that we'd be lonely. I giggled. Margaret couldn't help it. She giggled with me.

Margaret:

Well, aren't we just the lucky ones! I exclaimed getting into the spirit. Welcome home, Ruth!

Two women with children passed by our open door and peered in at us laughing. They only paused and moved on, but they smiled at what they had heard us say.

In a few minutes, they were both back with their brooms and buckets and soap, and best of all, they brought us cheery smiles of welcome. As if it were a game of competition, they beat and swept the rats and roaches from our room. Together, we swept and scrubbed the walls, floors, and the pitiful excuse for a kitchen. I was so grateful that I couldn't help myself. I began to cry. Ruth was delighted to meet them. She clapped her hands and sang us a song, while we worked. They didn't turn away from her like so many others had. If anything, they were curious and friendly at the same time. Who would have thought the two could go together in this strange land! Ruth answered their questions, while I cried and cleaned. I was just so tired. One of the women left and came back with two more women who had a pile of rags with them. They stuffed the cracks and holes to keep the bugs and vermin out. "This should keep those demons out for a minute or two," one of them said. Another lady brought us a bucket for relief. She warned us that it was too dangerous at night to go to the outhouse behind the house. "Days aren't much better, but at least you can see who's around." How dear and kind they were. Before they left, they offered us food, but I told them that we had some. They made me show it, before they would leave.

With everyone gone, and the room livable, I lay down on the floor next to Ruth. I was numb. I'd never been so tired in my life.

Ruth:

I told Margaret that this would be a happy place for us. It was obvious that the women who had helped us were good women. We were brought to this very place to be with these women. I told Margaret so. She sniveled for a bit, and then, she was very quiet and still. She could barely keep her eyes open. She was so bone-tired. She had been afraid to really sleep, because she was guarding me all the time. Making a little pillow for her head from some of our clothes, I put it on the floor and pushed her to lie down. She was asleep instantly.

I did a lot of praying that night...a lot more than usual.

Margaret:

It was midday when my bladder woke me. I was confused. Where was I? It took me a few moments to get my bearings. Ruth was asleep in the trunk. She looked so sweet. She would be hungry when she woke. There was only a small amount of food left.

I must make this place a home. I needed things: a broom, bucket, coal for the stove to say nothing of food to cook. We only had two thin blankets, and it was chilly. Ruth had put them both on me as I slept. Now, I put them around her pitifully thin body. She cooed and snuggled down deeper into her sleep. I unpacked our bowls from the trunk putting them on the shelf with our cups from the night before. The small pot and kettle, I placed on the top of the cold stove.

I read Granny's Bible until Ruth waked, and then I tended to her needs. Two of the ladies from the night before stopped by to check on us. They invited us to come out to the stoop. We did. Children played all around us. A few were cruel to Ruth, but Ruth was as always tolerant. Me, not so tolerant; I ran them off. She was just happy to be outside and among people.

Ruth:

Oh yes, how nice to be invited to go outside and to have friends! They accepted us as we were. Margaret fetched our blankets and wrapped them around my shoulders in the pram when the weather turned cool. The sun was going down. The streets were emptying of the women who had to cook supper for their men. We stayed where we were. Both of us were watching for Da, but neither of us would say that we were.

Margaret:

Lo and behold, there came Da swaggering towards us grinning!

"Maggie, me girl, what's for dinner?"

Afraid of his anger, I ducked my head mumbling. He laughed his loud bellowing laughter, and he handed me money. "You go round the corner and fetch us whatever we need. I'll be back in a bit."

I took Ruth back inside and tucked her into the trunk. She was reading when I left. The rags were holding the rats away and most of the bugs. I killed a few bugs, and then ran all the way to the grocery.

Coal, candles, matches, a bigger pot, potatoes, carrots, cabbage, milk, cheese, flour, honey, oil, a beef bone, salt. I collected my things and I was on my way. It didn't take long and our meal was simmering. When it was done, Da wasn't there. We waited, until the smells mixed with hunger were driving us crazy. We stole a few bites; we had to! But we didn't dare eat until after Da had his fill, so we waited with our stomachs growling. The room, at least, was warmer because of the stove, and we fell asleep.

I woke to Da's boot in my backside. It was still dark out. I filled his plate. He ate, but he didn't say a word. I could smell the whiskey on him. I washed and dried his bowl, covered the pot, and sat it outside on the window sill to keep it cool. When I turned back, Da was curled up on the floor asleep.

Ruth:

Da had no use for me. Not only did he avoid looking in my direction, but he never even referred to me in his conversations with Margaret. Being ignored like that by my own father was very hurtful. As old for my years as I was, I was still only a little girl. But that's the way it was, and since I'd rather be ignored than stir his wrath, I'd survive. After all, I was here with Margaret and not in an orphanage. That was my blessing.

Next pay, Da bought us cots. Shortly after that, he gave Margaret money to buys us blankets and pillows. Back in Ireland, he hardly ever came home with money or gave us anything, but he was doing it now. That was the important thing. Maybe Granny was right; maybe he would change for the better. He was working every day, but he was still drinking every night. Oh, there were still plenty of bad nights, when he came home so drunk he could barely find the door to Number 4. Those nights were full of ranting and verbal beatings, but there were other kinds of nights now as well. I recall nights when he brought home penny candies for Margaret. He could be charming and friendly, even nice.

Journal Entry VI
What Now?

Margaret:

Da was nicer to me. He spent more time at home. More often now he would bring his whiskey home. He took to patting me and smacking me on the backside when I moved around the room. Sometimes I caught him looking at me with that "purring cat" look, but he didn't get mad when I looked away. He chuckled. Da liked to be taken care of at all times. If it wasn't his meals, it was shaving him, cutting his hair, washing his back. When he was home, he wanted all my attention. To him there was no Ruth. She kept very quiet to accommodate him. It was their unspoken truce.

Ruth:

It felt pretty bad when Da came home to Number 4. Margaret and I were happy when he was gone, but when the sun began to set every evening, we had a tightness in our bellies. We talked about it, but nothing took the feeling away. We were just grateful that he wasn't hitting Margaret any more, and the cursing and screaming was less. We were glad that he was still working and able to pay the rent and give Margaret money to feed us. He had mellowed a bit from our point of view. We were hopeful.

I started keeping records of all the money Da gave Margaret, and I subtracted what she spent. What she didn't spend wasn't much, but we had a plan for a rainy day. Out of the money left after expenses, Margaret took a few pennies and hid them. The remainder went to a safe place. Sometimes Da ran out of money before the next pay day. When he did, he went looking for the money that he was sure Margaret had left from groceries. He'd slam things around and pitch a fit, until he found something, anything! So, we made sure that the pennies were hidden in different spots for him to find at different times. Sometimes, we put money in one of the cups. Sometimes, we hid it under a pot. Once he found money, he was satisfied, and he would leave to buy his whiskey. It didn't occur to him that we would have any more money anywhere, because we were only females after all! We counted on that. Fairly certain it would never occur to him that I might have hidden money, I stashed our loot. He deemed me so worthless that he wouldn't have thought that I might have value of any kind. On those nights, he looked for money and ranted, I stayed curled up feigning sleep on my cot. Surrounding me, in my batting protection, was our money!

I kept an eye on Da and the way he touched Margaret. She was almost fourteen now, and she had filled out some. Her skin was beautiful and smooth. Her eyes were green in the middle with a bit of brown and golden flecks around them. She was very pretty, but it was her hair that was her most beautiful feature. Red, but a dark sparkling red mixed with dark brown, it fell in big, bouncy curls just past her shoulders. The looks he gave her and the way his fingers lingered on her body made me uneasy. She was torn. On the one hand, he was being nice to her (and to me by default). He hadn't really beaten her in a long time. He talked sweetly to her most of the time. It was probably the fact that he now wanted her to sit on his lap when he was home that made me worried for her. She just thought it was the way he was, but somewhere in the back of her mind, she must have known it wasn't quite right, because she'd already told me that she felt dirty from his looks and touches. If she avoided him, he would get angry and give her less money to buy our groceries. If she was nice, he was kinder and would give her more money to spend. As he began to spend more time at home, I worried more.

Margaret:

I tried pretending to be asleep when he came home late, but he would always wake me up saying "Come sit with your ole Da. I've missed ye Maggie girl." I began sleeping in my clothes, because when I wore my nightgown, he could touch me easier, and touch me, he did. At first, it was like it was accidental, but after a while, he stopped pretending. He became more direct. Instead of bumping into me, he'd just reach out and touch my growing breasts making some nasty comment. If it wasn't that, he would pinch me. And then there were other times, when he would just rub my back or arms. That felt good. I didn't mind that touch so much. However, when he was into his cups, he wasn't gentle at all. He was rough, and he hurt me. Pulling away from him at those times could bring a sharp slap or a fist to my back, as I skittered away from him.

It wasn't all bad. When I shaved him, he was playful. He liked having me shave him. Of course, it was practically impossible to shave him and not bump him with my body, and he made it "impossible". He would pull me to him and cuddle me, and that was how the whole thing of sitting in his lap got worse. He pulled me into his lap and gave me a kiss, but it wasn't a kiss on the cheek or even a peck on the lips. He kissed me hard and long on the lips.

"Did you like that Maggie girl?"

"No, it hurt."

"Well, let me kiss away the hurt. With that, he pulled me closer to him, and he kissed me long and slipped his tongue into my mouth. I couldn't help it. I spit! "Don't you ever spit again when I kiss you girl, or I will hurt you so bad that no one will ever want to kiss you ever again!" With that he slapped my face and shoved me to the floor! I hit the floor hard. He left and was gone for two days and three nights.

Ruth:

We were glad he was gone! But we were afraid he wouldn't come back, and then again that he would! We couldn't decide which we were more afraid of! One of the women that we had become friends with came by daily to check on us. She saw Margaret's bruised face. She was our closest neighbor, and she could hear everything that went on in our place, just as we could hear hers. I saw her hug Margaret and whisper to her, but Margaret wouldn't tell me what she had said.

Margaret:

I couldn't tell Ruth that the neighbor had said "It won't be long now. He'll make you spread. It's the way life is. Don't fight anymore."

What should I do? Wild thoughts ran through my mind. How could I love my Da and hate him too?

The third night, Da came home. Not uttering a word to me, he ate his dinner and went to his cot. I heard him snoring, so I put on my nightgown and curled up next to Ruth. I was just about to fall asleep, when I heard him stirring. He rolled off his cot and crawled across the floor to mine. I pretended to be asleep, as I felt his big hammy hands rubbing my breasts and stomach. He curled up with his chest to my back. I could feel him begin to move his body against my bottom. I didn't move. His breaths were short and loud. His hands moved to my belly, and then down, until his fingers were rubbing my girl parts. I could feel his male parts still against my bottom. He shuddered, and soon after, he rolled to the floor and returned crawling to his cot. I didn't move. I was afraid to move. I prayed Ruth had slept through this. I wished I really could have.

The next morning after Da left for work, there was sticky stuff on the bottom of my nightgown. I washed it out before Ruth woke, so she wouldn't know.

Ruth:

"But I did know. I knew it all. I'd known there was danger for Margaret, but I didn't know what to do to help her. The only way I could help was to pretend like she was that nothing had happened.

We played the game for weeks. The same game over and over. Da pretended to be asleep. Margaret pretended to be asleep. All of us pretended.

Margaret:

Da was more aggressive in his touching and kissing me all the time now. He said it was his right. Where would we be without him? It was his right, and I guess it was.

There was no stopping Da. When he came home to eat, he wanted me sitting on his lap, so he could feel me, and run his big sausage fingers on and into my girl parts. It clearly didn't matter anymore to him whether I winced in pain or begged him to stop. It didn't even matter that Ruth was awake. She didn't count as anything but a stack of rags to him, and he said as much. His breath stunk; his teeth were rotten. He smelled of old garbage. I hated him, but I had to pretend otherwise when he was there. He told me that I couldn't fool him. "You know you like it Maggie girl. You like the way your ole Da makes you feel. Say it now. Say it!" I said it, and when he let go his sticky man business, he left me alone for another few days.

I couldn't talk to Ruth about it. I was too ashamed. I knew she loved me, and she knew what was happening. When she was awake, she would turn away. We didn't speak about any of it. We went to the stoop with the women to watch the children play. We gossiped with our women friends. We laughed when we could. Maybe this was the way all families are. The neighbor had told me what was coming. She knew, and she'd been right about most of it.

What I wasn't expecting was the night he came home with flowers in his fist and candy for Ruth and me. He actually said for me to share the candy with Ruth. I didn't know what to think. Had his conscious gotten the better of him? I gave Ruth some candy. I fixed Da's supper and sat on his lap when he was ready for me.

I can hear him now whispering in my ear, as he massaged my breast through my clothes. "Tonight is going to be special Maggie me girl. Tonight you become a woman. You'll be a woman just like your beautiful mother was to me." He kissed me then. I heard his breathing change. This time, there was no pretending to be asleep or even pretending to just be close while sitting on his lap. This time, he picked me up and carried me to his bed. He started taking off his clothes. "Take your clothes off Maggie, I want to see your body...all of it. Take them off."

I didn't know what to do. Ruth decided for me.

Ruth:

"You pig! Leave her alone! Maggie, get up! Run, get out, run!"

Margaret:

Da exploded with rage. I'd never seen him so furious.

"I'll kill you, you freak! I should have done it years ago! I'll kill you!" He turned away from me and was moving towards Ruth. I jumped to my feet and grabbed the iron skillet from the stove. As he moved towards her in a blind rage, I struck him. I struck him again and again. I have no idea how many times I hit him, but there was blood everywhere, and finally, he wasn't trying to get to Ruth anymore. He was still.

I ran to the neighbor and begged her to help us. She had heard everything. We threw our things in the trunk, and Ruth went into the pram. Ruth was crying. I'd not seen her cry since she was a small baby. It had a strange effect on me. I was in charge. I was like a rock with no feelings. I was intent on getting us out and to safety somewhere, anywhere else. Our friend's husband came and carried the pram with Ruth in it to the stoop, and the two of them walked with us for many blocks, until we felt sure that Da wasn't following.

Where could we go? What should we do? What could we do? Hide was all I could think. Hide somewhere Da wouldn't look. And that is how we came to the Catholic church. We hid ourselves in one of the alcoves. For the first time, Ruth and I talked about what had been going on. It was in the silent dimness of the church that night that we prayed. We came up with a kind of a plan.

Ruth:

Our plan was that I stay here the next day, and Margaret go back to Number 4. She would collect the rest of our things and all the food. She planned to talk to our women friends to see what they advised us to do. It was simple and short, but sufficient. (We hoped).

Margaret:

I waited until the sun was straight up and made my way back to what was no longer our home. Da had locked the door, but there was nothing to picking the lock. That's exactly what I did. He was gone. I hadn't killed him. Glory be! I had been so afraid that I had killed my own father. What a relief! I let our neighbor lady know I was there. I asked her to get our friends and come to Number 4, while I gathered the rest of our belongings. As I picked through the smashed remnants of what had once been our home, they advised me.

"You could get a job as a maid, but then what do you with Ruth?"

"Perhaps, she could hide her," another volunteered. If she closes the trunk, no one would know she's there."

"You could be a barmaid, but then, there would be more men just like your Da pawing you, and you'd still have the problem of Ruth."

"Ruth's a problem. You should put her in an orphanage, until you can find a job and get a place of your own."

"There's a brothel on Pearl Street. Maybe they need a maid. I hear those women make good money."

I thanked them all, kissed them, and left Number 4 behind.

Journal Entry VII
The Next Stop

Ruth:

It was an eternity before Margaret returned. My mind ran wild. I imagined Da there waiting for her, hurting her, maybe even killing her. Or maybe, someone had found him dead, and the police were going to arrest her. In any case, I was so afraid that I would never see her again. I couldn't concentrate. I watched the door. Each time it opened and it wasn't Margaret, my heart sank. The priest found me hiding in the shadows. He was a very kind man. He prayed and tried to comfort me. I told him that my sister had left me here, but that she would be back soon. I don't think he believed me. He said he would check on me again, before he went to the rectory for the night.

It was almost dark outside. I could tell because each time someone came inside the light was dimmer at the doorway. I prayed for Margaret's safety. I prayed for help for me to be able to be a good sister and a helper for her. I prayed for help from above.

The church door opened, and in rolled my pram carrying our food and belongings. There was Margaret smiling and searching the darkness for me.

Margaret:

It's me Ruth. I'm back. Where are you? Oh, there you are. Are you all right? We're going to be fine. Da is alive. He wasn't there, so I know he's alive. Let's eat.

There was a little bread left. It tasted so very good. After we'd eaten, it was time to decide what we should do. I told Ruth what our friends had advised. This was serious business, and we had to make the right choices.

When the priest returned to check on Ruth, he found both of us. We asked him if we could stay where we were until tomorrow. He assured us that we could. He left. Within a few minutes, he came back with hot tea and blankets for us. Warm tea had never tasted so good.

Ruth:

See Margaret, God is letting us know that we did the right thing. He is watching out for us. We slept that night with angels watching over us. We were safe.

Margaret:

Morning arrived on shiny wings of hope. The priest came by to say good morning. He brought more tea and biscuits. He was so nice. Ruth asked him if she could remain here a while longer. We told him I was going to see about a maid's job. It didn't seem right that Ruth should go with me, I told him, while I made application. He agreed. We didn't dare tell him the whole truth.

Birds were singing outside as I left the church headed for Pearl Street. It was a good sign. Ruth and I had discussed our options. We decided that wherever we could make the most money seemed to be the best idea. That was the brothel. It seemed the most reasonable thing for us to try first.

Once I located the House on Pearl Street, I went to the back door and spoke with the cook. At first she thought I was begging food, but when I explained that I was looking for work, she had her little boy run for the mistress of the house.

Mrs. Fitch owned the house. She was a tall, large woman with flaming red hair. She wore beautiful clothes. She wore lots of rouge and lipstick, but it looked pretty on her. She brought me inside and set me down by her desk in a big room with heavy drapes. It was noon, but her lamp was already burning to lighten up the darkness of the room.

"Where have you worked before?"

At home, I replied. I'm here from Ireland three years almost.

"Can you clean? I mean, were you taught properly how to clean?"

Oh, yes Mam, my Granny taught me, and everything was spotless.

"Do you know how to make a bed?"

Yes, Mam. With two sheets even.

"Are you a scaredy-cat if you hear loud talking or loud noises? Have you been around men who drink and raise hell?"

I'm not afraid of anything anymore. My Da tried to force himself on me, and I beat him with a skillet. It just tumbled out of my mouth like water from a split barrel! I had to hit him. I hit him until he stopped moving, but he was gone when I went back to get my things.

"How old are you girl?"

Thirteen, I fibbed. (I was fourteen, but instinctively I knew, younger was better with her).

"Are you broken in?"

Mam? Broken in?

"Did your Da stick his thing in you?"

No Mam, No, he didn't. I was surprised she would ask me such a thing.

"Are you sure you will be a hard worker? I need a good hard working girl."

Yes, Mam. I'm sure. I will work harder for you than any maid you've ever had. I promise I will.

"You'd better. I like your scrappiness. Sunday's noon until Monday afternoon, you're off. You will take all your meals here except on Sunday. You do as you're told to do. I have ten girls here, and you do what they need for you to do. You answer your bell night or day. Do you understand? Do you want to see your room?" Everything was very business-like.

Yes, Mam. I'd love to see my room, but how much exactly will I be making?

She laughed at that. "Business woman, are you?"

She quoted me a figure that was a few cents more than Da had given me to feed and clothe the three of us. I was excited, but I did my best not to look too happy. She told me that if I did extra things that I could sometimes earn more money from guests, but that I would have to give her half of whatever I got extra. She added with a raised eyebrow, "My rule is I trust you to split fairly. You do, and you're my friend. You don't, and you don't have a job or a friend. Understand?" I nodded that I understood. She instructed the cook to show me to my room. "Once you return from getting your things, there is plenty of work to do."

Sumee showed me my room. It was the highest room in the house. Actually, the room was in the attic. It was a perfect place. There were two windows; one had a view of the bay; the other, the city. Ruth would like that. It was big too. There was a bed that would serve us and a chamber pot with a lid. Yes, it would do nicely. Now, I thought to myself, I just have to smuggle Ruth in and go to work.

Ruth:

Margaret was all smiles. "I have work! We have a room all to ourselves, and you can see the big ships and the city all from the same place! We left the church.

As we approached the House on Pearl Street, we hid in an alley. Margaret took me out of the pram, and she packed me into the old trunk. Our extra things were in the bottom of the pram. The trunk with me inside was set atop our belongings. It was precarious at best, but it was the only way to get everything and me inside the house.

Sumee greeted Margaret at the back door, and she helped her to carry the pram up the stairs. Margaret told her she'd found the pram in an alley, and thought it would be good to move her belongings. (It was kind of true!) I wondered what she would have thought if she had known there was a seven year old girl inside that trunk! I had to giggle more than once, but they were making so much noise in their struggle with the pram on the steep stairs that they couldn't hear me.

Margaret was right. It was a beautiful room. It was big across where our bed stood. The two windows opposite each other were close enough that I could sit in the pram and see out of both. We would make it work for us. As long as no one knew I was there, we could save money and plan our next move, but it would take some time.

We were free. Or so we thought at the time.

Journal Entry VIII
Now, To Work

Margaret:

My day started very late in the morning usually, because the girls (as Mrs. Fitch called them) were up taking care of customers until the early morning hours. Around eleven, the bell started ringing for me. There was a rope attached to a bell on my wall. When the bell rang, I had to run downstairs to take care of whatever it was that was needed. The girls put a towel on the doorknob, so that I knew who had rung for me. I changed the sheets when the girls got up for the day and collected any towels or clothing that needed to be laundered. Then, I took the washing in big baskets downstairs to be tended by the laundress and her helper. Sumee and her little boy, Tad, fed Mrs. Fitch and the girls at the huge dining table in the room by the kitchen. I'd already eaten in the kitchen hours earlier. From my plate, I smuggled (in my apron pockets mostly) Ruth's half up to her. After the noon dinner that happened to be around one o'clock, cold snacks were delivered to each girl's room. They dressed for the evening. I busied myself running from room to room to make sure that I was doing whatever was needed. When things were slow in the daytime, I could spend time with Ruth, but I was always waiting for the bell to ring.

The evenings, on the other hand, were frenzied. I sat in a chair in the hallway outside the girls' rooms waiting to be called. If they needed towels, a clean sheet, more soap, more ice, more drinks, I was there on the spot. Some of the girls in the house treated me kindly. Some acted like they hated me. There were big girls and tiny girls. Some girls had big breasts; some, small. Some were pretty, but not all. There was no accounting why men picked the girls they did. When one of the guests would make advances to me, the girls would step in and take them away. Usually, they made the takeover sound like a joke, and they would leave together laughing. There was a lot of laughter in the house and a great deal of drinking. There was some meanness too. Mrs. Fitch had a big man (her companion, the girls gossiped and winked); he was very tall and broad. When some fellow drank too much or hurt one of the girls, it was him who took care of the problem. But, even then, unless the meanness was really bad, he finessed the man, and he left to come again another time.

Ruth:

It didn't take Margaret long to settle into her routine. She was busy all the time. For me, it was more difficult. I had gotten used to going out on the stoop to watch the children play. I had grown accustomed to being with women who were my friends and laughing and gossiping. Now except for Margaret, I was even more isolated than before we left Ireland. But there was no Da, and that was better. The worse thing was that there was no end in sight for my new style of life to change. Trying to focus on the future, when it seemed so very far away, just made me sad. Margaret was off every Sunday afternoon until Monday afternoon, but we couldn't go anywhere together. I was a prisoner. I was lonesome. The newness of the big room wore off. I spent my time trying to figure out a plan to get us into a different situation. Unfortunately, Margaret had to work so much that I found myself trying to organize a plan for our future by myself. I say that, however, I wasn't truly alone. I never was. Granny and Mother shored me up. They were my close companions. "It will work out" was the recurring message from them. I knew it would work out, but still, it was hard.

Margaret:

I knew it was tough on Ruth being so secluded. I felt bad about it. I spent as much time with her as I could, but I just couldn't be everywhere at once. My first pay day came. Without telling Ruth, I slipped out of The House taking the money with me. I wanted to buy her something special to cheer her up. The only shop open on Sunday morning was one for boats and sailors. It was meant to be that I was led to this store, because I found the most special gift of all for Ruth. It was a telescope. It was small, but it would be perfect for her. It was. When she saw it, her eyes lit up. It succeeded in opening her world again, if only just a crack.

Weeks drifted by. We spent our Sundays together playing card games that the girls had taught me. Early Monday mornings, I went to the shops to find food that would tide us over until the next pay day. As a treat, I would bring back discarded Sunday newspapers, and anything else that I thought Ruth might enjoy. She saved them for when I was gone. One week she asked me to get her a ledger and some pencils. I was very surprised to see her begin to keep books on how much money we had saved. Each week we decided together what we needed and how much we could spend. In her book she added what we saved, and we dreamed as young girls do of having a place of our own and a way to earn money without having to be separated, but for now, this would have to do.

Ruth:

Margaret taught me how to embroider and tat. Surprisingly, my tiny fingers were perfect for the intricate stitches. Thus, I began to make fine embroidered lace and linen handkerchiefs for the girls and Mrs. Fitch. They were beautiful and delicate, and not free! Margaret checked shops on Monday mornings to learn how much a fine handkerchief would cost. We sold ours for less. Everyone downstairs thought that Margaret was the one making them, and that was fine with me. They liked them so much that they special ordered more to match their new dresses, and we were able to charge a bit more for those.

All the work helped to pass my time. I felt useful for the first time in my life. I was actually making money for us! It was a grand feeling. I smiled more and hummed as I worked next to the window of my choice. Margaret would move me from window to window. She had to carry me now, because I couldn't walk anymore, not even a few steps. Just putting pressure on my legs to stand splintered them and broke them you see.

Margaret:

All of them wanted our hankies, and they often squabbled over them. Most of the girls were nice to me however, now that I had something they wanted. And yet, there were a few who were cruel and said terrible things to me. Three were awful to me. They were close friends. They didn't like me at all and did their best to make my life miserable. I couldn't understand it. I tried so hard to make everyone like me. They picked at me calling me "Maggie", because they knew I wanted to be called Margaret. I never wanted to be called Maggie by anyone, ever again. It brought back everything bad that had happened with Da. I hated the sound of it. I hated the thoughts that came with the name! One day after a particularly nasty encounter with the threesome, Sumee caught me cowering in a corner trying to stay out of sight.

"What you doin in dere Miss Margaret? You come on out. You got to stands up for you self wid dem girls! Til you does, dey gonna be even worse. Dey just 'fraid Miss Fitch gonna put one of dem out and move you in her room. Dat's all."

What do you mean? Me...one of the girls?

"Sure 'nuff. You prettier than de prettiest one of dem, and dey all knows it."

Me? I'm just a nothing little girl maid.

"You mo dan dat Miss Margaret!" And with that, she drug me out of my corner and pushed me to the front hallway depositing me in front of the big mirror. She made me look at myself.

What I saw surprised me! My shape was full and pretty even without all the fine corsets like the girls wore. I wasn't a child anymore. Sometime since we had come to Mrs. Fitch's I had turned into a young woman. My hair hung shiny about my face in little curls. Even gathered in a bun like I had to wear it for work, it was pretty. My skin was white and flawless; my eyes, startlingly green; my lips, pink and full. I looked like Mother. How had that happened? When? I stood in a trance. I look like Mother!

"Now, child no mo runnin way from dem girls. You plant you feets, and come on into you self."

Ruth:

Margaret opened the door, and asked "Do you see anything different about me?" I didn't have any idea what she was talking about. I looked her over. She was just Margaret to me.

She told me about Sumee talking to her and showing herself to her in the mirror.

"Ruth" she said with a hint of reverence, "I look just like Mother."

Of course you do. Didn't you know that? Looking at you is like seeing her!

Something changed that day with Margaret. She was still sweet. She was still practical, but she had a new walk. Her head was up instead of down all the time. Her shoulders were straighter. Her steps firmer.

Margaret:

I changed. The girls still made fun of me, but I think they began to think better of me. What was interesting to me was that for the first time in all the months that I'd been working in The House, it really didn't matter to me whether they liked me or not. No longer did I react in any way when they called me "Maggie". As a matter of fact, I pretended that they hadn't said a word. I did nothing they wanted, until they called me Margaret. It was funny. I overheard the terrible threesome whining to Mrs. Fitch about my lack of responsiveness to their needs. Peeking around the door frame, I watched as she looked each of them over head-to-toe, and then matter-of-factly said, "Did you ask Margaret or Maggie?" She was a smart woman, and nothing ever got past her…well, almost nothing. I did my work well. I was proud of what I did, but more importantly, I was proud of myself inside and even how I looked outside now.

Journal Entry IX
Venturing Out

Ruth:

Our little attic business was doing well, but a woman can only use so many handkerchiefs. We weren't selling so many anymore, and I found myself spending more time looking out at the city with my telescope and thinking.

There were so many people moving in the streets below. They looked like ants working a nest, as they moved in and out of shop doorways, and stopped and started at market stands to haggle over vegetables and fruits. As I was so engaged one afternoon, I clearly heard Granny say, "Why not sell those hankies to those fine folks down there?"

Why not? I couldn't think of a reason. Margaret and I discussed it, and she said that she couldn't believe we hadn't thought of it before. I laughed. We still hadn't thought about it. Granny did!

From some of the newspapers that Margaret had brought me to read, I had found pictures of the latest fashions. I thought if that was the way the dresses looked these days that I could do better. I certainly couldn't do any worse. Margaret bought me some paper and drawing charcoals, and I played around drawing pictures of dresses, until Margaret really like one of them in particular.

I began sewing a fancy dress for Margaret out of some of the girls' discarded dresses. I finished it over the weekend, so that Margaret could wear it on Monday, when she went to find us a buyer for our hankies. She looked absolutely beautiful dressed in her new and very first fine dress. I had made her a white linen embroidered collar and cuffs to match her fine handkerchief. Off she went very early into the streets of New York City looking like a right proper young woman.

She did look splendid, if I must say so myself.

Margaret:

I did it! What a day! I sold every handkerchief I had taken to the shops. The most amazing thing was that the shop owners treated me like a real lady. I kind of fibbed and told them that my husband had passed. Furthermore, I shared that I made these hankies to take care of my baby and me. It was just a little white lie, but there was some truth in it at that. Da was dead to us. Ruth was pretty much my baby. Of course, I dared not to ever say that to her! Halloo! I may be the worker, but she's the boss. The more I talked and smiled, the more orders I was given. And that wasn't all! Ruth was going to be wild.

I couldn't wait to get home to tell Ruth!

Ruth:.

We're in business, a real business, with real buyers! I clapped my hands and kissed Margaret's face and hands. We were so happy!

Margaret:

I saved the best for last for Ruth. One shopkeeper asked me where I purchased my dress. When I told her that I made it myself (I was getting good at fibs), she asked me if I would make one for her daughter. She would supply all the material and thread, but she wanted it to look just like mine. Besides that, she would pay more than ten times what one of our finest handkerchiefs went for! I didn't even have to ask Ruth. I already knew her answer. I took her daughter's measurements right there on the spot. Upon returning to the attic, I showed Ruth the brown paper package holding everything needed to make the dress! It was a day to celebrate, and we did.

I bought chocolate for us.

Ruth:

Margaret and I had our own little party, until it was time for her to go to work again with the girls. It was grand.

Within a month, we were sure that we had stumbled into a gold mine. The business was going great, and the shopkeeper was very happy with her daughter's dress. In fact, she was so happy that she told Margaret she would buy every dress we made as long as we didn't sell them to any other shops. Our savings grew by leaps and bounds. We gave thanks.

Journal Entry X
The Showdown

Margaret:

Mrs. Fitch called me to her desk. She didn't appear to be pleased. She wanted me to know what I was doing in my free time. It seemed that one of the customers had recognized me.

"He told me that you have been selling dresses and handkerchiefs to his wife and that you have a thriving business. Is it true Margaret? Have you been deceiving me? Have you been doing this behind my back? Have you forgotten our deal?"

I've always given you half if a customer gave me extra money for anything, Mrs. Fitch.

"I don't recall ever getting half of this dress and hanky business!" Her lips pulled tight in a line. "After all I've done for you, how could you cheat me like this?"

I didn't know what to say. It had never occurred to me that she might expect half. She'd not taken half of the handkerchief money when I sold them to her and the girls. She had seemed rather amused that I was trying to better myself. Now she was livid!

"I should throw you out of my house, you little cheat!" I was on the verge of tears. Suddenly, her whole attitude changed. "Come here Margaret, don't cry. There, there, maybe we can work something out."

Ruth:

Sure! She wanted to work something out! She wanted Margaret...body and soul. She told Margaret how beautiful she was, and that she had lots of inquiries from customers wanting to know when she would be ready for her first time. Telling Margaret how she had protected her, and how much she owed her for everything she had done for her, she said she would be willing to forget the dress business and putting her out, if she would let her sell her virginity to the highest bidder. Margaret, head hung low by then, told her she would think about it.

Margaret:

"That's right Margaret, you think about it, and let me know, if you want to be in a nice warm house with only the best clothes to wear, the best food to eat, and the best men making a fuss over you, or if you want to be in the street when the first snow flies, because that's about how long you have to decide. I've done everything for you. I have a right to have your loyalty!" And with that pronouncement, Mrs. Fitch turned her back on me, and I knew I was dismissed.

Why is it that when Good Fortune smiles, she always seems to get a few teeth knocked out!

Sumee had overheard the entire conversation. She caught me as I was going upstairs. She told me that she would help me no matter what I decided to do. She had truly become a dear friend to me.

The girls must have heard something about the talk I had with Mrs. Fitch, because even the nicer ones were acting weird. Nobody looked me in the eyes. They weren't asking me to help them very much either. I definitely noticed a difference.

The more I thought about the things she said to me, the more it sounded like Da telling me that he had a right to me! No one has a right to me! No one!

Sunday came around, and we knew we had to come to a decision. I had just turned sixteen. Ruth was nine. I had seen enough to know that I didn't want the kind of life the girls had. I wanted to have a husband and children of my own one day. I wanted to have a place where Ruth could have a big room of her own, a wheelchair, and a big soft bed to comfort her.

We could have a shop of our own. We could make dresses. We had been. Why couldn't we do it all the time? Did we have enough money to do that?

Ruth:

I began to look through newspapers to see how much it would take to rent a shop. Our rainy day had arrived. I added up on the ledger what I thought it would take for Margaret and me to feed ourselves, get the household things we would need, and the materials for the dresses. I even added the possibility of another person to work with us. We just might be able to do it. I prayed about it. I checked with Mother and Granny. They said "Do it. Do it right away."

Journal Entry XI
The Best Laid Plans

Margaret:

While Ruth did the sums and worked out the particulars in her mind and on paper, I had to keep working. Not only did I keep working, but I allowed Mrs. Fitch to think I was seriously considering her offer, but that I just needed a little more time to be ready. I never actually said "No", but I made sure that I never said "Yes" either. She just assumed that I would do what she wanted.

One week went by. Come my time off, I looked for a place for us to set up shop. They wanted too much money. A woman alone, a well-dressed woman at that, and the men thought I was an easy mark. If they didn't want too much money, they wanted fringe benefits, and that just wasn't going to happen!

Ruth knew exactly how much we could spend, and I knew that I couldn't go above that limit. She was accounting for three months for us to sew enough dresses before we could officially open our shop. I kept looking. It was tiring and very disappointing.

The third week went by without an agreement. Mrs. Fitch was beginning to press me. "Too much time Margaret, and you make it all more than it is. It's just a business deal." I was feeling desperate. It was all on me to find the place, and it had to be soon.

Sumee had enough of watching my erratic behaviors. Early one morning at breakfast, she turned to me and said, "What you doin Miss Margaret? Is you gonna be one of de girls, or is you getting out of dis place?" I was under such a strain, I broke down crying. It was then that I did what I never thought I would.

I put my finger to my lips and motioned for her to follow. Up to the attic I went. Sumee followed. Once inside the room, she saw Ruth and gasped in surprise! "Who be dis Miss Margaret?" I introduced her to Ruth and explained to her how we had come to be here. She couldn't believe that Ruth had been here all this time without her knowing. The three of us talked, until there was no more time for talking. Lunch had to be served. My work had to proceed. "Let me think on this," she said.

Ruth:

After lunch was served to Mrs. Fitch and the girls, Margaret had to go about her normal duties. Sumee came up to see me. She was a delightful woman and very smart. It was obvious to me that she loved Margaret.

"Not so many maids come here and don't wind up one o' de girls here or somewhere else. Yo'r sister is special."

I know. I'm worried for her. Do you have any ideas what we should do? We haven't found a place yet, and Mrs. Fitch is becoming more and more demanding. I'm afraid.

"Don't you be 'fraid, Miss Ruth. We think o' something." And it was then that we conspired to make changes. Sumee and Tad were going with us when we left. "I can cook and clean," she said. "I a fast learner at most anything you might need. My Tad can run errands. He a good boy, respectful, and know his place." The deal was struck.

On faith, she packed up our belongings. She took them downstairs to her room. On faith, I let her.

"I find us a place to stay, til we get de shop. I do it, when I go to de market dis afternoon." That very day, she found the four of us a small room. I gave her the money to pay in advance for a week. When Margaret came up to check on me later in the evening, I explained it all. Sumee was moving her belongings and ours right away. Once done, she would come back, and she and Tad would hide me in the trunk and carry me downstairs on top of the pram and out the kitchen door. If anyone saw her, she would say that she had discarded clothes that she was taking to the church for the orphans, and that she would be right back. But, of course, she would not be right back. I told her the cross streets, but the actual apartment number, I would leave on the window sill. When Margaret's duties were over, she was to follow, and we would be done with The House on Pearl Street.

Margaret:

It was a good plan.

Close to midnight, Mrs. Fitch summoned me to her room. She couldn't have been nicer to me. "How pretty you look tonight, Margaret. I hope you're not too tired, because I have a surprise for you. Follow me."

We walked to the room next to hers. It was a big bedroom...bigger than all the girls had, but not as big as Mrs. Fitch's room. It was only used for rich customers. It was beautiful with fancy wall hangings and a goose down comforter. There atop the bed was a delicate white dress with a very low neckline and dainty little blue flowers in the hem and sleeves. "This is for you Margaret. This is your coming-out dress."

I thanked her stuttering. My face flushed red. She touched my cheek and told me to get in the bathtub standing in the corner of the room. "I fixed it myself just for you. It was sweet smelling salts in it."

But what about the girls, Mrs. Fitch? They'll be needing me.

"Don't be silly. I hired another maid today, and she will be tending them. You won't be a maid after tonight...in many ways." She smiled her sweetest smile.

I felt sick to my stomach. How was I going to get out of this? Well, I thought, best to play along, and at my first opportunity, run. So, that's exactly what I did. I began "oohing and aahing" over the dress and the room and bath. Instead of leaving me to bathe and dress, however, Mrs. Fitch stayed and began to help me undress. She was enjoying this too much. She eyed my body as I tried my best to maintain my modesty. She seemed to think that was funny. She clucked and told me that I would get over my shyness and not to worry.

"I picked you a very nice gentleman. He's an older man, and he has his eye set on you since the very first time he saw you over six months ago. He has assured me that he will be kind and take care with you, so don't be afraid." She handed me a drink of whiskey. I took it and sipped it slowly while in the bath. On the sly, I poured a little of it into the bath. I had no idea how it would affect me, but I knew I would need my wits about me to get out of this.

I put on the dress, and indeed, it was beautiful. It showed off every curve to full advantage. Once on, she heaped compliments on me while stroking my arms and back. I was calmer now. She began to brush my hair commenting on how she could see the flush of readiness creeping up my neck and into my cheeks. I could see it as well in the fancy mirror, but I am quite sure that it was not the same flush she thought she was seeing. Mine was all about the urgency to run! There was a knock on the door. The big man, Mrs. Fitch's companion, told her he needed to see her. She didn't seem pleased to be leaving me, but she went. Now was my opportunity. I waited until I heard their footsteps moving away. I went to the door and peeked out. Two girls were gossiping in the hallway, so I had to wait until they left. It seemed like hours, but it was really only minutes. I slipped from the room and made my way up the hallway, downstairs, and through the kitchen. I looked for Sumee, but she wasn't there. Hastily, I continued up the stairs to the attic. I'd made it. I opened the door.

Ruth! Ruth! I called out.

"Hello Maggie," Mrs. Fitch sneered. I cringed. "Do you think I don't know what goes on in my own house? It's all over! You will do what I want, or you will never see Ruth again! Do you understand?"

I took in the room. Thrown against the wall was the pram. I saw several pieces of Ruth's clothes strewn on the floor. There was her trunk with the padded lining ripped out. It was lying open on the floor. Oh, Ruth, my Ruth! What happened here? No, no, no, I moaned.

Oh please Mrs. Fitch, please don't hurt Ruth. I'll do whatever you want. I promise. Just please, please, tell me where she is. Is she all right?

"She's in a safe place, but you won't likely ever see her again, unless you take care of business!" With that she took hold of one arm and the big man took the other. With one mighty shove, they pushed me towards the door. "Get back downstairs! Get your hair and face fixed now!"

I went.

I washed my face and brushed my hair. The worse had come to pass. I had waited too long to move us to safety. If only I had paid more money for the shop, I could have gotten us out of here. Where was Ruth? What had they done to her when they moved her? She most certainly had broken bones. She was in pain somewhere in this house and terrified or worse! If only we had run away from here when Mrs. Fitch first made her demands. If only I had been braver. If only I could have taken better care of Ruth. If only…If only…and then, it was too late.

Mrs. Fitch arrived with her companion carrying several decanters and ice. She informed me that my benefactor was here and impatient to see me. "You 'will' do whatever he tells you to do. You will be a good girl. Do you understand?" I nodded my head that I understood. She motioned for her companion to stand guard outside the door to the room to "protect her from herself."

The knock on the door…my heart sank. I would do whatever was required of me. I would obey, so that Ruth and I could survive. Mrs. Fitch opened the door, and the doorway was filled with a heavy-set man. He was balding and had piggy eyes that he squinted in appraisal of me. He let out a sigh and shook his head affirmatively to Mrs. Fitch. Following his belly into the room, he smiled at me. I was sickened. I forced a weak smile in return. That was the introduction. Mrs. Fitch left the room.

The man sat in the chair by the bed and motioned for me to come to him. He took my hands in his stroking my arms, my neck, my face. "Mrs. Fitch tells me your name is Maggie, and that you are ready for me. Is that right Maggie me girl?" I began to cry. I couldn't help it. I sobbed. He pulled me into his lap. It was like Da had hold of me again, only this time I knew that I couldn't escape. Ruth's life depended on me. The more I tried to stop crying, the harder I cried. The faster he began to breathe. He liked it. He liked me afraid and crying. Oh God, please help me.

"Get on the bed" he ordered gruffly. Half stumbling, I backed to the bed. He rose from the chair and pushed his belly into me, until he was on top of me sweating and panting. He spread my legs with his knee, and something happened to me. It was as if I left my body. I wasn't thinking. I wasn't seeing him. The room disappeared. He disappeared.

In the distance, I heard a door open and close. I lay there, and gradually I regained my senses. My body ached. The once beautiful white dress was torn. The skirt front and back were spotted with blood. My neck hurt, and when I had the strength to look into the mirror I saw why. There were reddish purple fingerprints collaring my neck. Bite nip marks dotted my breasts now exposed from the ripped fabric. On my wrists were rings of bruises. I must have been tied at one point. My girl parts hurt worse of all. Gingerly, I raised the stained skirts to look at myself. What I saw made me dizzy. I thought I might puke. He had brutalized me. He must have used me for a long time. I could barely walk without crying out in pain. I stripped off the clothes and lowered myself into the cold used bath water. I scrubbed as hard as I could trying to wash the filthiness and pain away. There was not enough soap and water. There would never be. Daylight peeked at me through the drapes. Dressing myself in my maid clothes, I tried to make myself as presentable as was possible. Brushing my hair was even painful, but I managed.

Mrs. Fitch opened the bedroom door. "Well, how's our woman this fine morning?" She was all foul smiles. "Did you enjoy yourself?"

Glazed eyes stared back at her.

"Answer me!" she demanded.

Where's Ruth? I want Ruth. She needs me.

"Well, isn't that too bad. Get used to it Maggie! You could have had it so much better. You did this to yourself. I lost money on you, and it's your own fault. I knew you and Sumee were up to something yesterday, when you took her up to your room. Now she's gone, and you're here. You and your precious Ruth! I had a fine gentleman just for you, but when I found out you were up to something, I changed my mind and you got what you got! You will be ready to do whatever and with whomever tonight and every night, until you are right…I mean right! And until you are right, nothing will change. Don't ask me about Ruth again, until you are right! Understood?"

I ducked my head. Yes, Mam, I understand.

I was moved to one of the smaller rooms. Now I was like all the other girls. No one spoke to me. The guard, the big man, was at my door. I did what I was told and after four days, I learned what no one should ever have to learn. I could laugh. I could make jokes about the marks on my body. I would wink and say "Oh, we just got carried away. It was so good!" I found the faster I made my customers feel good, the faster they left, and the happier Mrs. Fitch was. When the next Sunday rolled around, I no longer had a guard at my door, but I was pretty sure that I was still being watched. Mrs. Fitch promised me that if I stayed a good girl and made her lots of money that I would soon be reunited with Ruth. "We'll make arrangements for her to stay with you, but only if you behave."

I behaved, and I behaved, and then, I behaved some more.

Journal Entry XII
Time to Move On

Ruth:

It had been almost three weeks since Sumee, Tad and I made our escape. Sumee had seen Mrs. Fitch's man looking in the kitchen from the dining room, as she went up the stairs to bring me out. She knew he would tell Mrs. Fitch, so they moved as quickly as they could. The pram was too unwieldy and would take too much time. That big man was a mean one. He would cause trouble if he caught us trying to leave. He would kill us all. Once Sumee ripped the padding from the trunk, she wrapped it around me, rolled me in the floor rug, and slung me over her shoulder. We hurtled down the stairs and out into the street.

Where was Margaret? I was frantic and so was Sumee. We had a sleepless night waiting for Margaret, but she didn't come. As best we could, under the circumstances, we set up our room. Days passed, a week, more, and so slowly. For something to do I began to teach Sumee how to sew. She was right; she was a fast learner. She used scraps from Margaret's fine dress. I thought it would be a good thing for her to do something small to learn. Sumee's first dress was a fancy dress for me. With my dress done, we started sewing in earnest. When Margaret found the shop and came for us, we could move and start selling our wares. I couldn't even allow myself to think that I might never see her again! Granny and Mother told me "Hold fast. You can endure." I didn't know if that meant Margaret would be coming soon, or if Margaret was dead and I'd never see her again. We kept ourselves busy sewing as if we had a deadline.

Sumee took good care of me, and Tad was a sweet boy, but no one could take the place of my sister. I wanted my Margaret. I had never been without her…not even one day in my whole life until now. I needed her. I wanted her. I was lost without her, but I had to be strong.

When the first week stretched into the second, the third, and the fourth, and still no Margaret, something had to be done. Since no respectable landlord would make a deal for renting a shop to a black woman, free or slave, I had to do it. I had to find us a shop, but first things first. I sent Sumee out into the city to find me a wheelchair. She tried to find a child sized one, but the only one available was an adult chair. Once again, lots of padding had to be wrapped everywhere to protect me. I was still suffering from a broken foot that happened during our escape. The chair was a huge unwieldy contraption, but with a thickly padded belt around my mid section, I could sit upright. It certainly didn't look like the ones advertised in the newspaper, but it would do.

Sumee packed a few of our new dresses in a suitcase that Tad could manage. She dressed me in the dress she'd made. She'd done a fine job. The design was mine. The thing is that I felt on me that it must look horrible. I could hide my body beneath the blossoms of material, but there was little I could do about my face and hands. My face was skull-like; my body skeletal and deformed. My hair was terrible. It was short unlike Margaret's, and it was a dull and lifeless straight black. It had to be short to keep it clean. Sumee saw me fretting. I tugged at it like I could somehow make it longer or prettier. "Don't worry Miss Ruth, I fix it." She pulled out one of my collars and a hanky, and she fashioned me a bonnet. How very clever! What a Godsend she was.

I had to find us a shop. Money was precious, and it was dwindling. If we didn't find something soon, we would be penniless.

We formed a little parade down the streets. Tad led the way with the suitcase full of clothes. I was next…a tiny vision of high fashion snug in my wheelchair, and lastly came Sumee struggling to push me. We inspected shop after shop. One landlord after another rejected us. I was exhausted and about to give up, when who should I see on the street walking towards us…the Priest, the kind one from the church where Margaret and I had hidden so long ago. He recognized me despite my finery (what a surprise!), and he came to greet me. I told him what I was trying to find. He told us to follow him.

By nightfall we returned to our little room. We had a shop. The priest talked to the landlord (and I suspect worked on his Christian charity), because the man rented the shop to us for even less than I had expected to pay. There were two floors. We could live and do our sewing on the top floor and have our office and displays and fitting rooms on the bottom. We were so excited and relieved, but our joy was tainted by not being able to share the news with Margaret.

Margaret, Margaret, I called out in my sleep. She was always in my thoughts and prayers.

Sumee decided to take the matter of our missing Margaret into her own hands. She asked a friend to visit the laundress of The House. Since Mrs. Fitch treated the laundress very badly and paid her little, there was no love lost between them. It was the laundress who told Sumee's friend that the new maid said that she had replaced Margaret who was now one of the girls and living in high style.

"She's laughing it up and having a good time," the new maid reported to the laundress.

Sumee told me all about it. She ventured that maybe for money, the laundress would deliver a note to Margaret. I thought it was a good idea. I wrote a note and enclosed some money for Sumee's friend to give to the laundress. I gave Sumee money for her friend as well. When the laundress was asked to pass the note, she said she would, but that she would need more money to give to the maid. "I don't like her very much, and I don't really trust her. She seems a bit too attracted to that way of life for me, but I think if you give her enough money, she'll deliver the note. She's a greedy one I think, likes the money. Besides, I can't go in the house. I ain't allowed. The maid though, she's there all the time. Make it good money for her, because if she gets caught, she ain't gonna have no job." That made sense, so I made up another envelope with more money for the maid. I had done all I could; so had Sumee. Bless her. At least we knew that Margaret was alive and well. It had been six weeks since we left. There was nothing to do now but wait some more and pray.

Margaret:

I saw an envelope slide under my door.

"**Dear Margaret, I am well and with our dear friends. I know something terrible has happened to you. I am enclosing money in case you need it to pay someone to help you get out of there. We are where we discussed for now, but if you can't come soon, go see the Priest from the alcove, and he will bring you to us. I love you. Come as soon as you safely can. Your loving sister, Ruth**"

Glory Be!!! Ruth is alive. She's safe. I don't know how, but she is. I could barely contain myself. God is good. Ruth is safe!

Journal Entry XIII
Our Time to Move

Ruth:

It was a very long night that first night after the envelope was sent. The next night was even longer. Did she get the envelope, or was it intercepted? The next day was Sunday. I hoped against hope that she would walk into the room, but it didn't happen. I was devastated, but she would come one day. I was holding fast like I'd been told to do.

Sumee and Tad spent Friday and Saturday scrubbing the shop and making it presentable. On Sunday they packed our meager belongings, and they began carrying our goods to the shop. By Monday, all that was left was our bedding. Sumee dressed me in my fancy dress and put me into my wheelchair. While she and Tad toted the last of our things, I sat reading Granny's Bible in the hallway.

I heard running footsteps; the door opened. Margaret rushed into the building! She all but fell over me. Never was a reunion sweeter! Thank you God!

But I saw her bruised face! She was a mess. No time to lose! I all but shouted, "Push this chair! Let's go! We have a shop now Margaret. Hurry! Let's go! We have a future. Get us out of here! No one will ever hurt you again. I'll kill them first!

We moved as one through the streets of New York, but this time we had somewhere to go that was "our somewhere." Run Margaret!

Margaret:

Ruth, Ruth, I can't believe it! I'm here! You're here! Oh Ruth!

Ruth:

I feel the same, I yelled. Push faster! We've got to get you off the streets. Her clothes were dirty, rumpled, torn. Her hair was a mess. Her eyes were a deep bruised blue; her lip split. But she was here with me again.

Hurry! Margaret, faster! Faster! Run!

Margaret:

I am, I whispered gasping in short little grunts.

Around the corner, down six streets; another corner...I could barely catch my breath. Something was sticking in my side. I hurt, but I kept moving. The sight of Ruth and her voice hurrying me frantically kept me going. The stones hurt my bare feet. I kept going. They could be coming. I kept going, and then, I fell. The wheelchair careened forward and turned over. I heard a scream.

Ruth:

It wasn't me screaming, nor was it Margaret. Margaret fell and didn't move.

It was Sumee running towards us screeching at the top of her lungs.

She righted my chair, and then she went to Margaret. People stopped around, but no one offered to help.

"Tad," Sumee barked. "You stays right here by Miss Margaret. Don't you let nobody touch her! I be right back!"

In a dead run, she wheeled me down the street and into our shop. Lifting me out of my chair, she said "I be right back Miss Ruth. You lay right here. I be right back with Miss Margaret."

Bless her heart, she took my chair and wheeled the still unconscious Margaret to me. She laid her on the floor next to me, and then brought blankets for us. She sent Tad running for water and salve. As soon as he returned, she sent him to fetch her friend to help.

Everything will be all right. God will take care of us Margaret. Can you hear me? I'm here Margaret. I'm going to take care of you. We're all going to take care of you. Oh, Margaret, hold fast. Listen to me. I need you. You're my strength. Margaret! Don't leave me! Margaret!

I pleaded with her to hear me…to move. I prayed out loud. I begged Mother and Granny to talk to her and tell her to come back to me. God, Help Us!

Don't die Margaret. Please, please, don't die.

Journal Entry XIV
Margaret's Escape

Margaret:

The door to my room was viciously slammed open against the wall. Before I could move, Mrs. Fitch was all over me, grabbing the envelope with the money and note from me. Her eyes were huge as she read the piece of paper. Stuffing the money down the front of her dress, she came at me like a wild, crazy woman. She was spitting vile obscenities within an inch of my face.

"I told you I know everything that goes on in my house!" Mrs. Fitch was totally out of control. She yanked my hair and slapped my face. "Stand up you ungrateful whore!" She knocked me down twice, as she hit me in the face with her fists. I pulled myself to my feet just in time to feel the weight of her fist in my stomach. I fell to the floor trying to catch my breath. She kicked me…again and again. When I stopped moving and tried to roll myself into a ball, she straddled me. She grabbed my hair and began to slam my head repeatedly onto the floor. Somewhat out of breath, she stood up and began to kick me again.

This time I grabbed her foot. Startled and off balance, she fell to the floor backwards. I pulled myself erect and tried to get out of the room. She grabbed my skirts and pulled me back down to the floor. I panicked!

This woman would either kill me or make me wish I was dead, but she wasn't going to stop, until she was too tired to hit me again. Fueled by her rage, I might be dead by then! Now that I knew Ruth was safe, there was no reason for me to buckle down to her. I was back on my knees again, while she struck at me with her fists. I grabbed at a small table. The pitcher and bowl on it crashed to the floor. I used the table to get to my feet. With all the strength I could muster, I reached for the nearest thing and swung it.

The chamber pot slammed into the side of her head. She lay still. She and I both were splattered in night soil. I took my chance, and I ran just as I was. I ran! I felt no pain, only the blood pumping in my temples. I had to get to Ruth. I had to get out of here, before she came to or someone came to help her. I ran!

People couldn't believe their eyes…this half dressed barefoot woman running wildly down the street. They moved aside probably thinking I was an escapee of an asylum.

I didn't stop. One more block to go. I didn't hear anyone running behind me, but that didn't mean that they weren't following me. Help me God. Help me get to Ruth.

Bursting through the door, I practically fell into Ruth's lap. She was sitting in her wheelchair, as if she was waiting for me! I kissed her. I tried to speak. I couldn't stop touching her face and hands. It was really her. I was here. I'd made it. Ruth told me to push her chair. We were out the door tears streaming down our faces. We were moving as quickly as I could run. The street turned from oyster shell to cobble stones. The chair was hopping the stones and slamming into others. My toes were screaming.

Ruth yelled "Run faster"! My side hurt so badly. With every short breath, I felt a sticking pain, but I didn't stop running. It was really Ruth. I was here with Ruth. I called her name out, because I wanted to hear her answer me. I needed to know this was not a dream!

I have no idea other than the good Lord pushing me, how I made it all that way, but Ruth would say "faster", and I kept moving.

Then I fell. The last thing I recall was hearing a scream followed by a crunch as the side of my head hit a pavement stone. Blackness enveloped me.

Ruth:

Sumee and her friend took Margaret and me upstairs and put us side-by-side in our bed. They were so tender with her. Tad ran up and down the stairs helping to bring things to care for Margaret.

He brought up water for Sumee and her friend to wash her bruised and battered body. Except for his big eyes, you would have thought he toted bloody water and torn and filthy clothing every day. Margaret had lost a lot of weight since we'd seen her last. She was pitiful with her darkening swollen eyes and the deepening bruises forming all over her. I put the salve on her face, but I couldn't stop shaking. Sumee chided, "Now, now Miss Ruth, you just hold her hand and talk to her. We do all de rest. Maybe she jez sleep a while. She be aw right." Margaret's breathing was ragged. She was limp moving only when moved.

I talked to her. I said all the things to her that I would have said had she had the time to hear me in years past. How sad it was that she always worked so hard to take care of us. There had never been enough time for me to tell her how much I loved her and appreciated everything she did for me. I thanked her for never hitting me or leaving me behind, when it would have been the easier thing to do. I thanked her for all her sacrifices. I promised her that our lives would be different if she would just come back. I was nine, but I was smart way beyond my years, and I could do a lot more things now to take some of the load off of her. I promised I would. I said many more things as the night closed around us. I told her how lucky we were to have each other, and that she had to come back, because our lives would be better from now on. I called her name over and over. I prayed. I fell asleep exhausted with my hand on top of hers. Things would be fine. She would wake; things would be fine.

Margaret:

I drifted in a golden light. It was warm and peaceful. There was love all around me. I wasn't alone. Someone was there with me, but I couldn't see them. I felt them. There was no time, no urgency in this most comforting place. We moved as the wind moves over the tops of greenery in Ireland. I floated upwards. There floating I saw Mother and Granny. Within that illumination, I knew there were others, but I couldn't make out their faces. How beautiful! Someone moved towards me all dressed in white.

Behind him were swirling rays of multicolored lights, but around him was a glow of pink, gold and white lights. I felt (rather than heard) "Ruth is waiting for you. You have much to do. Go back."

I didn't want to go. I wanted to stay with Mother and Granny. I wanted to stay wrapped round in this exquisite and safe love. I pleaded. Very softly, I heard a voice saying "You may stay if you choose." But in that instant, I knew that I was going back. I heard Ruth calling my name. How could I leave and not tell her how wonderful it was here. I felt myself withdrawing.

The early morning light filtered through the small windows. I peeped through the slit in one of my damaged eyes. How beautiful dawn is. It's a taste of what heaven is like…a blessed reminder of our real home. I lay there feeling my body come excruciatingly alive bit by bit. From my throbbing head to my agonizing breaths, life returned on the wings of pain. It was so difficult to breathe, but I knew that I would do whatever I needed to do. I knew what it was like on the other side now, and I would go back there someday.

Ruth? I called her name, and instantly, I saw her tiny face above mine. She stroked my forehead tenderly.

Ruth:

Margaret? Oh, Margaret, thank you for coming back. Thank you. I love you so much. Please don't ever leave me again.

Margaret:

I won't leave you ever again Ruth. I love you too. I'll always take care of you. With that I fell asleep, and I slept deeply.

Ruth:

Margaret slept around the clock, but it was real sleep this time, and she would heal. Mother and Granny reassured me of that. God answered prayers.

Her body was a mess. Handfuls of hair had been pulled from her head, but hair would grow back. Her face would heal. I worried about her breathing, but Sumee wrapped some long pieces of fabric around her ribs. She said it would help her "be all better soon". Her feet were pathetic. They were cut from running on the oyster shells of Pearl Street, and she was missing several toenails, but her feet too would heal. We would just have to keep them clean and have her stay off them.

Little did I know that keeping Margaret in bed and off her feet would be the easiest part of her healing.

Margaret:

I awoke the next day hungry and thirsty. Mush never tasted so good, but after a few bites, I realized that I wasn't really hungry at all. I was glad to be with Ruth and Sumee and Tad and hear their chatter, but I couldn't seem to focus on what they were saying. Abrupt noises and sudden movements (no matter how small or well meant) thrust me into a strange place that demanded I run or hide!

I heard bits and pieces of how Ruth acquired the shop. I heard the story of how they ran away with Ruth slung over Sumee's shoulder. They had done well, and they had done it without me. Ruth was overjoyed and full of hope for our future. She didn't seem to be able to stop showering me night and day with talk about the business and what was ahead.

I didn't want to hear it. Well, I did, but I didn't. I wanted to sleep. I wanted to fly away and see that wonderful place again, but I couldn't. I dozed off in the middle of conversations. I told them only that Mrs. Fitch made me believe that she had Ruth hostage. When Ruth asked for more information, I would reply "Not now". What I was thinking was "Not ever". I didn't want to talk about anything that had gone on in The House on Pearl Street. I didn't want to ever think about it. An odd thing happened, the more I tried not to think about it, the more prominent it became in my mind! It pushed out everything else…all the joy of being back with Ruth. And so I slept as much as I could. And when I couldn't sleep, I went to a safe place in my head to keep from thinking.

Ruth:

Sumee gently told me "Don't worry, she be fine. She just healin, and dat take time." But I did worry. She wasn't right. Not even close. We'd been through bad times before, and she had bounced back and been happy again. She couldn't even manage a smile any more, and this bothered me the most. I prayed and begged God to send her back to me so much that I hadn't considered what it would be like for Margaret to come back. I guess in my selfishness I had just thought of how awful life for me would be without her...not how terrible life would be for Margaret living with what she had been through! I did everything I could to make her waking times pleasant, but nothing seemed to help.

Margaret:

There was a lot of sewing going on, but I didn't help. At first, it was hard for me to try to sit up, because of the sticking when I breathed, so I was excused.

Sumee and Ruth began sewing early in the morning, and they didn't stop until an hour or so before dark. A month passed. I didn't even know it, until Ruth mentioned it one night. It's time you get up and help us sew Margaret. What do you think? How about tomorrow? It'll do you good."

LEAVE ME ALONE! I shouted at her. I'd never raised my voice to Ruth. As soon as the words were out of my mouth, I felt terrible. I couldn't say I was sorry though. I didn't want to get out of bed. I was too tired. I didn't feel well. Couldn't she see that? I just wanted to be left alone. Ruth withdrew into herself. I was left alone.

A few days later while Ruth was downstairs, Sumee came to me with a scowl on her face. "It time you up. 'Nuff of dis!" I knew she was right. I let her help me dress. We went downstairs together. I began to sew. That night when it was time to stop and go upstairs, Ruth remained with Tad. She was working on the books. Tad was sweeping up. I knew Ruth didn't want to talk to me. She was still all but silent to me since my outburst. I'd hurt her. I was ashamed, but not repentant. Sumee helped me up the stairs. I thought she was going to give me something to eat before she returned to Ruth, but I was mistaken.

She had something else on her mind. There was no supper. Sumee put me to bed, and she sat next to me. "I knows you thinkin nobody know what you done been through Miss Margaret, but I knows. I been through something like you. You scared. You mad. You hurt. You shut you eyes and it happen all over ag'in. Ain't dat right? You hear someone on de stairs or you hears a door open, and you done think dey comin fer you ag'in. Well, I ain't goin to tell you bad things never goin to happen ag'in, but I is goin to tell you, it time fer you to get on past it, live ag'in, find you self. You done did it once or twice already, so you knows how to do it." With that she patted my cheek and said, "We love you; you jez needs to love you self. You didn't want none of dat to happen. We he'p you wid our love if you lets us, but we can't he'p if you shut us out." With that she turned and went downstairs.

I had to think about this. She was right. I couldn't just let Mrs. Fitch and those others win. I'm stronger than that. I got away. I'm here. If I stay in this bed, or even this shop, and never get back to being me, then they've won, and I might as well still be in The House on Pearl Street.

The words were easy. The work on getting back to me was the hardest I'd ever done.

Journal Entry XV
Our Grand Opening

Ruth:

It took time for Margaret. She was not herself for quite a while, but little by little, she emerged a stronger butterfly and even more beautiful than she was before. Sumee and and I made sure that she had time to gather herself together. We carried the load of the shop. Margaret decided that she would attend to pattern cutting and piecing the materials together. This worked for her. She was with us, but still separate with her thoughts. Before long, she was taking a keener interest, and the day I caught her making a little joke, and she laughed out loud, I knew that she would make it all the way.

We discussed our plans for the shop as we were sewing. Each week we put a new dress in the window. Interest was growing. A little sign on the door read "Opening Soon", but it wasn't until two weeks before that door came open that we put our official opening date. We agreed to supply our original shopkeeper who had faith in us with two special dresses a month for the next year. She was pleased. "If folks don't want mine, I'll send them on to you." We were set.

On the day of our Grand Opening, we had a good stock of dresses laid by, or so we thought. We had no idea that so many people would show up! There was a steady stream of customers and nosey rosies from early morning to late night the first day, and the next, and each day thereafter. Margaret and I were in the shop together. She flattered the women, helped them get fitted, and took measurements. The dresses sold themselves. I took the payments and orders and kept the books. Sumee treated the customers to tea and little cakes. Tad carried their packages home for them if they bought straight from our stock. We almost immediately had a booming business!

What brought so many to our door! I knew our dresses were exceptional, but it wasn't just the wares. I think it was Margaret who ran near naked (in our day's standards) and then passed out, and me and my peculiarities. (I have always been a curiosity.) Every old biddy who'd heard the gossip came. The thing is…once they met us and saw what we were like, and how beautiful our goods were, they were sold on us. They told their friends who told their friends, and in a short while, we received invitations to parties and teas just like the rich people. For once, people saw us for who we are instead of who they thought we might be. Dreams do sometimes come true.

They came true in multiple ways. After a week, I showed the books to Margaret. It was clear to us both that we needed help, or we would not be able to keep up with all the dress-making. Sumee agreed. We hired her friend who had helped with getting word to Margaret and the laundress. They were both fast learners. We had them cutting out material in no time at all. That wasn't enough however.

Margaret went back to the house where we had lived in Number 4. She sought out the good women who had befriended us so long ago, and two of them came to work for us. How wonderful life was! A business making money, friends at our side; what more could we ask! We were helping others and creating beauty in the world. It couldn't get much better than this, but it did!

Margaret began to bloom.

Margaret:

We earned ourselves a wonderful reputation. Before long mothers asked for help with their daughters' trousseaus. They wanted something different for their daughters…something that no one else had. We could do that! Ruth was nothing, except a one-of-a-kind designer! She enjoyed creating wedding gowns and evening dresses. It was fun for her. We had quite a mix of customers, from the very wealthy to the ordinary people like us. It soon became clear that we needed more space. We spoke with the landlord. He saw the success of our business and was more than willing to rent us his adjoining shop. He and his workers knocked out the walls. Our friend the Priest was very proud of him and his benevolence. We were pretty pleased ourselves. We hired more workers. Unlike so many of the other shops, we paid a fair wage. We knew firsthand how difficult it is for a woman to make it on her own. As a result, we had loyal and cheerful staff.

Ruth:

People still stared at us and pointed when we went out, but they also waved and spoke kindly. The women smiled and nodded; the men tipped their hats. Who would have thought that this day would have ever come? Margaret grew more beautiful each day.

It was a rare day that men came to our shop, but it did happen. Fathers and brothers came with their wives and mothers and sisters. One of those days remains a special memory.

Margaret:

I can see him now, his sister's hand on his arm. He was tall and slim. When he spoke to her, he bent over and talked softly into her ear. His hair was blond and shiny. A lock of it fell over his eyes as he bent to her. With a pitch of his head, it returned to its place. What blue eyes! And he had a pouty lower lip that accentuated white, straight teeth. What a handsome man, I thought. He caught me looking at him and smiled. I could feel the blood rushing into my cheeks. Trying to ignore his twinkling eyes, I turned quickly to his mother and began talking about her requests.

The threesome left. I was relieved.

The following week, he and his sister returned to pick up the dresses made for their mother. A few days later, they returned for his sister's dresses. Ruth talked to him, as he paid the bills for both. I envied her doing the books for the first time ever.

Ruth:

He was a polite gentleman. Margaret was smitten. It was obvious to me. She couldn't stop blushing when he was in the shop. What she didn't know was that he had inquired about her of me. Who was she? How long had she been selling for me? Where was she from? Was she married? I answered every question. I was amused that he thought I was the owner of the shop and my older sister was my employee, but I kept that to myself. It made me laugh.

On his next visit, I had questions for him…my own and Margaret's. His name was Alexander Morrison. He was twenty-one, unmarried and studying to be a lawyer. In a year when he finished his education in New York City, he was returning to Chicago where his family lived. His mother and sister had come for a visit.

Margaret:

He came again and again, and I could not stop blushing when I caught him looking at me. At last he spoke directly to me. He asked me for a glass of water. I could barely hold the glass to fill it. He spoke of the weather. He said how very much his mother and sister loved our clothing. Then, it was as if we both ran out of things to say. He left.

I thought I had made a fool of myself and that I would never see him again, but the following week, he returned with his mother. She asked us to make her a gown with a matching cloak. She brought the most beautiful velvet fabric I'd ever seen. It took us two weeks to finish it, but they came back frequently to see the progress. Each time we traded pleasantries. I managed not to be so red in the face at last.

The time came for his family to return to Chicago. He came with his mother and sister to pick up the last of their purchases. He smiled at me, and as they were about to leave, he took my hand in his, and he asked me if my father was available.

My father isn't here, I replied hesitantly.

"When might I meet him?" he inquired.

With trepidation, I explained that I had no idea where he was. I felt doom closing in around me. No self-respecting man would want a young woman who had no idea where her father was.

"Then, I guess I will just have to speak with your sister."

Ruth:

Alexander came to my desk asking if he might have a word with me. I saw Margaret standing off to the side of the shop. She looked as if she might cry. I motioned to Sumee. She wheeled my chair into the back of the shop. Alexander followed.

"Miss Ruth, I would like very much to court your sister, but since there is no father available, I would like to ask your permission."

Do you promise to treat her kindly? I authoritatively inquired as I drew myself as tall as possible.

"In all respects," he replied.

Then, you may court her.

Margaret:

And court he did! It was wonderful. He wrote me lengthy letters when he was at school, and on Sundays, he would arrive in a carriage to take Ruth and me (and sometimes Tad) for rides. We had picnics on the green. We listened to music. We ate in fancy restaurants. We attended plays. Another dream come true! The months flew by. Alexander completed his studies. It was time for him to return to Chicago to begin his practice. He asked Ruth (who had grown to love this kind and gentle young man) for my hand in marriage.

Ruth:

I was happy for Margaret when Alexander asked to marry her, but there were so many "if's". If she married him, she would leave New York and move to Chicago. If she married him, she would no longer be there to help me with the business. If she married him, I would be without her. I didn't know if I could bear it, but Margaret deserved to have love, and I said "Yes, yes, yes" and clapped my hands in joy for the two of them. I would figure out the rest later. I was eleven, and Margaret was eighteen.

Margaret:

Alexander proposed. I accepted. We were ecstatic, thrilled, even rapturous! It would be a spring wedding. Alexander would return to Chicago and get his affairs in order while setting up his practice. He promised to write every day; I vowed to do the same. We would all come to Chicago to live as a family. We would have children. Ruth would have her own bed with a big comforter.

Ruth:

We had a business to sell. We had a trousseau to make, and never was a trousseau made with such love and care by so many fingers. After the wedding, we would take a few months to decide what we wanted to do about opening a new business. Sewing machines were all the rage now. We would have to consider our possibilities, but for now, we were busy with our own future opening, and it was grand!

Journal Entry XVI
CLOSED

Ruth:

Time was running out. I had talked to Margaret about telling Alexander the truth about everything, but she was terrified that she would lose her only chance for happiness. I understood her fear, but Granny and Mother told me to tell her to talk with Alexander, and "tell him everything".

I thought she should be truthful with him. I couldn't tell him. It wasn't my place. I told her, but I couldn't and I wouldn't make her. She had been through so much.

Instead of selling the business, we became partners with the two women from where we lived at Number 4. They would take a month off to build up their stock, and then they would open again. They would send us ten percent. All of our employees would still have work, but this time, they would have sewing machines with which to do their work. Times were changing.

Margaret:

I knew I should tell Alexander, but I was just too scared. What would he think if he knew the things Da had done to me? And that would seem like nothing compared to being a maid and then one of the girls in The House on Pearl Street! I didn't sleep well. I lost weight. Many times I tried to write to him about it all, but I tore up the letters and threw them in the stove.

What if he told his father? Worse than that, what would his mother and sister think of me? They certainly would not want such a woman marrying into their fine family. What am I going to do? What should I do?

I was happy about my upcoming marriage, but I was tormented by my past.

"You jez leave it 'lone Miss Margaret. Men folk don't got to know everythin," Sumee proposed.

I leaned in her direction on this one, instead of Ruth's.

Ruth:

It was our last night in the shop. Everything was packed and ready for shipping. The four of us were completing our tasks before sleeping in New York City for the last time as residents, when there was a pounding on the front door.

Sumee ran downstairs. She saw a big man leaning on the door tapping it with his cane. He demanded to be let inside.

"We closed Sir," Sumee offered. "Come back tomorrow."

"COMIN IN T'NIGHT! He replied, and he slammed his body into the door. It flew open. "MAGGIE ME GIRL! Maggie, I know you're here. Come see your ole Da!"

Margaret:

I couldn't believe my ears. I felt as if time had turned backward. My head was spinning. I felt sick.

I could hear the clump, clump, clump of feet and cane moving up the stairs. Sumee was calling out. "No, Sir, ain't no one here by dat name. Sir! Come back Sir! You in de wrong place!"

He stood at the top of the stairs looking around. Tad was at the other end of the room. Ruth lay in her bed. I was cringing behind a chair in the corner.

"Maggie! Maggie me girl! Come on out of there. Your ole Da is here to see you. I've been looking for ye all these years, and just today, I saw the little freak on the street. I followed her home. I knew where she was, you'd be. Come on out!"

How dare he! How dare he come into our home and call Ruth a freak! How dare he think he could ever come into our home!

I rose from the corner and stood up straight. My eyes flashing, I walked toward him decisively.

Get out you sorry excuse for a man! Get out you worthless piece of shit! You aren't fit to wipe the filth from Ruth's shoes. HOW DARE YOU CALL HER A FREAK! YOU'RE THE FREAK! A FREAK WHO TRIED TO BED HIS OWN DAUGHTER! A FREAK WHO DENIES HIS OWN FLESH! GET OUT! DON'T EVER COME BACK! YOU'RE NO FATHER! YOU'RE NOTHING!

Ruth:

With that he could contain himself no longer. He swung his cane towards Margaret's head. She fell to the floor stunned. He advanced on her his cane in the air! I raised myself and aimed my gun at his head. I pulled the trigger. He plunged headlong over Margaret's body. I was about to fire again when Margaret began moving out from under him.

He was dead. My practice for a day such as this had paid off. Long ago I had obtained a gun. Sumee would take me to the cellar to aim and shoot while Margaret was out. He was dead. I had killed our father, and I had no remorse whatsoever. He was never a father to me. I had promised to kill to protect Margaret. I had.

Margaret was shaking. She came to me and hugged me.

Margaret:

Thank you. Thank you, Ruth.

When we were calmer, Sumee, Tad and I rolled the body into a rug. (Funny somehow, Sumee saved Ruth by rolling her in a rug, and now we were all being saved by rolling someone else in a rug.) Sumee hired a buggy off the street, and we loaded the rug and went to the Hudson River. I told the driver we needed to dispose of some trash before leaving for Chicago. That was the truth. The trash went splashing into the river with the help of the burly driver. He received a generous tip.

Ruth:

That part of our lives was forever closed.

Margaret:

I knew now that I had to stop worrying about telling Alexander everything. I didn't fear Da anymore, and I would not spend my life fearful of my past being discovered and losing the man I loved…the man who said he loved me. We would find out if it was real love when we arrived in Chicago.

Journal Entry XVII
The Ride

Ruth:

We boarded the train early the next morning. Four of us: Margaret and me; Sumee and Tad; sixteen trunks, and my wheelchair! We sent a telegram to Alexander that we were leaving New York City and when we would arrive. It was really happening. Margaret was very quiet. Sumee was busy taking care of the trunks and me. Tad, well Tad was a typical ten year old boy entranced by the train. He was worthless to any of us, but he was having the time of his life. He was a good boy. He deserved to have time to himself. Sumee made herself the queen of the trunks and my chair. She saw to it that everything was stowed carefully. We had prepared for the ride, and now there was nothing to do but rock with the rhythm of the train and think.

Margaret:

I was thinking of how I could tell my love of my sordid past. I was thinking of what the outcome might be. Everything I had ever wanted for me and Ruth was in Chicago with my young man, but it was right that I should tell him and give him the opportunity to make a decision for his own happiness. I had no right to trick him into marriage, love or no love. If his future didn't lie with me, then so be it. Ruth and I had been on our own before. We would manage. No lies to this man. No lies, not white, but especially not these, the blackest of them all.

I was afraid, but I knew it was the right thing to do.

Ruth:

The train conductor shouted "All Aboard". The train lurched forward. We were on our way.

I talked with Granny and Mother. How would Alexander react? What would happen to us?

"Hold fast," was the answer. And so, I would.

Margaret:

The train was moving. Ruth and I sat face-to-face. We didn't speak. She was reading Granny's Bible. I was rehearsing for Alexander.

How slowly the train moved at first. It swayed, and my thoughts moved in unison.

I would say: I love you Alexander. I believe you love me. There are things you must know about me. My Da touched me in ways a man shouldn't touch a daughter. He was mean, especially to Ruth. He called her a freak, and one night when she was trying to protect me, I beat and bloodied him, and we ran away. Just before we left New York, he found us, and Ruth shot him dead.

That wouldn't do. What about this? He was a cruel man never acknowledging Ruth. He wanted to use me. One night he put me into his bed. No, no! There's just no way to say it that makes it sound any better.

How about? We ran away from Da, because he was touching me, and he was going to hurt Ruth. Yes, that's good. Now what?

I became a maid in a brothel at the age of fourteen, so that I could take care of Ruth and me. Oh my, that sounds terrible, but it's the truth. But what about, I lost my virginity at the age of sixteen, because I thought the madam of the House had kidnapped Ruth, and I had to protect her. I did whatever she told me to, until I received a message that Ruth was alive, and then I ran away from there. Oh my, oh my! This was it without the sordid details, but he was a man, and he could fill them in himself. Oh, my!

How will I ever say these things to him? Oh, my!

How will I ever be able to look into his eyes. Oh, my!

How can I do this?

Ruth:

I could feel the pain in Margaret. The tears would well in her eyes. She would turn her face to the window to wipe them away thinking I wouldn't notice. Silly girl, I noticed everything about her. She was so afraid, but she was now determined to tell Alexander, and no matter what happened, I was proud of her.

If I had been in her position, I am not sure that I could have told him.

Margaret:

The train rocked Ruth and me to sleep, but when I awoke, I had dreamed of Alexander. We were together walking in a field. We were smiling, and then, he fell to the ground dead. I was left standing over his dead body not knowing what to do.

Ruth:

Margaret shared her dream with me. I told her that dreaming of death was a common thing. I had dreamed of her death and mine many times, and look at us Margaret, we're still here. Granny had told me that dreaming of death often means an end to one thing and the beginning of another. That didn't bring her much comfort. We ate; we passed the time as best we could, and we slept.

Margaret:

It wasn't just about telling Alexander that I was fretting. What about his family? Would they all be there at the train station to meet us? Could I fake being a happy and excited bride-to-be? How would I get him alone to tell him?

Thoughts rambled in and out of my restless mind. Memories of the times we spent together in New York came sweetly and brought fresh tears. Dreams of our future now so uncertain brought tears as well. The question was, "What didn't bring tears at this point?" I felt like an endless fountain of pain. With each spurt, the tears fell.

Ruth:

We were one day from our arrival in Chicago. The train had stopped many times, so that travelers could come and go. We were very tired, and yet the tension was building. Sleep had deserted both of us. I pondered more "If's". I was very good at "If's".

If only, Da had been a good man, how different our lives would be now.

If only, we hadn't run away to The House on Pearl Street, there would be nothing for Margaret to tell.

If only, we had just stayed in New York City, perhaps, we could have lived a quiet and productive life together. Now we were uprooted, and we would have to start again.

If only, and it was about there, that the door to our compartment opened. In ducked the tall, handsome man of the hour, Alexander!

Margaret:

Alexander! You're here! We embraced. Neither of us wanted to let go, but the train jerked forward, and we were forced to sit. He took my hands in his and kissed them. Oh, my, how difficult this was going to be!

Do you have a compartment of your own Alexander?

"No, but I can get one if I need to do so. I thought Ruth here a good chaperone for the remainder of the journey," and he bellowed a hearty laugh.

Alexander, I stuttered, I am so very pleased that you came ahead to greet us. There are some things that we need to discuss.

"I couldn't wait," he explained. "Besides, my whole family will be waiting at the station. I didn't want you snatched away from me by all those women the first moment I saw you again! Oh, Love, how I've missed you."

I've missed you as well, I began. I have some things I must tell you.

Ruth:

And Margaret began. She began from the very beginning of when I was born, and how Granny had cared for us. She told him about Da, his pain, his anger, and his drinking. She included his calling me "Freak" and his disdain for me. Periodically, he would wipe her tears away, but he let her speak uninterrupted. He glanced from her to me and back to her again.

"I love you Alexander. The things I am about to share with you are hard to hear, but I have to tell you, and you must let me." She ducked her head, and then from somewhere, she gathered her strength. Sitting upright, she looked into his blue eyes and began to share about our life in America with Da. She told him about the touching, and how it escalated until one night, he demanded she become his woman. "It was Ruth who shouted and turned his wrath towards her to stop him from hurting me. He meant to kill her. I had to stop him, so I beat him unconscious, and then Ruth and I ran away."

He kissed her on the cheek. She took a deep breath and continued. "I went to work in a brothel as a maid. I was fourteen. Ruth had just turned eight. I had to smuggle her upstairs; we lived there three years almost. We started our business there, and it was with the money that we put away from my work and selling handkerchiefs and dresses that we were able to plot our escape. It didn't work out just like we wanted. Ruth, Sumee and Tad escaped, but when I ran to our room to grab Ruth, her bed was still there and her pram. The madam let me think that she had Ruth. She told me the only way I could save Ruth was to work for her."

"When you say work, what do you mean?" he ventured.

"Work, as one of the girls." Alexander, now completely deflated, hung his head and tears slid down his face, but he held onto Margaret's hands. "She sent every bully to me to punish me. I did everything I was told. I had too. Ruth's life, I thought, depended on me." She hesitated. She was sobbing now. Alexander was trembling like a hurt animal. "I'm so sorry to tell you this. I didn't want to, but something happened before we left New York, and I knew you had to know. Whatever you decide, I'll understand."

I was choking on tears. I felt like a peeping Tom. She had bared her soul to him. The last was for me to tell.

Alexander, I sputtered, I must tell the rest. Da found us. He was after Margaret. He hit her with his cane. I shot him dead. We wrapped him in a rug and dumped him in the Hudson River.

The silence was deafening. He raised himself from the seat and walked out the door.

Margaret and I were devastated. We held hands. An hour passed. We hadn't spoken at all. There was nothing either of us could say.

The door opened, and Alexander came inside. He sat across from Margaret and me. Through red swollen eyes, he searched our faces, and then he took our hands and held them in his.

He was a stricken man. His chin quivered as he began to speak. "I love you both so very much. You are my family now. No one will ever hurt either of you again. You two are the bravest people that I've ever known. No one should have gone through what you have. Look at you! You are the best, kindest and most loving people I know. Margaret, I would be proud to have you as my wife and the mother of my children. Will you marry me?"

Margaret:

It was done. Glory be! Halloo! He knew the worse, and he loved me. He loved Ruth. Joy spilled over, and the tears began again from the three of us, but this time, they were tears of happiness.

Ruth:

We were giddy. The train stopped. We disembarked, and as Alexander had predicted, there in mass was his huge family, our new family They were there to "Hold Fast" to us.

Journal Entry XVIII
Coming Home

Margaret:

Our wedding was held in the garden of Alexander's family home. There were blooming flowers everywhere. The fragrances were heady. My Ruth, sweet Ruth was my Maid-of-Honor, and she had a new custom made wheelchair for the occasion. Alexander had it built just for her. My gown was incredible. Ruth had outdone herself with the design. Sumee and Ruth stitched it themselves. I hadn't even seen it until the week before the wedding for the final fitting. It was the most beautiful gown I had ever seen. Alexander's younger sister stood with us, as did his father as his Best Man, and his friend from school. A huge gathering of people came to see us take our vows, and their joy swept over us.

Ruth:

Never had there been a more beautiful bride than my Margaret! When she walked down the aisle, Alexander and I both had tears in our eyes. She had no idea how truly beautiful she was, but then, she never had. There was a glow about her, and not just the glow from her. Granny and Mother were there standing in the air behind the two of them as they said their vows. There were others that I didn't recognize, but I knew they loved her. I could feel the love radiating from them. What a fantastic ceremony!

Margaret:

The party after the wedding was glorious. We danced, and we enjoyed ourselves. I remember my face hurting from smiling so much. But what a wonderful pain to have! We left and went to our own home for our wedding night.

How gentle Alexander was with me. I cannot begin to say how love transformed what I previously thought was the most ugly of acts into the most beautiful, but Alexander's love for me and my love for him did it. He was tender and caring. There was no rush. There was no selfishness. I am loved. Glory be! I am loved, and I am capable of loving.

We left the next day for our honeymoon.

Ruth:

Never had I seen such happiness, as when they left on their honeymoon, nor when they returned a month later. Alexander vowed that their honeymoon would never end. A month or so after their return, Margaret was sick in the mornings, afternoons, and evenings. Yes, she was expecting. We were all thrilled.

New clothes were a must. Sumee and Margaret and I began to sew again with renewed joy. There were dresses to accommodate Margaret's growing form, and there were baby dresses needed. Blankets, also, for the cold winters ahead. As February arrived, so did our boy!

He was named after his father. He was a fine happy baby. Margaret's milk agreed with little Alex, and we watched him grow into a laughing butterball. Since he was the first grandchild, we perpetually had a house full or relatives. It didn't matter, there was plenty of love to go around in our home.

Margaret:

Oh, how I loved to cuddle Alex, and I loved to watch his Papa holding him. Alexander was a wonderful father. He slept with us, which surprised many, but we couldn't bear to have him away from us.

One day in May, he woke with the sniffles. Then, he had a fever, and two days later, we woke, and Alex was cold. He had left us. There is no sadness to compare with the loss of a beloved child. There is no pain like it. We were dazed. We didn't know what to do with ourselves.

Alexander made arrangements with the pastor at the church for a service. Together we picked out a family plot, so that one day we could all rest together. Ruth, Sumee, and Tad were inconsolable. The rest of the family took over the house. They brought food, but none of us wanted to eat. They helped us dress. They insisted we drink something, even if we didn't eat. Me, I cried all the time.

My husband was strong for the world to see. He tended to business. Once the lamps were out, I felt the bed shaking with his sobs. We held each other in the night. Once the plot was chosen, I took to my bed, and I might have stayed there, but I overheard Alexander's mother talking about how she was going to dress Alex. I got up. I dressed. Ruth and I chose what Alex would wear. I asked Alexander's mother to go with me, and together we dressed little Alex. It would be the last time. He was such a handsome little boy, just like his father. I couldn't help thinking…his little eyes are closed to the world as I know it, but they are open to the world of Granny and Mother. I knew they were holding him now. Still, I wanted to be the one holding him. How would I go on? How could I? How could any of us?

Ruth:

How could we indeed? Why? Why? I asked God. No, I demanded God tell me "Why?" It made no sense. Hadn't Margaret suffered enough? I would have gone in his place. I would have gladly gone. The answer came. "I know best. Haven't you learned to trust me yet? I only loaned him for a short while. Look how much love he brought to you all."

Margaret:

We buried my baby in a tiny dark hole in the ground on a beautiful sunny day. Alexander and I hunched by the graveside holding each other. We told him goodbye. We told him that we would see him again in a better place.

Days passed. I cried every day for the longest time. The days became weeks. The sadness was at times unbearable, but love won out, time healed. We spoke of better times when Alex was with us. We laughed and were happy to have had him with us, and we realized that he had breached the gap for all of us. He was love from all of us personified. In August, I realized that I was once again with child. Even though we were pleased, I found myself being guarded. I was reluctant to be too happy for fear it would again be snatched from me.

Ruth:

Well, enough was enough. We owed it to this new life to welcome it with open arms as we had Alex! Sumee and I made new clothes. As the weeks passed, Margaret's fears dissipated, she became joyful with the prospect of another child to love. The "expectancy" grew if you will! She couldn't have been healthier. With this baby, there was no sickness morning or otherwise. In March, we were blessed with a beautiful tiny girl who had rosy cheeks and a hint of red hair curling about her face.

Margaret:

How happy I was to meet my new daughter! Secretly, I was glad it was a her and not a him. I was afraid that I would pass my sadness over to a him, but with this darling little girl, every day was new. Her name was Ruth, of course! Her middle name was Maureen after Granny. We were so pleased. Ruth doted over Ruthie. Her little smile was contagious. She grew strong and healthy. She loved all of us, but it was Ruth that she favored, and naturally, Ruth favored her. They developed their own secret society. They could communicate with each other without speaking a word. It was sweet to watch.

Ruth:

Needless-to-say, we weren't starting a business in Chicago. We were living life and loving it. Wild horses couldn't have dragged me away from little Ruthie! Having her in my life was as close to having a child of my own, as I had ever dreamed. Thankfully, Margaret and Alexander shared her with me unconditionally. There were nights when she cried out for me, and one of them would dutifully bring her from their bed to mine. Her coming brought happiness back into our home. She was sunshine. Within a short two years, there was yet another child on the way, and most welcome.

Ruthie and I played together. I had never had an actual playmate of my own when I was small. Oh, yes, Margaret was there, but it wasn't the same. I was Ruthie's playmate even if others might think me too old. It didn't matter to me. We had puppet shows and played with her doll house together. I told her stories. She told me things too. She knew about heaven. We saw spirits together. She was as comfortable with them as I.

While we were thus engaged one afternoon, she informed me casually in her tiny girl voice, "Aunt Wuth, they say, come home." I knew exactly what she was talking about! Hadn't I been two when I told my Granny to get ready to go home? I kissed her little sweet cheeks. I smiled at her. "I'm going to Heaven, but I will be watching over you and your mother and father and all your little brothers and sisters to come, until the day that all of you come home to be with me. You know that you can talk to me anytime, don't you?

"Aw wight, Aunt Wuth, I talk you." And with that said, she scampered away.

Margaret:

Ruth passed within the week. She went to all the love and peace that I'd felt so many years before. I couldn't even be unhappy that she was gone, because she was never really too far away. I've had a full life, and I've felt Ruth at my side often, good times or bad. As a very old woman on my own deathbed, I recalled the words of Granny as she prepared to leave us, **Always take care of Ruth, and Ruth will take care of you.**

JOHN'S TESTIMONY

Prologue

Within this story of John's, you will find words, and the accents and colloquialisms which were used back in his lifetime. They may be offensive in our day and time, but during John's life, these were commonplace. Please accept them for what they were as a sign of the times, his times. It is not my intent, in any way, to demean or offend him or a race of people who helped to build this country into what it is today. Having said that, I hope you will enjoy "Railin" with him.

Chapter One
Fair is Fair

Hello, my name is John. I'm a mulatto man of 48 years, but no one would know I was of mixed blood, unless I told them, because I am very fair. My hair is more like my father's (or so Mam says), and I am baldin a bit, as it begins to turn gray. I could pass if I wanted. I never aimed to do that though, even though I have at times. It would be dishonorin to my mother and grandmother. I'm a conductor on the M-K-T. For those of y'all who don't know what that is, it is the Missouri-Kansas-Texas Railroad. I take care of the passengers and the like. I call "All Aboard!" and the train gets to moving. That feels powerful to me.

It's a good job mostly. People are almost always happy to travel on the train. Sometimes, however, you get them sad folk that are goin home to funerals, or even worse, they are carryin someone they love home to bury. Pretty much though, I like my job. I enjoy workin. I like folks. I guess I come by that natural from my mother. I love children, and that's a good thing, because there's always children runnin wild on the train. They want to know about everythin from the engine to the caboose. I do enjoy tellin them about it, as long as they're respectful. If they aren't respectful, then they don't get much of anythin from me. "Fair is fair", my Mam always told me.

I was born in 1859 on a plantation in Western Louisiana. In those days, we were all slaves. My Mam was a pretty young thing. She worked in the main house with her Mammy. Mammy was in charge of cookin everythin for the white folks. We all ate pretty well from their table leavins. That was a bonus. My Mam shared with me that when she was fourteen, one of the Mast'r's boys told her he loved her. She loved him too, always had. They'd played together as babies. Next thing, "I was 'spectin' you. My young Mast'r sent off to school. Never saw him no more. That's jez the way it be. I loved him. He loved me, but it don't matter. You's mine, so you's colored. I knowed it would be dis way, but it don't matter none. Fair is fair. You give, you get. Or, is dat you get, you give. I's never quite sure how it go," she giggled.

After I came along, I spent most of my time in the main house with my Mam and Mammy. The two of them told me that I was born smart. "You was borned a-knowin when to be seen and not seen. Same wid hearin." Mammy said. When I was old enough, I helped out in the kitchen fetchin things and such. I was their "Lil Nigger." They called me that all the time. Come to think of it, I'm still a-fetchin. (Makes me laugh. I guess I've been a-doin just that all my life!)

The Civil War exploded all around us. We heard about it, but it didn't touch us much, until the soldier boys from the Texas Legion cut through our land headin to Vicksburg. We were afraid, because we didn't know what to expect. Mammy said "Soldiers is soldiers. They's always hungry and wantin anything they sees." She made Mam and me hide out in the woods with what food and livestock we could haul with us. I was just a little feller then, but I can remember how stinky those soldiers smelled, as they marched past our hidin place. I can remember how scared I was too.

Mam said they wouldn't hurt us, but I didn't think she was "a-tellin true", because I heard lots of "hollerin" at the main house after she and I took off to hide. There were no chickens on the place after they left. They killed a hog too. They made Mammy give them everythin she had cooked up. She was mad as a hornet, and she called them "down-dirty names". The Master told us that we had to help the soldiers, because they were doing God's work, but when he didn't have his "Mammy" fried chicken dinner on Sunday, he didn't seem too happy to have helped.

I'd turned six just before we heard that the war ended. We'd been touched by all the goin's on, but it wasn't really too very different for us on the plantation. We didn't have a lot of food, because we couldn't grow as much, but we made do. Me, bein little, I hadn't really noticed, but when the soldiers drifted down the roads, things began to change a lot. Most of them soldiers were in rags. I mean, real rags barely held together enough to cover their bodies. Very few of them had shoes or boots. Their feet were either bare or wrapped in rags. That was if they even had both feet. Some were missing arms or legs. It was a terrible sight. Some were blind. Some were just plain crazy and couldn't talk straight. Young soldier boys much older than their years, and old men alike begged at our place. We fed them soup, sometimes not much more than a watered down gruel, but we tried. Food got scarcer and scarcer. Mam and Mammy would send me down the road with somethin to feed them every day. They were always thankful for what we could share. It made me feel good, but it made me feel awful to see how bad off some of them were too. For the men who were just plain sick, the Mistress and Mam and Mammy would take care of them, until they were ready to pass on or move on down the road to see what was left of their homes and families. Mostly, they were beaten, sad men. They were defeated inside and out. I've felt that way a time or two in my life, but that's getting ahead of myself.

The summer after I turned eight, Mam told me "We's a goin to Texas. We cain't stays here no mo. There ain't no mo work fer us here. Mast'r say he cain't feed us. He cain't pay us. We jez cain't live here no mo. ...Don't you be a-cryin! ...Mast'r, he say he cain't even make 'nuff to pay fer de plantin. He don't know what he gonna do to take care o' his family. ...Shush now boy! We's free now. The President done say so. Nobody cans sell us no mo. We's got to make it on our own. We's free Johnny. We gonna be happy. We gonna go where we want to go. We gonna have our own place someday. You jez wait and see. It be good, jez you and me Johnny. We gonna be fine. You gonna make new friends. ...Stop cryin now... No, Mammy not comin wid us. She too old. Mast'r say he gonna keep de old folk who is too worn out to make it on de own. She stayin here. She be cared fer. ...Don't you cry now. You makin me cry. ...We gonna be happy. You gonna see."

I couldn't see. I didn't want to see! It just didn't seem right to me, not then, not even now. We were born there, me and Mam both. We didn't want to leave. Why couldn't we just be free there and stay with Mammy? I didn't want to go. I told them both so, often and loudly.

I thought it would be terrible to leave Mammy and all I'd ever known, but I didn't know how truly terrible it would be. At 8 years of age, how could I understand that there was no comin back to be rocked by my Mammy! I didn't have any idea how I would feel when she wasn't there to fuss at me, and then turn around and give me a big hug to make sure I knew things with us were all right. How I would miss her givin me little stolen sweet treats in the years to come! There'd be no more fishin in the creek out back. No more swingin and jumpin off the rope into the cool water with my friends on a summer afternoon. All them little children that I played with were leavin too. I'd seen them every day of my life. It wasn't right. We wouldn't be catchin no lightenin bugs together ever again. No more rides on the hay wagon. No more catchin grass hoppers fer fishin. There'd be no more ever of Mammy's biscuits to share at the creek! How could life go on!

Mammy and me put mine and Mam's clothes in an old tater sack. What little food we had, we put in a flour sack. The day came we had to say our goodbyes. My heart still hurts; the tears still stand in my eyes when I thinkof it. Mammy pulled me into her enormous lap for the last time. She said "Johnny Boy, you a man now. You gots to take care of yo momma. She ain't got nobody else but you. She got no mo' Mammy to help her when you leaves here. You's a good boy. I's always gonna love you. It don't matter none how fer you and yo' Mam go, you is my chillums. You's both always gonna be my chillums. Even after I's gone from dis old world, I's gonna watch ov'r you. You take good care of yo' Mam. Don't cry now. It time fer you to go be a man. It time for you and yo' Mam to be free. You go be free fer me." With that, she gave me a big hug that lasted a long, long time. I wished it could have lasted longer. She slipped some cookies into my shirt pocket, she kissed me, and gave me a swat on my behind.

Mam was outside waitin with the others who were leavin. She came to Mammy as we stepped outside. They hugged and cried. I didn't hear what it was they were sayin. I didn't want to hear. I couldn't stand much more of this. It hurt to swallow. I couldn't speak. I wanted my Mam to see me strong; Mammy wanted me to be strong. I turned away from them and ran down the road to catch up with my friends. I was all cried out.

Mam caught up. We trudged along the road quiet for a while, and then our group of twenty or so began to sing.

"**Swing low, Sweet Chariot. Comin fer to carry me home. Swing low, sweet chariot, Comin fer to carry me home.**

I looked over Jordan, And What did I see, Comin fer to carry me home, A band of angels comin after me, Comin fer to carry me home.

If you get there afore I do, Comin fer to carry me home, Tell all my friends I'm comin too, Comin fer to carry me home."

There was strength in numbers. The spirit of adventure soon took over. I had my friends to play with along the way. Singing made the time past faster, and that's how we traveled at first…on a song. We sang work songs and gospel songs. At night we slept on the ground with our sacks for pillows. We children caught fish and crawfish. The men killed snakes and frogs. Mostly, the women folk cooked our bounty over the fire at night. We ate berries and grapes straight from the vine as we walked. We dug roots. In short, we ate whatever we could find. It was summer and damp and hot. We welcomed the rain, but too much was a test. Still, we were surrounded by trees that gave us some shelter. Fires at night gave us a safe feelin. When we piled green leaves on it, the smoke drove the skeeters off for a little while. Not long though. We kept movin farther away from home every day. Our feet hurt and bled. We didn't know where we were a-goin, but we figured someone did. Wrong! What we children didn't know was that even the older folks didn't have any idea where we were headed or what we would find when we got there! Two of the babies passed away. They just weren't strong enough. By the time we crossed the Sabine River, we were starving and filthy like none of us had ever been before. Most of us were sick in one way or the other. I myself don't even remember crossing the river. Mam filled me in later on how she'd tied me to her with her shawl and half-carried, half-drug me through the muddy waters.

I remembered little or nothing about that. My playmates left with their families. I was too sick to say goodbye. We stayed in a small settlement on the banks of the river. There were only a few families, but Mam went to each of them beggin for covered shelter for her and her sick boy in return for work. No one wanted us. No one except for the Blacksmith. He took us to his barn. Mam took care of his two children and his house, so that we could stay there dry, while she tried to heal me. Mam said that I had the ague. I was pretty bad sick.

There are only a few things I remember from that time. I have a brief memory of Mam proppin me against a huge tree and givin me cool water to drink. I remember feelin the shock of the water all over my body (probably when we crossed the river). My fever was so hot that my eyes hurt. I thought I was too close to the oven in Mammy's kitchen sleepin. I was talkin out of my head accordin to Mam.

My very first memory of being in Texas was Mam spoonin hot soup in my mouth. She put a little in the spoon, blew on it, and then poured it into me. At first, it dribbled out as fast as she put it in, but she persisted and got it down me. Slowly, I began to feel better. Once again, we were eatin someone's scraps. There weren't too many. Mam said "These is really po' folk's scraps." Still, they were good. When you're hungry, most any food is good food, and best to be grateful. We were.

Weeks after we crossed the river, I was finally well enough to understand that Mam was gone takin care of the Blacksmith's children durin the days, and just with me in the nights puttin poultices on my chest and pourin root tea down me. I'd been so out of my head, I thought she was there all the time. "All dem folks dey acted scared of me when I went lookin fer work," she told me. "It were only de big smithy dat took us in. He pretty good man," she rattled on. The Blacksmith was a burly man who towered over Mam. He was hairy everywhere and ugly. He talked gruffly, but he didn't feel mean to me. Actually, when I was better, he was pretty nice showin me how to help him. Mam must have done a good job fer him, because it wasn't too long, and she was tellin me how "he jez over his limit wid a-knowin what to do wid no woman! His wife done run off to New Orleans, and left him wid dese two babies." The boy was four years old; the little girl, barely weaned. They had no manners at all, until Mam got hold of dem. It wasn't a bad life. Next thing I knew, the Blacksmith made Mam his woman. We ate better then, got castoffs too. "Fair is fair" as Mam said. I guess so. Mostly I did whatever he told me. So did Mam. He used to come to the barn to be with her at night. I knew when not to be seen. We were free, but not really. Still, it was considerably better than the swamps and skeeters!

We stayed there nigh onto two years before the Blacksmith took him a wife. He told Mam that we had to go. Go where? We didn't have any idea! The Blacksmith and Mam discussed our options, and it was decided we should go to Galveston. Mam was sure that in a bigger place she could find work. In her words, "We's got to make it on our own. We's free, Johnny. We gonna be happy. We gonna go where we want to go. We gonna have our own place someday. You jez wait and see. It be good, just you and me; Johnny, we gonna be fine." The Blacksmith gave us a stake, and he let us have his mule.

We set out. It was just the two of us.

Chapter Two
Galveston

We were on our way. We were goin to be happy. Mam said so, and this time, at least, we had a destination. We were headed to Galveston, Texas. Once again, we were movin along an unknown road to a place unknown to us. At least, it had a name this time, so that was a good thing. We were delighted to have the mule, because we could ride once in a while, and we didn't have to carry everythin (such as it was). We now had four bags instead of just two. It was early spring. Flowers were bloomin. The weather was still cool, but not cold. It didn't yet rain every day. For the first couple of days, we moved through swampy land that was just like Louisiana land. Then we came to a big river, the Trinity River. We had to go a ways down to find a place to cross over. On either side, the woods were incredibly thick. It appeared to me that the trees didn't have any trunks, as they erupted as afterthoughts from bushes and plants of every size and description. They were just part of the bushes, but taller and bigger around higher up. Mam and me and our mule struggled through the brambles, but even the sunlight had a hard time cuttin through that brush! Later in the night, we could hear panthers screamin. They sounded just like a woman screamin. How any animal could maneuver his way through that denseness in a run, I will never know. We barely could in a slow walk. Still, in the night, the noises around us were deafenin, and ten years old or not, I was scared. Maybe, one of those panthers would just drop down off a tree limb on top of me! Maybe, one of those wild pigs squealin and gruntin within earshot would charge his way past the brush to eat me up! Needless-to-say, there wasn't any grumblin from me when the sun came up! Mam couldn't quite figure out why I was so cheerful and ready to get walkin again. I didn't tell her. There were a whole bunch of things I never told Mam. After all, I was the man.

Galveston turned out to be an island. Who knew?! We had to ride across the water on a big flat boat that the man called a ferry. It was a "big" town compared to where we'd lived before. Big wooden ships from all sorts of foreign places lined the docks. There were people sellin their wares in the street all the time, not just Saturdays. There were saloons where I watched men stumble out doors to fight one another. There were two hotels for white folks. There were other boardin houses for people not quite so white or wealthy. And, then, there were places for poor colored folks like us to stay. Most of these were just a few boards slapped together, but they were covered and had walls. We didn't have much money, but we had the mule. Mam sold the mule. We got us a room and had money left. We were rich. The room had a pail for water, a bed, and a stove for cookin and heatin. There was even a floor in it. I wasn't goin to have to sleep on the ground or in hay! I could make my pallet on a wooden floor. The only other time I'd ever slept on boards was back in Louisiana in Mammy's main house kitchen. I was thrilled. Mam was smilin. Was this what being free was all about?

Mam went out lookin for work the very next day. I tagged along with her. We met a nice man on the street who told her that for four bits, he knew someone lookin for a cook. He was right friendly. He said it was a "fer sure" job, but "I's got to make me a lil somethin out of dis." Mam promised him the money. We went back to our room and returned with the four bits. He took it, bit at it (to make sure it was good), and pointed "three streets down. It be the second store on de right. Good luck."

Elated, we headed down the road. When we arrived, the second store was a barber shop. "That don't look right to me," Mam murmured under her breath, but she went up the steps and stuck her head in the door. "A man done sent me here to see 'bout work, Sir. You gots anythin I can do here, Sir?" The barber shouted at her to get away from his door. "Maybe we didn't hear de man right Johnny. Lets us go back and talk to him."

Back to our startin place we went, but the man who helped us out wasn't there. We found a couple of short keg barrels in the alleyway and sat waitin for him. Hours passed. The sun was hot. We were hungry and tired, especially me. We returned to our room. "Maybe we sees him tomorra" Mam stated while openin the door.

Our belongings were everywhere! The bedding was turned over. The coffee pot where Mam had hidden our money was overturned, and the money was gone! Mam threw herself on the floor and cried hysterically. I'd never seen her like this. I was furious. I couldn't help thinkin what I'd like to do to that man who robbed us. We were just too trustin. "He'd better hope I don't find him!" I shouted to no one in particular. Night fell. Mam was still on the floor sobbin. "Come on Mam, let's us eat. Let's eat and get a good night's sleep. We'll figger out what to do in de mornin." She couldn't eat. I ate for both of us.

I could hear Mam whimperin softly in the night, but come the mornin, she was all better. She washed up. I peeked at her as she smoothed her dress. I stretched "Good mornin" to her and rubbed my eyes. This was the Mam I knew. "We gonna be fine. Do you wanna go wid me, or do you want to sleep a bit mo'? You can get in de bed if you wants. We gonna be fine Johnny. I'll find somethin to do, or we'll jez sleep outside like we done afore. Won't be no worse off than we already been. Meanwhile, why don't you climb yo'self up in dat bed. We done better enjoy dis place as long as we cans." I grinned and hopped up into the bed.

When I knew Mam was out of sight, I got out of bed, cleaned myself up and went to town. People were friendly to me. They greeted me with a smile or a hello. These were white people mostly speakin to me. I was a little surprised. No one had said anythin or smiled at me yesterday, and then it dawned on me. They thought I was a white boy today! They weren't nice to me like this when I was with Mam, and they saw me as colored. No one I'd ever been around thought of me as anythin but a darkie until now. How different this is. I nodded, the white folk nodded. I smiled, they smiled. So, being a boy, I took it a step farther. I followed a family into the general store. When the woman behind the counter gave the children a penny piece of candy, I put my hand right out there; she handed me one thinkin I was one of them! What is this! It was like I'd crossed into another world the way they were treatin me. I took my candy and found a bench on the boardwalk to sit a spell. I knew we were treated differently. That's just the way it is, but I don't like it. I never did, but I really hadn't spent any time thinkin on it. I liked being with my folks. Colored folks, of course. Today is strange. Whites get candy for free! I do like candy. I like smiles and hellos. Why can't it be that way for everyone. It sure feels better. How fair is that?

Well, life ain't always fair then, is it? I determined right then and there that I would not let people think I was white, "unless" it helped both me and mine. How far I would go with that I would have to think on later. I sure wouldn't pretend to be white again for candy. That was beneath me, but I would maybe if it was something serious. I live in a "colored" world. My Mam and Mammy both live in a "colored" world. I want a better life, but not at the expense of hurtin the people who love me. I wouldn't ever want them to think I was ashamed of them. I don't want to hurt them; I never want to hurt them. Reason told me however, that I could use this asset (this fairness of mine) to my advantage, and why shouldn't I? Maybe I would let these white folks get to know me and like me, and then I would let them know who I really am outside, as well as in. In my ten year old mind, it seemed so reasonable.

Finishin my candy, I slurped a drink of water from the horse trough, and I continued explorin. I looked through the dusty windows of the shops where women things were sold. I drooled at the bakery window. I sat on the fence and watched the blacksmith work. I strolled along the docks. There were people on the streets of all colors. I saw a yellow man with slanty eyes. He had on a funny funnel kind of hat and clothes that hung loose on his body. He didn't smile or wave at me. There was a dark reddish-brown feller who was dressed in buckskins. There were all kinds of colored beads on his shirt, but the most impressive thing about him was his long straight black hair. It flowed past his waist. I thought he was beautiful. He didn't smile or wave at me either. A multitude of white folks were gettin off one of the ships. I expected a nod from them, but no chance. They spoke very fast and in words that I couldn't understand. They had very light hair and very red cheeks, and isolated themselves in tight groups. I saw coloreds everywhere I went. They were busy, but not what I would call overly friendly. If I spoke to them or waved, they would acknowledge me, but they didn't say hello first. How odd, but then it hit me, they thought I was white! It works both ways! That hadn't occurred to me. These darkies were my people, but without my being in the presence of my dark mother, they didn't know that I was just like them. Now, how was that going to work? I am so confused. I wish I could talk to Mammy about it all. I miss her.

Well, on with it. I could think about all of this later. Right now, I had to find a job. That would make Mam happy again. I stopped at every shop askin if they needed a boy to help out. There were "no's" and more "no's", but at the end of the day, I had a job. I was goin to work at the white folks boardin house sweepin and moppin up, carryin water and dumpin chamber pots, but in return, I would be fed breakfast and lunch. I worked from dawn, until the work was done, and then I could leave. Any fish I caught, the landlady, Mrs. Bea, would buy from me. I made eight bits a week. I worked six days instead of seven, because the landlady boss said "All God's children should honor the Sabbath."

Mam didn't find work that day. She was tired and discouraged. She smiled at my news. "You's such a good boy, and here I done thought you was jez a-sleepin all day. I'll find somethin tomorra." We ate our potatoes for supper and went to bed early. Mam woke me the next mornin, and for the first time. I left before she did.

I was good at doin the chores at Mrs. Bea's boardin house. I found out that there were all the kinds of things that I was good at. Mammy and Mam had taught me well, and workin for the Blacksmith had made me even better. It didn't take me long to finish up. I ate my lunch and helped clean the pots and pans. Mrs. Bea told me I was "dismissed" for the rest of the day. The mornin had gone quickly. I didn't feel like I'd done much of anythin.

I'll bet you're wonderin if I told Mrs. Bea I was colored. Nope, I didn't. I let her think I was white. It wasn't a real lie, because she didn't ask. Besides, it was to help Mam.

I took off for the dock to look at the ships. I saw the waves crashin and rollin over the sand, and the big fine houses at the water's edge. It was a glorious place to be a young boy on a spring day. Meanderin down the beach, I came across an elderly darkie a-fishin. He was a wiry feller, not tall, but not short either. He had a scruffy beard with some gray hairs peekin out. His clothes were tattered. He was barefooted like me. I struck up a conversation with him. His name was Bo. He offered me a line and a pole. We baited our hooks with hard-head fish he'd caught earlier. We stood together with our lines in the water. First thing I snagged a crab! Bo belly laughed watchin me try to get rid of the thing! "Dems good eatin, but you'd need a passel mo of dem fer a meal." He showed me how to weight my line to get it further out into the water. Within a few minutes, I was playin tug-of-war with my very first Galveston fish. When the fight ended, I was somewhat surprised to see that my fish had whiskers just like the catfish we caught back home in Louisiana. We put him on a stringer so he could stay alive in the water next to our feet. Chucklin, the old man advised, "Watch out fer yo fish, or Mr. Crab will eat him fer dinner instead of you eatin him!" Patiently, Bo instructed me in the art of cleanin salt-water catfish, but not before I caught three more to go with the first.

Hmmm, I thought, what do I do about these fish? Do I sell them all to Mrs. Bea? I could make more money to take home to Mam. Nope, not goin to sell them all. First catch will always be for Mam and me (if it's big enough); I'll sell the rest. I figured somewhere along the line, we should come first with somethin. That decided, I thanked the old man very much. He told me to come back any time. I told him I would every chance I had. We had enjoyed our time together, and to tell the truth, it was pretty nice havin a man who wasn't orderin me around and just wanted to spend time with me. I took my stringer and headed for Mrs. Bea. She wanted them all, especially the biggest, which just happened to be mine to keep. It was the first one. I told her I was savin it for me and Mam's dinner. She smiled at that. I sold her the other three. She paid me six cents. Mam would be so proud of me.

Mam was proud of me. She took the money and stuffed it into her pocket, but first, she handed me one cent tellin me, "You's a workin man now, and a man should have a part of his earnin's to spend on whatever he wants." While she cooked our fish, I ran as fast as I could to the store and bought me a piece of candy! That became our routine. Some days I would get me a piece of candy; somedays, I'd get somethin for Mam. Other days, I tucked it away. It was nice havin a choice. I did feel pretty grown up.

When I returned from the store that day, I found Mam weepin. I couldn't understand why. She hugged me and said "Now, Johnny, don't you worry none. Yo'r Mam jez bein silly. De fish almost ready. Go wash up." It's a hard thing to be the man in a family. I thought Mam would be happy, but she seemed sadder than ever. That was the best fish dinner! Mam didn't eat much. She said she just wasn't hungry.

"It'll be a good day tomorra." Muttered Mam as I was dropping off to sleep. It was a good day today! I thought, but I was way too tired to say anythin. Besides she didn't really seem to be talkin to me, as much as she was to herself. I worked and fished with my friend Bo, and Mam looked for work every day. On Sunday, I got to sleep late, and then the two of us went to the First Gospel Church of Texas for colored folks. We carried us a little lunch and stayed there all day. The singin and preachin lifted us up. Mam, for sure, seemed to take to it. It was nice to see her happy. She could "sing all day and night" she bubbled. Mam loved the Lord. Me, I didn't know Him, but Mam and Mammy did, and that was good enough for me. I sang too, but not like Mam. She sang with her heart, and sometimes her heart would break, and tears would stream down her cheeks. Still, even cryin, her singin made her smilin happy.

The next week was pretty much the same, as was the next and the next. I'd earn my eight bits every week and give it to Mam, along with the money from the fish, except for my penny a catch. We didn't spend much on anythin at all, except for a little flour and fatback, but we didn't have enough money to pay the rent on our room when the time came. We had to leave that nice room. I was sad, but Mam was even sadder. She didn't laugh much anymore at all. We stopped goin to church. She hadn't found work. "There's jez plenty of womenfolk here, colored and white, to cook and take care of folks' homes. Most people here is po as we is." The light went out behind her eyes, when we took our four bags and began lookin for a place to sleep.

It was the middle of June, and it was cooler by the water. The sun was heatin things up pretty good. On the beach, the bugs and skeeters weren't quite as bad as everywhere else. The wind blew them away, but the sand was awful. Sand gets into everythin, and there's sand fleas that bite and sting, until they just about make you crazy. I could leave and go to work, but Mam stayed there all day long to protect our belongin's, such as they were. We weren't the only Negro folks livin on the beach, but we'd already had a taste of being robbed by trustin, so we knew better than to leave our things unprotected. When I came back from fishin each day, I would stay with our things, and Mam would go into town to look for work. I would cook the fish right about dark, eat, and go to sleep. Mam ate whenever she came back from town.

Mam seemed to arrive later and later from lookin for work. Mostly I'd be asleep. The food I left her would be gone when I woke in the morning sometimes; sometimes not. She didn't wake me up at dawn anymore. She was asleep when I left for work, and usually she was asleep when I returned in the afternoon. She looked tired all the time. There was no life about her. She was either sleepin or gone. In between, she was pretty nasty talkin to me. I couldn't do nothin right. She just stopped tryin to ever make herself look nice at all, much less talk nice. I didn't know her. But I did notice how bad she stunk. I told her she needed to clean herself up. That made her pretty mad, but I charmed her into walkin in the water with me. She was afraid of the waves, but eventually we got past that. From then on, we bathed in the gulf, but the smell never left her. Summer ended. Fall came. Winter that year blew in with a norther that nearly froze us to death. We were still livin on the beach. Mam had no work. She left every night to look for work, or so she told me. Somethin was drastically wrong with Mam. She sat starin at nothin in particular. I'd talk to her, but she didn't look at me. I never knew if she even heard me. She used to hug me all the time, but not now. She was either dead to me or just plain mad. I didn't know what to do.

One April day, Mrs. Bea called me to the kitchen. I thought I was in trouble, but instead, I was surprised by her and two of the staff singin "Happy Birthday" to me! "I know you don't know exactly when your birthday is, but from now on, today's the day!" She'd made a pretty cake all for me. I took some to share with Bo, and with Mam. She wasn't interested, but I was excited, and I wanted her to be. I reached out to hug her. She slapped me. "Leave me alone! I'm late!" Stunned and hurt, I watched her drag herself towards town. She didn't even look back.

I waited until dark. There was no moon. I scraped out a hole in the dune and buried our four shrinking bags. I tied a piece of cloth to a stick and marked the spot. I went to town. I found Mam. I am sorry that I found Mam, but I had to know what was goin on with her. She was sittin in the dirt leanin back against a water trough in front of a saloon. She looked pitiful. She looked like a little girl the way she was curled around herself. I was about to approach her, when a red-faced fat man came out of the bar and gave her a little glass with brown stuff in it. She gulped it down, and she gave the man a kiss. I gagged. He touched her in a familiar way, and then he went back inside. I was twelve. I was old enough to know what that meant. He was a white man dressed in rags worse than ours. She sat head down, vacantly staring at the door of the saloon. I couldn't speak. I turned and ran back to the beach. Sittin there atop the dune, I waited for her to return. I felt like someone had beaten me up.

So many emotions surged in me. This was my Mam! What was she thinkin? What was she doin? She smelled like one of those old men that lie in the dirt full of whiskey. Mammy, oh Mammy, I need you! Mam needs you. You're her mother; you'd know what to say. You'd know what to do! I don't know! I'm just a boy! I'm not a man. I'm a boy. What's the matter wid her! I want my Mam. No, I don't. I hate her! I hate her so much! How can she do this to me? I want my Mam the way she used to be. Somebody! Help me. God, if you're there, help me! If I could've, I'd have drug her by her hair all the way back here! I just want to scream at her. She nothin but a trifling ho! (I sat quiet now looking out to sea). She's my Mam. I love her no matter what she been doin. I want my Mam. And with those last words, I crumpled. I lay curled on the beach cryin myself to sleep.

When I woke, the sun was high. Thank you God, it's Sunday. I sure can't lose my job now. What would I do? I searched, but Mam was nowhere to be seen. What was I to do now! Had she deserted me? Did she see me? I can't think about her now. I took my pole and went to the water's edge. I let my mind drift atop the waves. Towards me and back, towards me and back. I felt a peace settlin over me. Mam was doin the same in her own way. Even if she tried to come to me, the misery drug her back. It was up to her to come on back and fight the misery. I just need to be here when she comes back.

Evenin came. The sun was down. I sat alone with a heavy heart, but a more peaceful one. I saw an old woman comin towards me on the beach. I thought my eyes were playin tricks in the dusky light. Short and round she advanced on me; her feet weren't touchin the sand. I heard her say, "You needs to fetch yo'r Mam. Tell her I say 'Mammy love you, Johnny love you. Be brave. Come on home to be loved. Dat all dere be'." Mammy faded from view.

I went to find Mam. To my surprise, she was stumbling up Main Street. When she saw me, she waved and called my name. I ran to her. "Johnny," she paused catching her breath, "Did you see Mammy? She say you love me, her to, and come home to be loved. I sorry Johnny. I sorry." She fell in a heap. I couldn't move her. I ran for Bo to help me.

She was sick, real sick. Bo said she was sick of mind and body, soul too. It wasn't easy to tell which was worse. I left Bo and Mam together and let Mrs. Bea know I couldn't work Monday. "My Mam's real sick."

"That's fine Johnny, you take good care of her. I'll expect you Tuesday."

Bo stayed with us all night, and the next day too. Mam puked and puked. She shook. Bo said it was the drink demons comin out of her. He held her body down. I was so scared. She was crazy. If she wasn't callin for Mammy or me, she was a-scratchin her skin raw or fightin off bugs and spiders. If she wasn't doin that, she was tryin to run away from us. By late afternoon, even I could see she was just gettin worse. I went back to Mrs. Bea.

"I don't know when I can be back to work. I'm a-thinkin my Mam might die she so sick. I needs to stay wid her. Please don't fire me." I begged. "I needs dis job, but I needs to take care o' my Mam."

"Of course, you do Honey," she patted my back. "You stay and take care of your Mam, until she is better. Your job will be her for you. Give me a minute. You just wait right here, and let me get you some sandwiches. You're going to need something to eat, so you can take care of her." When she returned she had a basket with big thick sandwiches in it. "You're a good boy John. Go take care of your mother."

Chapter Three
Judge Not

Mam was jerkin all over when I got back to the beach! White stuff was comin out of her mouth. Bo tried to hold her up, but she was so stiff, it took both of us. He demanded, "Give me any money you got!" Why was he askin that? Mam's sick. "She got to have a drink of whiskey. She need it right now. It de demon in de whiskey makin her sick." I gave him the few cents I'd saved. "I'll be right back" he shouted as he ran towards town.

I didn't know what to think! Bo was my friend, but I have to tell you that when he left and took all the money I had in the world, I was worried. Mam was sicker than anybody I'd ever seen. I didn't have no one else. What if he just kept the money and never came back. He could do that.

I need not have worried. Bo came back right away just like he said he would. I held Mam up, while he dribbled a little whiskey into her mouth. She grabbed at his hands holdin the bottle, but he took it away. She fell into a restless sleep. Bo built a fire. Mam was shivering, but she was sweatin at the same time. "Best you keep dis," Bo volunteered the whiskey bottle. "Dat ole devil in dat bottle done knows my name." We kept watch.

When Mam quietened down, I asked him if he still drank whiskey. He said he didn't, but then he added, "Well, I ain't in a long time. Dat's why I fish. I sells my fish, and I has a few cents here and dere fer food, but I don't has 'nuff to drink no mo. Anyways, dat what I tells myself." He looked down at the ground. "I had me a family once a long time ago. My woman and me, we had us two babies. They was sweet lil boy babies. My woman was a good woman. I loved dem babies and my woman too. I grew corn in de fields for my Massa, and he done let me make corn squeezins. Thing was, I liked to drink what I made. Dat wouldn't have been so bad, but when I drank, I be mean, real mean. I done beat on my woman and my babies too. The Massa, he didn't like me messin wid his property, so he sold me off. My new Massa, he liked the devil drink too, like me. Thing is, he liked to drink wid me, and then, he blamed his meanness on me. He beat on me likes I'd beat on my family. I deserved it and mo. No doubt 'bout dat! When de war ended, and Mr. Lincoln sent out dat Proclamation dat we was free, I jez took me up and walk away. I been here in Galveston ever since. I found lots of jobs, when I first done come here, but I couldn't keep no work, because I had money, I had whiskey. If I didn't have no money, I begged. When I couldn't get it beggin, I get straight, and get another job. It start all over a'g'in. Pert soon, no body hire me no mo. I's tryin hard not to drink no mo. I don't like who I is when I do. My boys grown by now, if'n dey ain't dead. I don't know what happened to my woman. Old plantation burned down to de ground. I ain't got no family. I ain't got no one. I ain't never even had no friend til you boy. Is you still gonna be my friend now dat I done told you all dis?" He stared intently at me waiting for my answer.

I looked into his red eyes. I looked at my fallen mother. Who was I to pass judgment on them? Besides I loved them both more than anyone else in the world. "Of course, you're my friend Bo. You'll always be my friend." Bo moved to my side and put his arm around me. No man in my life had ever put his arm around me. I couldn't help it, man or no, I cried into his chest. I felt his tears falling on to my neck.

"We's gonna take good care of yo'r Mam. We gonna do all we can fer her. She have to do what we cain't." Together, we sat watching Mam all night. When she began to shake and talk out of her head, I held her up and Bo gave her a sip of whiskey. She begged for more, but he told her "No, yo boy don't need to see you like dis no mo! You jez shush now. Let old Bo take care o you." She laid back down like a scolded child.

During the vigil, Bo and I talked about what to do next. He said that I should go back to work. "What yo Mam need now is somebody like me to take good care o' her. I cans do dat. I needs to do dat fer you and fer her, but most o' all, fer me." He convinced me to go. "When you done wid work, you come on back here, and you can stay wid yo Mam, whilst I fish. We can sell dem fish, and buy a bit of food to stick to yo Mam's skinny ribs."

So that was our plan. I returned to Mrs. Bea's Boarding House. She gave me a blanket and a dress for my Mam, and a few other woman type things. I didn't tell her we were on the beach, but I did find the courage to tell her that I wasn't white. "John, it doesn't matter to me if you're purple. You're a good boy and a good worker. Take that broom, and get to sweeping." I was so glad to know it didn't matter, but I couldn't help wondering if I would have gotten the job had she known I wasn't white from the beginning. I shook that thought from my head. I had sweepin to do.

Mam did get better. Her body got better first. Her mind was another thing altogether. She had all kinds of reasons that she needed to go to town. Bo told me whatever I did to not let her go. "That old devil drink done stuck in her head. It got to come outta dere. That take time, and wid some folk, time don't even do it." When Bo would go fish, Mam would try her best to leave. I told her everythin I could think of to keep her put. She could be nasty and say "down dirty" words to me, but even when she hurt me in my heart, I wouldn't let her go. I was bigger than she was now, and if I held on to her, she wasn't going nowhere.

With Bo, Mam tried her womanly things, but Bo didn't budge. He'd just push her away, and tell her "Johnny love you woman. Behave yo'self fer dat boy!" That would usually stop her.

Fall was coming on in Galveston when Mam was at last her old self again, if that were even possible. (Sometimes I think it's better if we don't try to fully go back to our old selves. I've never met anyone who really could go back, but I've met plenty who tried and failed miserably. I think it's just better to go from where you're at, and move forward to a new you, but that's just me.) Mrs. Bea gave me a trunk full of woman's clothes and shoes that had been left behind at the boardin house by one of the summer folks. "You take these home. They're just taking up room here. Maybe your mother can use some of them." Mam's eyes lit up when she opened that trunk. I brought a bucket of water and a piece of soap for her the next day. When I woke up to go to work, Mam was just finishing dressing. She was wearing one of the nice dresses from the trunk. She went lookin for work. This time, she found a job. She was to be the cook for a rich lady that lived on the Strand where all the fine houses were. Mam was in her element. She was feelin good about herself again. She was cookin in a Big House. The people liked her food. They liked her. My Mam came back to me just like the waves on the beach, and she sent that misery out to stay. We was "gonna be happy" after all.

With Mam's money and mine, we found us a little place again, and it had a floor. It wasn't big, but it was two rooms. Bo came to live with us. He was part of our family now. He handed over almost every penny he made sellin his fish, and he cleaned up after us all. Mam was glad of that, because she worked long hours. She didn't come home until very late, but she brought us left-over food when she did. That's not all. The most important thing was that she brought us a smile. That made me and Bo happier than all the pecan pie in the whole world! It didn't stop us eatin it though.

Chapter Four
Christmas

We had a wonderful Christmas that year, even if we did have to wait until the day after the holiday to celebrate Jesus's birthday. Mam had to work. We were grateful that Mam was workin and that she was well. Bo and me popped us up some popcorn and stitched it together with a needle and thread. He found us a big branch of driftwood to serve as our tree. We hung the strings of corn on it. It was the first Christmas tree of our own that any of us had ever had. Bo cooked up some sweet potatoes and cornbread. Mrs. Bea gave us some fried chicken that she'd made for her table and some biscuits. I thanked her for that. She reminded me of Mammy in so many ways, and this was just another one. I couldn't help but think that Mammy had a hand in that particular gift of food. Made me laugh. When Mam came home from The Strand, she brought a whole pecan pie. She knew it was mine and Bo's favorite. She said that her Mrs. gave it specifically to her for us to have, since she had worked on Christmas Day. She liked her Mrs. almost as much as I liked Mrs. Bea.

Mam saw what Bo and I had done. She cried. I just don't understand why women cry so much! They cry when they're happy. They cry when they're sad. By George, they even cry when they're mad! I was pretty sure that these tears were happy tears though, and I much prefer that kind. She had worked straight for the past day and a half, and Bo and I told her to go to sleep. We would have our dinner whenever she woke up rested. We took our poles and went fishin.

After we sold our catch, we went to the General Store. Bo took off on his own. So did I. The man in the store wrapped our purchases in brown paper and string, and we went home to Mam. She was awake by then. It was almost dark. She put little candles on some of the branches of the driftwood tree, and she hung a few pieces of ribbon on it too. Our little tree came to life. The table was set for our fine Christmas dinner. We each had a plate, a regular kind of glass-like plate, not a metal or a wooden one. They had a few chips as I recall, but we were so proud of them. That was Mam's gift to us.

Dinner was delicious. Mam said it was because we were eatin it on fine china. We agreed and chuckled at her. She'd put all the food into the warmer of the stove, and it was waitin for us. We pulled up our boxes to sit. We were more than ready to eat, but Mam stopped us. "Who wants to say de grace?" I looked at Bo; he looked at me. Mam smiled and giggled, "Don't you worry none. Dis time I's gonna say grace."

Dear God, I hopes you is a-listenin to dis wretched sinner woman tonight, cause I's got a bit to say. I wants to tell you Lord dat I love you. I thanks you fer my boy Johnny, and fer our dear friend here, Bo. Dey is special blessin's, and I loves You fer sending the two of dem my way in dis life. I thanks you fer sending yo'r little baby boy Jesus so long ago. Jez like us here, He didn't have so much worldly things, but He had love, and He gave it away. We has love here fer each other. Dat de most impo'tant thing, next to You. I love you Lord Jesus. I wants dese men here to knows dat I do. I done axed forgiveness fer all the wrongs I did to dem and to me, but mostest to You. I knows you done fergived me. I thanks you fer dat kindness. I ax you to bless my Johnny and Bo fer savin me from dat evil drink, so dat's we's could all be here tonight to praise Yo'r name. Please God, watch o'er dem, and keep dem safe. Bless me too, and if You see Mammy round dere, tell her I good wid You now, and things is fine. I's a-axen a special blessin on dis food that You done provided fer us. This be the best birthday dinner ever fer you Jesus. Yo'r Will be done. In Your Name, Amen.

Tears spilled down Bo's and my cheeks. We couldn't help ourselves. Mam had cried throughout the prayer. What a night!

Dinner over, Mam cleaned up. Instead of helpin like he usually did, Bo went outside. When he returned, I saw him slip two brown packages under our tree. This was my cue. I pulled my two packages out from under my bedding, and put them under the tree as well. Then, we helped finish clearin up.

I couldn't wait any longer. "Come on Mam, Come sit." I took my gift for her and placed it in her hands. She cried again! (Is there no stopping her?) She pulled me to her, hugging and kissing me on the cheek.

"You's de best gift I ever got, but dis may be de second best!" She opened it, and inside was a sewing basket full of needles, all different colored threads, a thimble and tiny pair of scissors. She hugged the basket to her chest, and pulled me to her once again. She was so happy. I hadn't seen her that happy in a very long time. Danged, if I didn't feel a tear or two creepin out of my eyes.

I went back to the tree, and picked up the other gift. I handed it to Bo. "Oh no, Johnny, you didn't get me nothin. I ain't ne'er had no gift. Not one, not from no one."

"You has one now. Just open it and shush." I answered him grinnin ear to ear.

Inside was a knife that folded inside itself. It was a pocket knife. Bo couldn't speak. He hugged and hugged on me instead. I didn't really want him to say anythin, because I couldn't. He showed it to Mam. Then he grabbed me ag'in. When he composed himself, he went to the tree, and brought out the packages that he'd gotten for us.

He gave Mam a blanket. It wasn't a scratchy one like we slept under, but a soft knitted one. "It's jez big nuff to cover you when you sittin and rockin," he told her. Mam laughed.

"I cans use it when I sit right here on dis box fer now. It's de nicest cover I ever did have Bo. I thanks you."

"Oh!" Bo shouted as he bolted out the door. Returning in just a minute, he was haulin a little sewin rockin chair. "How could I's ferget dis!" and he grinned broadly. If there hadn't been tears before, there were now! Mam was beside herself! I hadn't known what Bo was gettin her, and he hadn't known what I was. I guess it's true. There's no such thing as coincidence!

"Ain't you gonna open yo'r present now? Bo looked at me expectantly. I looked down at my lap. This was all too much. We were just like folks in a big house tonight, with a tree and a big dinner and gifts and everythin.

"Bo, I think I'm gonna cry again. Why you gonna make me cry?" He laughed and motioned for me to open it. I felt the package. It wasn't hard, but it wasn't really soft either. I picked at the corner being silly, but all I could see was that it was dark inside. They were both fussin at me to hurry up and open it. I borrowed Bo's new pocket knife to cut the string. Then, I carefully knotted and rolled the string up. It was fun teasin them. The suspense finally got to me. I couldn't play around anymore, no matter how much fun it was. I tore off the paper and lyin in my lap was a pair of long trousers. My very first long trousers! It was the first new piece of clothin I had ever had. I was overwhelmed. I squealed with happiness. My first long pair of pants! In my head, I heard Mammy say, "See Johnny, I tolds you. You's a man, and now a man done sees it too!" I could never repay Bo for what he'd given me!

Mam rocked in her rocker watching me strut my stuff in my new pants. Bo whittled with his new knife. Mam began to sing. It had been a very long time since I'd heard her sing. We hadn't been to church since the early days after we first moved here. When the light went out behind her eyes, the songs left her as well. Now, they were back. In her beautiful voice, she sang.

"It came upon a midnight clear; Dat glorious song of old, From angels bendin near de earth, To touch der harps of gold. 'Peace on de earth, good will to men, From Heav'ns all gracious King.' De world in solemn stillness lay To hear de angels sing.

And then, from out of nowhere...

"Mine eyes has seen de glory of de comin of de Lord, He is tramplin out de vintage where de grapes o' wrath is stored. He hath loosed de fateful lightenin of His terrible swift sword, His truth is marchin on. Glory, glory, hallelujah, Glory, glory hallelujah, Glory, glory, hallelujah, His truth is marchin on."

I recalled her voice from the past. "We's free now. Nobody

cans sell us no mo. We's got to make it on our own. We's free Johnny. We gonna be happy. You jez wait and see. It be good, jez you and me Johnny; we gonna be fine. We gonna go where we want to go. We gonna have our own place someday. You jez wait and see. It be good, jez you and me. You gonna make new friends."

It had all come true. I looked around the room. We were free. We were makin it on our own in a place of our choosin. We had made new friends. We are happy, not only Mam and me, but Bo too. It had come true, just as Mam had said. To top it all off, I knew for certain that Mammy had come with us after all. Mammy was free. She was in Heaven, but she was with us too. Everythin we'd been through to get here was worth it tonight.

Chapter Five
She Went One Way

The holiday was over, and it was time to get back to work. There would be another big holiday comin in just five days. New Year's Day, 1872. Lots of folks would be arrivin at Mrs. Bea's, and there would be a lot of extra work. Mrs. Bea said she would pay me extra if I'd stay on for the next few days to help with luggage and folks' wants. That would be a nice way to start the New Year I figured, since I'd spent every cent I had for Christmas gifts. I was up early and arrived as always with the dawn at the boardin house.

Mam and I left at the same time now every mornin. She gave me a hug and kissed me goodbye. She went one way; I went the other.

Bo was still asleep. He would wake later and straighten up while he had his coffee. After that, he would go fishin. Of course, he never had to ever straighten up a thing again if he didn't want to, because after that rocking chair present, Mam would let him stay on with us if he never swept another floor!

It was an unusually busy day. It was a little more excitin with so many people arrivin at Mrs. Bea's Boarding House. She hired an extra person to cook with her, so that she could be there personally to welcome and assist her guests. They were so needy. Mostly, it was couples, but some of them brought their small children with a grandmother or a nanny to watch over them. It made for a lot of noise in the house. About midday, Mrs. Bea asked me if I could run to the bakery and the store for her. She needed some things. I wanted to get out of there. I enjoyed the children runnin and playin hide and seek, but I wasn't used to it. A little went a long way. Besides, I was a man in long pants now, and somehow it didn't seem quite right for them to be wantin me to play with them.

I escaped. Workmen were busily placing more cobblestones on the main dirt roads. It would help the carriages and wagons when it rained to still be able to navigate. Cotton was being sold again, and there were more people comin to Galveston all the time. Galveston was better than havin to go all the way to New Orleans to sell, even though the prices were higher there. Guests were arrivin on the ferry to see the fireworks over the water on New Year's Eve night. I found myself listenin to the noises in the city. There were women shoutin about sellin fish. I heard a boy calling from the corner; he was sellin newspapers. Fruit and vegetable vendors lined the streets with their associated racket. Cattle waiting for slaughter mooed their complaints. I heard the chaotic chatter of people meetin on the boardwalks. A definite excitement was in the air. People tended to stay to their homes for Christmas, but New Years was a party in the makin, and obviously a good time to travel.

I traveled to the bakery first. "I'm here to pick up Mrs. Bea's order." The feller behind the counter told me that it would take a few minutes. "I'll be back. I'll just leave her order here," I said as I placed her notepaper under a rock on his counter. "I need to go pick up another order from the General Store." I wandered casually into the sunshine on this brisk winter day. I was in no hurry.

The weather was cool and crisp. A strong wind was blowin from the Gulf. It was the kind of day too good to be inside. It felt good being out here. I sat down on a bench on the boardwalk, the sun bouncing off my face. I watched the people go by. Some of them were dressed in their best finery. A lot of it looked like it was new, so I guessed that maybe they had received it as Christmas gifts. They may have more money than we do, I thought to myself, but there's no way that any of those finely dressed strollers had a better Christmas than we did.

In front of me, there were two men dressed in worn-out work clothes standing at the hitchin post with their horses. I watched as their conversation grew louder accompanied by gestures. The taller of the two suddenly landed a fist to the other's head knocking him backwards forcefully into his horse. The horse spooked, rearing up and backing into a horse pulling a small buggy up the street. Now the second horse spooked! In response, the frenzied buggy horse bolted jerking the buggy sideways into a water trough. The buggy tipped, the driver lost his balance and was tossed to the street. Now totally disoriented, the buggy horse lurched forward at breakneck speed. Like a thunderbolt he dashed up the street in a dead run. With no one holding the reins, the buggy tipped to and fro threatening to overturn. I was on my feet watchin this show, when I suddenly had a sinkin feelin in my belly.

I didn't know why, but I ran. "Stop him! Stop him!" I screamed joinin my cries for help with an already swelling chorus.

She was carrying boxes stacked one atop another. Her Mrs. walked in front of her crossing The Strand. Mam looked towards the commotion. She saw the wild-eyed horse and the careening carriage comin directly towards them. Droppin the boxes, she leaped forward pushin her Mrs. out of the way, but it was too late for Mam. I watched as the horse charged her and she went down under his hooves and the wheels of the buggy. I couldn't believe my eyes!

"Mam!" I screamed helplessly. A long piercing cry escaped my lips as I saw her lying lifeless in the road. By the time I reached her, her Mrs. was kneelin by Mam holdin her head. She was white as a sheet; Mam, on the other hand, looked a dusty gray. She didn't move.

"Help! Someone help me! Mrs. screeched. Men ran to her. "Not me, you fools! Help her! Get a doctor quick! You two, help me get her in the house!" she demanded.

The men were already pickin Mam up as I reached for her. "Get her legs Boy!" one of them ordered. I took her feet. How heavy they were for such a tiny woman! I would have never thought. We carried her inside. The Mrs. had us lay her on the sofa. I hovered near her feet tryin to see Mam's face through the bulkiness of men. They left. I didn't. The household was in an uproar. The maid brought water and smellin salts, but Mam didn't open her eyes. The man servant was sent for the doctor, but as he reached the front gate, the doctor rushed past him bounding up the stairs. I heard him askin where the Mrs. was. He thought she was hurt, until he saw Mam lying there.

"Are you all right?" he inquired of the Mrs. She replied that she was, but that her servant wasn't.

"She saved me. She pushed me out of the way." She was anguished. "Save her. I'll pay anything. Just save her."

"She's alive" he offered as he pulled Mam's eyelids open and peered inside. "Barely alive. How long has she been like this?"

"Minutes, I don't know. Since she was run over by that horse and carriage. Long enough to get her out of the street and here!"

"We need to move her to a bed and get her clothes off. I have to examine her. I have to do it now. Come here boy," he pointed to me. I moved to catch her feet again. The man-servant took her middle, the doctor, her chest. "Let's keep her straight as we can." Her Mrs. held her head and we moved in unison to the nearest bedroom. Gently, we laid her down. Motioning for the Mrs. to stay, he stated "Do you have scissors? We've got to get these clothes off." The man servant went for scissors. Mam didn't move. I didn't either. I could see her barely breathing. She wasn't dead. Thank you God. I must have said it out loud, because the Mrs, looked up at me.

"Are you all right boy?" she asked. "You look a little peaked. Thanks for your help. You best be going now. We've got work to do here."

Stubbornly I declared "I AIN'T GOIN NOWHERES!"

"I beg your pardon. I don't need any smart talk!"

"No, Mrs. I ain't goin. That there's my Mam."

"What? Your Mam, you mean your mother, but you're white." The doctor glanced at her as if to tell her to hush. "Sure, you must stay. We'll take good care of her. Step outside just for a bit, while we get these clothes off her, and Doc takes a look. Then, you can come back in."

"Just til then," I spoke hesitantly backing out of the room. I didn't want to take my eyes off Mam, not even for a second. The door shut. I was standin in the hall lookin at the closed door. The man-servant took my arm and moved me to the kitchen.

"Sit down son. You look likes you gonna fall down." He brought me water. "Put yo'r head b'tween your knees." I did. In a short while, I felt somewhat better. "I's heard 'bout you Johnny. Yo'r Mam mighty proud o' you. You works down the road at Mrs. Bea's Boarding House, right? What was you doin up here?" I told him my story about having to go to the bakery and store for Mrs. Bea, and then, there was nothin more to say. I could feel that pain in my throat, when you're close to cryin, and it hurts so bad. I couldn't swallow. I was afraid to talk any more. I was tryin so hard to be strong for Mam. I looked up. Mam's Mrs. was cryin softly. The doctor looked grave.

"Her ribs are broken, but she's still breathing. It appears that the horse's hooves went over her twice. Her head was stomped. She's got some fluid leaking from her ears and nose. I'm afraid her skull is cracked. I've bandaged her best I can; but we'll have to wait and see if she comes back. Right now, I've got to do some surgery. I'm not sure she can stand it, but she's going to bleed to death if I don't. When the buggy ran over her leg, it broke the big bone. That I could fix, but it tore the leg up inside pretty bad, and now that leg and her belly are filling up with blood. We need to clear this table and bring her in here to open up that leg."

The Mrs. told me to come back to the bedroom. "Spend some time with your Mam, while we get things ready in here. Talk to her boy. I'm sorry, what's your name? I knew she had a boy that she was mighty proud of, but I don't remember your name."

"It's John. She called me Johnny. Mam always called me Johnny." I whimpered and felt tears building.

"Your Mam's going to be all right. She will be John. We'll take care of her. We'll make her all right. You go on in there now, and talk to her. Tell her how much you love her. Tell her how much you need her to fight to be here." I did.

I could hear the sounds of preparations being made for the doctor to operate. Dishes clattered from the table. Pots of water rattled loudly as they were placed on the fire. Sheets were torn in strips. They came for her with the table top, and after she was placed on it, four men carried her back to the kitchen. My heart ached. I wasn't allowed to go with her.

I staggered blinded by tears to the front porch. I never felt so alone in my life. Okay Lord, I's countin on you. Help Mam. Please. Mammy, if you's there, talk to yo'r God and tell him I needs Mam." I was in agony. Bo, I needed Bo, but he was most likely somewhere fishin. He expected us both to be late, so there was no reason for him to come home like usual. Oh, no, I thought. Mrs. Bea must be frantic. I jumped up from the bench looking right and left! I didn't know what to do!

Hearing chair legs scrape, I turned. "John, what is it?" It was the man-servant.

"It's Mrs. Bea. She's gonna be worried out of her head!" I stammered.

"It's aw right John. I done sent someone to pick up her things from de bakery and de store and to tells her what' happenin. You cans rest easy on dat."

I thankfully collapsed back to the bench. "I appreciate that." Time drug by.

It was dark now and getting colder all the time. The man-servant was still on the porch with me. "What's takin so long? You heared anythin?"

"Yo Mam back in de bed, but she not doin too good. The Doc and Mrs. is wid her. She say she come get you if anythin change."

"I feels so helpless. What's yo'r name?"

"Ben" he replied sadly. He handed me a blanket to wrap around my shoulders. He wrapped one around his.

We sat there silently. It was the longest night of my young life. When the first rays of sun peaked on the horizon, the Mrs. came outside. "I don't know what to tell you John. She's still with us, but it's touch and go. Why don't you go back inside? Susie will fix you both something to eat. You must be starving by now, a big boy like you. I'm going to send the doctor home and clean up Mam, and then, you can come in."

I agreed. I didn't know I was hungry until I tasted that first drink of buttermilk, and then I ate everythin that Susie put in front of me. Ben gobbled his food right alongside me. He asked if there was anythin he could do for me. I told him about Bo. Bo would be wonderin where me and Mam were by now. Ben said he'd go right away and bring him here. I needed Bo. Mam needed Bo.

I was sittin beside Mam holdin her hand, when I heard quick steps on the front porch stairs. I knew they belonged to Bo. Ben ushered him into the room. Ben had given Bo a good scrubbin and some different clothes, shoes too. I figured they must be Ben's because of the size of them. They swallowed Bo, but he looked nice. As Bo encircled me with his strong arms, I broke down. I couldn't help myself. He let me cry like a baby, and then holdin me out in front of him, he looked sternly at me and said "Johnny, you gots to be brave for Mam. We all has. She need us to be strong fer her." He carried a chair to the other side of her bed and took her hand in his. I heard him whisperin to her from time-to-time, but I couldn't tell what it was he was sayin. The only time we left Mam was to eat or go to the outhouse, and of course, when the Mrs. and Susie came to clean her up and change her bandages. Mam never moved. She never blinked. Three days passed.

"I don't think she's gonna make it," the doctor shared. "Her breathing isn't as good today as it was yesterday. She's lost a lot of blood." I didn't cry. Neither did Bo. The Mrs. did. The three of us sat with her all night, and the next day. Mam was makin loud awful noises when she took a breath. It was just terrible to hear! I will never forget it as long as I live. People all over the house and porch could hear her. There was no gettin away from the sounds comin from my mother's poor little body. I wanted to run, but I couldn't. I owed Mam that. I owed her to pass with me holdin her hand.

The Mrs. didn't leave her bedside either. She and Bo and me took turns. "As long as she breathes, there's hope she'll open her eyes," she remarked. "She saved me you know. She threw herself in front of that horse to save me. We have to keep on hoping. Don't give up on her."

Bo and I didn't give up. We talked to her. We held her hands. We wiped her face. And then, somehow I knew. Mam was leavin. She was goin home to her Mammy. I told Bo. He shook his head. He knew too. I kissed her forehead goodbye. Just before the New Year, Mam's life ended. The fireworks began.

Chapter Six
I Went the Other Way

Nothin would ever be the same. I knew it in my achin heart. I saw it in Bo's face when he looked at me. Her Mrs. and us buried her in the colored folk's cemetery there on the island. Her Mrs. had a marker of stone made for her. It read:

Here lies Aida Mary Johnson

Born in Louisiana 1845

Died Free in Texas 1871

Loving mother of Johnny

Loved by Bo.

Died for her friend, Abigail.

She sings in Heaven for the Angels

Mam would have been so pleased with her headstone. I was, but I wasn't. I just wanted Mam. Bo and I stayed on in our rooms for a while, but then Bo told me that he just had to go. "Stayin here jez makin me sad. I gots to go Johnny. I cain't stays here no more." I understood. I wanted to go too, but I didn't have anywhere to go. Then, Mrs. Bea offered me a room all of my own in her upstairs. I took it. I didn't have to pay anythin. She loved me, even if she was a white woman. I saw Bo fishin sometime, but then one day I went to find him, and he was gone. I guess he couldn't bear another goodbye. I couldn't either.

I turned thirteen in the springtime, but there was no pleasure in it. Mrs. Bea made me a cake. I had a hard time chokin it down, because I couldn't help thinkin of my other birthday cake. She meant well. She was a good woman tryin to make me feel better.

Time passed so slowly, but it has a way of passin. Summer was over. Mrs. Bea asked to speak with me. I thought maybe I'd done somethin wrong. She wasn't mad. I worried all the time about her getting mad at me and makin me leave. I don't know why. She was one of the kindest women I'd ever known, but I still worried.

Smilin at me, she asked, "So, John, what is it you want to do when you're grown up?"

"I don't rightly know." I meant it. I didn't.

"John, do you know how to write your name?"

"No Mam, I never learned how. No need." I answered matter-of-factly.

"There is a need, and I want to teach you, but only if you really want to learn."

"I never figured on readin or writin, Mrs. Bea. Do you think a dumb colored feller like me could learn?"

"I don't ever want to hear you say a thing like that about yourself again, John Johnson!" She was fuming mad. "I mean it! You are not dumb. Get that out of your head. Question is whether or not you want to learn?"

"Well, if you think I can, then yes, I reckon I do. I think that would make my Mam and Mammy happy, don't you?"

"I certainly do. I think they'd be very happy, and you'll be happy too. School starts tonight," Mrs. Bea dictated. "You meet me in the kitchen after all the dishes are done. Here's a list of things I need you to bring from the store, so we can start your education." I took the list. I looked at it. I didn't understand any of the scribbles. I looked back at her. "Don't worry Johnny, pretty soon, you'll be able to read every word on that paper, and write it too."

Well, maybe so I thought, maybe not, but I was gonna give it a try. I picked up the supplies, and that night lessons began. It was hard at first. I felt stupid. I kept at it and pretty soon, I got the hang of it. Mrs. Bea was pleased with my progress. She said I was a fast learner. Anyway, that's what she said. I learned my ABC's in no time at all. I enjoyed learnin numbers. I was better at the numbers than the letters, but I was likin this learnin stuff. Once I learned how to do little words, I got excited. I wanted to learn more words. Mrs. Bea read to me in the beginning. Before I knew it, I was reading in McGuffey's Reader myself. I was proud of myself when I read the first page without any help at all, and I did it right. I couldn't stop grinning! Somewhere along the way, I realized that the way I talked wasn't the way things were read, and I determined to learn to speak and write in a more proper manner.

Becoming an educated man, as Mrs. Bea put it, took time and effort. Mostly it took a love of learning. I spent nights in my room with the coal lamp burning, so that I could read and do my sums better. Mrs. Bea told me that I surpassed all her expectations. "See, your Mam and Mammy were right when they told you how smart you were. You are smart. Be proud of yourself. John, books can take you anywhere. Knowing how to figure sums can make you wealthy." I believed everything she told me. I worked hard at my studies, but if I am honest, I would have to say that I worked hard partly to keep my mind off missing Mam and Bo, as much as to learn. It all worked together.

One morning I was out in the back of the house doing my chores, and I heard a familiar voice. "Johnny, how ya doin?" I turned. It was Bo. It had been well over a year. I joyfully threw my arms around him.

"I've missed you so much. Where have you been?" I asked. We stood there patting each other on the shoulders and hugging. It was so good to see him again, and he looked good. He looked clean and real good.

"Let's us go fishin dis afternoon," he ventured with a questioning look on his face. "You think Mrs. Bea'll let you?"

"I'll ask, but I'm sure she will. Where will I find you?"

"I be right down de street in front of de bakery waitin fer ya. It don't matter what time. I's gonna be dere. We's got a lot of catchin up to do."

Mrs. Bea was excited for me. "Let me make you two some sandwiches, and you get on outta here. There isn't a thing that can't wait until tomorrow." She sent me on my way in minutes with her wonderful ham sandwiches and pickles. She knew what I liked.

There Bo was waiting on a box. We hugged. "Where's your pole?"

"Come wid me. We gonna get it. What you got in dat paper dere? Smells like ham."

"It is. Mrs. Bea fixed us some ham sandwiches for us to take fishing. She said you feel free to stop by anytime." We walked fast and talked faster.

"You sure done shot up. You way taller dan me now. I jez cain't believe you so big! Guess you needin another pair of pants!" We laughed.

"Right here's where I stays," he remarked as he pointed to a little shack. By the door were two fishing poles, some stringers and a bag. "Just let me leave my shoes here." He opened the door and pitched his shoes inside. We walked over the dunes to the beach as we had a thousand times before. It was as if no time had passed between us.

After we wet our lines, we began to talk. At first, we were careful not to mention anything that might be upsetting, but as our comfort grew, so did our conversation. "What you been doin, Johnny? I think 'bout you all de time. I wonder how you be. I missed you."

"I've been learnin how to read and write and do numbers from Mrs. Bea. Can you believes dat?" Enthusiastically I continued, "A feller like me! I can read and write now. I like to read, but I cain't get hold of too many books. I wish I had more. There's a school here. Mrs. Bea said she'd see 'bout gettin me in there, but you know what, I just ain't (I mean, I'm not) the right color inside fer dat school house. Besides I got to pay my way by workin fer Mrs. Bea. She a good teacher anyhow. Does that surprise you? Me readin and writing and doin sums?"

Bo had a big smile on his face. "No, that don't surprise me none at all. I bet Mam proud of you. I is. You know I needs to tell you what happened to me."

Worried he might bolt and run again, I replied, "Nah, you don't need to tell me. It's enough you're back here with me now."

"Yes, Johnny, I needs to tell you. I needs to tell you fer both o' us. Let's plant dese poles and sit a spell."

We gathered up our things and moved to a washed up log. We sat down. I was feelin butterflies in my stomach. Did I really want to know? Well, I thought, I guess it doesn't make any difference whether I want to know or not, because Bo's made up his mind that he's gonna tell me. Trying to delay the inevitable, I unwrapped us each a sandwich, and we ate. That Mrs. Bea, she sure knows how to make a man a sandwich. Her bread's cut thick, and then she slathers butter on it, before adding a big slice of ham. Sometimes, she'll add tomato, but not today. Today, it was pickle. Yum. We make short work of our food. There was nothin to do now, but listen to Bo do his talkin.

"I's ain't old. I knows you thinks I is, but I ain't. I jez look dat way 'cause I took to de drink fer so long and hard. I's only 42 years old. That ain't old. But it old nuff fer me to know, you could be my boy, and then, I met yo'r Mam. She coulda been my woman. I guess somewhere in my head, I pictured us'ns dat way. I never did nothin 'bout it, but I thought 'bout yo'r Mam dat way. That why I never did say nothin. I were so 'fraid I would start dat devil drinkin and be mean ag'in. When I were a young man, my mamma done take me to church. I believed all dat stuff. I were a religious fella, til after me and my woman got together. Then, I fell on evil ways. I fell in wid devil drinkin evil peoples. My babies came, and I tried to be good ag'in, but I didn't last too long at it. They cried in the nighttime, and I was tired all de time from workin in de field. She couldn't make dem quiet, so I start drinkin ag'in just so's I could sleep. Anyway dat what I thought. Dat didn't help. I just got meaner and meaner, til Massa sold me off. I done told you all dat afore. I knows I's rambling.

Well, here de thing. I love Mam and you. I was 'fraid to, but I jez cain't he'p myself. She done showed me what love could do when she got over her bad times. She loved you so much that she let go her fears and worries and was dere fer you. When she did dat, I thought, well maybe, jez maybe, I's could do it too.

We had us a nice little home, didn't we? Weren't dat Christmas tree of ours somethin special? Mam,She was jez like them lil candles she put on dem branches. She lighted all us up and made us look better than we really was. Anyway, me she did. I had everythin I wanted there wid de two of you.

And then, that horse went crazy in de street, knocked her down, kilt her, kilt us. Afore she passed, I told her all dat, but it were too late then." He cried silently now, but ever so often his body would jerk with emotion. He had me cryin with him.

"I tried my best to stay Johnny. I really did, but de bottle, it called my name. I sure didn't want you a-seein me dat way. I never done want to hurt you, so dat's why I done left wid no goodbye. I tried to stay but I just couldn't. I didn't want to say goodbye to you, just like I didn't wants to say bye to Mam." He paused wiping his tears away with his shirt sleeve. "I hads to go."

Composing himself, he continued "I gots drunk. I gots mean. I gots on de ferry and took myself over to Harrisburg. I couldn't bear de thought of you seeing me de way my babies afore done seen me. I don't know how long I's drunk…long time. One day I wake up by a ditch. Bloody and beaten I were. Inside and out. I found me a puddle o' muddy water to wash in. Dat puddle jez happen to be by a little colored folk's church. They was a-singin. They was a-singin dat song yo Mam sang to us."

"The Christmas song? Hark the Herald Angels' song?" I inquired.

"Nope, twern't dat one. It de oth'r. You know." He raised his eyes to the sky, and in a clear booming voice he sang:

"Mine eyes has seen de glory of de comin of de Lord,

> He is tramplin out de vintage where de grapes o' wrath is stored,
>
> He hath loosed de fateful lightnin o' His terrible swift sword,
>
> His truth is marchin on. Glory, glory, hallelujah,
>
> Glory, glory, hallelujah. Glory, glory, hallelujah,
>
> His truth is marchin on."

"That be my bolt of lightnin from de Lord to me through Mam. I knew de glory dere all de time. He trampled all de bad anger out o' me. He let me know dat de truth o' his love done lay right dere in front o' me. I's been singin and preachin his praises ever since. Do you believe dat? Me, I's a preacher now. I's called to do de Lord's work, and dat's why I's here."

"That's wonderful, but I don't understand. What do you mean, 'that's why you're here?'"

"I's here to set you free Johnny. Free in a different way than Mr. Lincoln did. I's here to tell you dat God love you and me. So do Mam. She want us to be free in ev'ry way. I's here to ask you if you will let de Lord Jesus come into yo'r life?"

Stuttering, I managed to tell Bo that I would have to think about it, but that I was happy for him. Trying to change the subject, I inquired, "What about the drink Bo?"

"I's don't wants it no more. It done outta my head and my soul. I's got all I needs. I's got de Lord God wid me always. I been preachin all over Harrisburg fer dis last six months or so. The Lord done called me to go to Kansas and Missouri to set dem peoples free. I come here to see you, because I'd be mighty proud if you would come wid me. If you ain't ready to let Jesus come in, dat will wait. He done gonna wait fer you as long as you take. But you is as much my son, as if you was birthed to me, maybe more. What you think?"

"When do you have to leave?"

"I's got my place here fer a few mo weeks. Come September first, I's got to be movin on. The Lord done waitin. You thinks on it. I knows I done hurt you bad. I knows you's a thinker, and you's needs to think. Dat's good. It won't be easy fer me to leave wid out you, but if you cain't, I's gonna understand, and I ain't never gonna stop lovin you. You is my son Johnny."

"Let's us fish some more."

It was nice fishing with Bo again. We laughed and had fun like the old days. It was good to be with him. I had a lot to consider. I was thirteen years old, and I had to think about my future, as Mrs. Bea so often told me. I had a lot to think about. Bo was on a Holy trip. I am a good feller, but I didn't know if I wanted to be that good. Here I was with Mrs. Bea. I had a nice place to live. She loved me. She took care of me. I took care of her. It was kind of like taking care of Mam, but it was different too. I didn't have to worry if there would be something to eat or a place to sleep. Mrs. Bea was teaching me that I could do things that I never thought was possible. Why, I was able to read and write just like she did. I wrote out the shopping lists now, and it had only been a year since she started learning me. (I mean "teaching" me.) It would break her heart if I left.

I made enough money to buy my own long pants. What was I to do?

Mrs. Bea knew there was something on my mind. I caught her looking at me, but she didn't ask me about it. She and I just went on like nothing had changed. Only thing was that I spent more time fishing with Bo, instead of hanging around the house.

It was time for Bo to leave. He had one more day. I had to make my decision. Where was Mammy when I needed her, I thought to myself. And as quick as I thought it, I heard her voice in my head. "I's right here boy. You knows I is." I thought, I have to make a decision, and I don't know what to do. "Hardest choice a man has to make is b'tween two rights. If Bo hadn't left when he did, would you have stayed wid him? Or would you have moved in wid Mrs. Bea?"

My decision was made. I told Mrs. Bea that I was leaving with Bo. Pensively she said, "I've been expecting you to tell me that for weeks now. I know it was a difficult decision for you. When do you leave?"

"Tomorrow, early morning," I winced. "I'm going to miss you. You've been so good to me. I've learned so much from you. I can never repay you."

"You've been good to me. You've been the son I never had. You're going to do well in this life. I know you." With that she rushed from the room, and I knew she was crying.

Next morning as Bo waited outside the kitchen door, she handed me a basket full of food, and included in that basket were a number of my favorite sandwiches. She paid me a month's wages and gave me a carpet bag packed with all my clean clothes. "Johnny, the rest of your life is your adventure. Write me letters. I want to know what is going on with you. Now, you get on out of here, before I can't keep a straight face."

Chapter Seven
A New Chapter

It was cloudy the day Bo and I left Galveston. The crossing on the ferry was rough. I could see the dark clouds gathering. I hoped it weren't no omen of things to come.

As I looked back at the island, a pang of nausea swept over me. I would have liked to blame it on the rocking of the ferry, but I couldn't. I knew better. Mam was there. Mrs. Bea was there. It was even worse than leaving Mammy. I would like to say I didn't second guess myself, but I did. I caught myself looking at Bo, and wondering "What have I done?" He must have been picking up on what I was feeling. He squeezed my shoulder and looked me in the eyes.

"Johnny, it ain't too late fer you to turn back if'n you're a mind to."

"It's gonna be fine." I sniffed. "It's sayin goodbye again that hurts."

"Then, let's me and you jez say 'hello' from now on. Let's look ahead. Yo'r gonna take all those memories wid ya. They gonna be stored in yo'r heart. They stay alives dat way. Let's us go make some 'Hellos'!" Bo seemed to know what I needed to hear.

We moved forward with him leading the way. It was hot and muggy. I thought that I would fare better than Bo. Wrong! Bo led the entire way. He was a driven man. Even through the mud, he out-paced me. We walked on squishy wet earth that sucked at our feet, until our shoes had to come off. More than once, we helped each other out of the muck. Insects feasted on us. Trees and bushes clawed at us, as if to say "Stay here". Still, we pushed forward dragging our own personal thoughts reluctantly behind us. We didn't do much talking. We had to concentrate on putting one foot in front of the other.

The first day we only made about ten miles before hunger and exhaustion sat us down. We built a little green fire to run off the skeeters, but they had other plans. The rain was sprinkling off and on during the day, but as night fell, it began to pour down in sheets. (At least the mosquitoes left when the rain was heavy! I preferred the rain to skeeters!) We heard the thunder. The lightning flashed in the distance. Thankfully, it wasn't near us. We huddled together under a tree eating our wonderful ham sandwiches, and trying at least to keep them dry, until we had crammed every morsel into our mouths. We ate so fast that we barely tasted them. That was a shame, but we had no choice. Listening to a "riveting" frog chorus that lulled us pretty near into a trance, we dropped off to sleep.

The next morning, the sun broke through the low hanging clouds, but not for long. We sloshed in rain water throughout the day. First, we waded through standing puddles. Then, we tramped through weedy lakes of ever rising rain waters. No shoes today. Shoestrings tied together, each of us sported shoes hung round our necks. Our pants were rolled up above our knees, but still it was an easier day than the one before. It was cooler. We ate the last of the sandwiches, and once again, I thanked Mrs. Bea. Bo thanked God.

Finally, we were out of the water. We were on a road, not really, more like a rutted path for wagons. We took it slower. We were tired. On the third afternoon, we hitched a ride on a freight wagon coming from Galveston to Harrisburg. That's when I thanked God. I was worn out and hungry too, but more tired than anything. When we arrived at the docks, our ride ended. From there, Bo said it was a short walk to the little church where Bo had been "saved again and fer good" per him. Preacher was a very old man. He welcomed us with open arms. His wife fed us some beans and rice and sent us to the creek for a splash bath. We slept that night in the shed next to the house. It was clean. The bed felt good; the roof, even better.

Up early, I chopped wood and brought in the water. Preacher's wife cooked us up some grits. Nice old couple. She was a round shouldered large lady whose face was still beautiful, serene. He was a stooped old feller who'd probably been really tall and commanding in his younger days. They both had sweet smiles, and when they looked at you, you felt larger and better somehow. Just a very nice couple!

Bo and Preacher couldn't stop talking. It was all about where we were going and which way would be the best way to travel. Preacher told us places along the way that we could expect to be well received. "This church" he smiled knowingly "will give you refuge. They'll be happy to have you preach. Probably take up a love offering for you." He told us places to stay away from as well. "Dem white folks up past Huntsville, they've be havin a hard time. White folks ain't happy wid de ways dis Reconstruction things goin. Ku Klux Klan's all over in that neck of the woods. Get through there fast as you can." Heads together, they were busily drawing a map with notes all over it. I didn't quite know what to do with myself, so I grabbed a pole and went fishing.

In the midst of the cradling greenery on the bayou, I found a big tree close to the water's edge and situated myself. I leaned back feeling the tree strong behind me. For the first time since we left Galveston, I had time to think. I hadn't really been doing much of that lately. Mostly, I'd just been concerned with whether I left with Bo or stayed with Mrs. Bea, or if I wore my shoes on my neck or my feet! It was quiet here. All I could hear was the buzzin of skeeters, an occasional fish flopping in the water, a turtle diving off a log. It was a good time to do some serious thinking or sleeping, whichever came first.

Am I the kind of person that will grow up to be a good man? I've seen mean, but I've been lucky to have seen more good in my life than mean. I believe I've been a good boy, but I'm thinking it's harder to be a good man from what I've seen. I want folks to like me. I want to have me a family some day. Why else am I here, if not to have a family? Bo's my only family now, but someday, I'd like to find me a pretty girl and have lots of babies. I've been alone so much. I want my children to have family around. I want them to never have to worry about not having someone to love them or take care of them. I want them to have a home that's theirs, and no matter what, nobody can make them leave or take it away from them. I don't know just how to go about getting all that, but I guess I've got plenty of time to figure it out. I'm not really in a big hurry.

So, what do I want to do with myself? Now, there's a hard one. Right now, I want to lay on this bank and think. I want to fish whenever I want. I want to be happy, and this makes me happy. I know, I know, this is supposed to be serious thinking. I think I want to be smart, even smarter than I am now. I actually love reading and learning new things. I enjoy doing figures. So, I guess maybe I should put more schooling on my list of things to do. I want to be able to talk with folks and feel like they respect me for who I am on the inside. I don't want to be judged by the color of my skin, whether folks think I'm colored or white. I wonder if that will ever be possible. I just want to feel respected. That respect thing, that's big for me.

Shifting my position, I rolled over on my belly laying my head on the cool ground. What about this God thing? I do believe there's a heaven. I believe Mam and Mammy are there watching over me. Haven't they made that clear enough to me? Bo talks about heaven all the time. I'm just not too clear on how a body gets there. Bo says you just believe on the Lord Jesus Christ. He says He came here and died for us to set us free from our sins. I don't know about that. Plenty of people I've been around say all the proper things about God and church and stuff, but not many of them actually "Love one another". They don't even treat each other politely. They're one way on Sunday while they're singing and shouting, and the next six days, they say and do anything! I don't like those kinds of folks who say one thing to your face and another to your back. I guess I'm just going to watch and see if there's anything to this Jesus and God thing for myself.

An ant crawled over my out-stretched arm. I was still. Another followed. I guess I'm blocking their trail, just another stick in the way to them, I chuckled. Before I knew it, there were a whole mess of them making my arm a bridge to the tree. I heard a distant crack of thunder. Heavy black clouds hung above. Mam always told me that ants know when to run for cover, long before peoples do. I could hear her teaching me. "Dems purty smart creatures. God done teach dem how to takes care of dem selfs. Little boys gots to learn to pay 'tention to God too."

Think time over, I scraped the ants off my arm, grabbed my pole, and ran for Preacher's house. Heavy rains chased me the whole way.

Sunday morning, Bo was dressed fit to kill. I hadn't ever seen him in a suit. He didn't look so old all slicked up like that. The rain had stopped in the night. The sun was bright. I put on my other set of clothes and tied up my shoes. We walked together with Preacher and his wife to the church. Everyone was slapping Bo and me on the back and saying "Welcome Brother!" "Glad to meet Bo's son" was the common refrain of the day. A man prayed, Preacher said a few words. (A few words for a preacher is quite lengthy, of course. I could already hear my stomach growling. I'd only had a couple of leftover biscuits this morning). Then, it was Bo's turn at the pulpit for his "few words". People were clapping and cheering him on, yelling "Praise God" and "Amen" after almost everything he said. IT WAS LOUD!

"I's jez glad to be back in the bosom of the Lord here wid you good peoples." (They praised and amen-ed). We all has much to be happy 'bout dis Sabbath Day. (More praising). Me, I's got my son Johnny here by my side. The Lord He done blessed me to give me a second chance to be a right kind of father, just like He is a right kind of father to each of you. (Amen). Reach out to dat person next to you. Tell 'em you love 'em. Tell 'em God love 'em. (Much talking in the congregation, followed by more praising). It be a happy day. (Bo began to sing as he walked around that building that held maybe ten pews and twenty or so folks). His bass voice shook the walls.

"I can hear my Savior callin, I can hear my Savior callin. I can hear my Savior callin, Take thy cross and follow, follow me. Tis de old-time religion, Tis de old-time religion, Tis de old time religion, Good enough fer me.

When I rise to brighter worlds unknown, I'll behold my Savior on His throne. O happy day, O happy day, When Jesus washed my sins away. O happy day, eternal day When I shall go with Him to stay.

Where He leads me I will follow, Where He leads me I will follow, Where He leads me I will follow, meekly follow; He will give me grace and glory, I'll go wid Him, wid Him, all de way. Tis de old-time religion; Tis de old-time religion; Tis de old-time religion, Good enough fer me.

When I rise to worlds unknown, I'll behold Him on His throne, O happy day; O happy day; When Jesus washed my sins away. O happy day, eternal day, When I shall go wid Him to stay, in glory stay."

I couldn't help it. I was moved. Never had I heard such a voice or a song sung with so much feeling, and considering Mam's gift of song, that is really something for me to say. Other folks joined in singing. So did I. God lived in Bo's voice. God lived in Bo. Even if I wasn't ready to say I believed, I could see and hear God in Bo.

It was a long meeting, but it didn't feel long. I forgot about the growling in my stomach. I forgot how hard the pews were. I was wrapped in the moment. Bo glowed as he preached and sang. Bo's "few words" went on for hours. And yet, I felt a twinge of regret when his words were over. Hugs and tears and hallelujah's followed us as we trudged slowly back to Preacher's house.

Next morning, Bo and I packed our few things and went to breakfast.

We had a hearty meal. Preacher's wife gave us food to carry on the road. Preacher prayed over us. Preacher and Bo kissed each other on wet cheeks. We left walking to the Kansas wilderness. Bo and I didn't once look back.

Chapter Eight
That Thicket's Thick

We were in northeast Texas, the Piney Woods. Some folks called it the Big Thicket, and with good reason. We trekked through small settlements hollowed out in the middle of vegetation so dense that it was impossible to see six feet past where the land had been cleared. It had to be difficult to live in such a place and fight off wild animals and encroaching trees and bushes constantly trying to re-establish their dominance. It couldn't have been easy to eke out a living here. We ate what we could find and what people gave us. Most folks were generous, even though it was obvious that they had very little. For the most part, they were good people and kind, but there are always the others. There were those who called us names and drove us away. I was beginning to understand that this was the way the world was: good and bad, loving and cruel. It seemed to me that no matter how much good folks did, there was some kind of evil sprouting to push the good out!

The weather was clear that first week, but our friends, the skeeters, were everywhere. I would have preferred drenching rain! They were in my nose, my ears making me crazy, but nothing bothered Bo. He sang as we walked. He taught me his favorite gospel songs. I sang along. My voice was squeaky and it couldn't make up its mind whether it wanted to be high or low, but Bo didn't care. It made the time past faster. It helped us walk faster in time with the songs.

Negroes were pretty much happy to see a preacher stop by. We had little come togethers. Bo preached and sang to them and with them. Some were in churches, but most folks didn't have a church. The ones that could gave us a few cents; the ones that couldn't often shared their meager food. We seldom had a roof over our heads, but we didn't mind. It was round the fire at night, when we were all alone, that Bo and I talked the most. He had been my friend since that day we met on the beach, but it was different now. He was still my friend, but we were both acutely aware of his teaching and guiding me. He was my father. He was all I had in this world, and I was the same for him, except as he often reminded me, "You ain't never alone if you has de Lord wid you."

When we reached the town of Nacogdoches, we were cautious. People here were not friendly. Where we entered the town was the busiest road, and there were a great many white folks there for Saturday market day. To get to the colored folks, we had to walk through the town. Thinking back, it must have looked strange to see an old colored man leading a white boy. Both of us were dusty and weather-worn. Usually, a Negro would walk behind a white person, not the other way round, and to those Texans, I looked white. There were catcalls and awful things shouted at the both of us, as we hastily made our way eyes down through the town. It obviously was not a friendly place for Bo, and I certainly didn't feel welcome there either. They called me just as many names as they did him. They threw rocks and chunks of dirt at us, and it wasn't just the men. The children joined in, and I'll never forget a woman who spit at us as we passed by her. What a relief to get to the other side of town!

The colored folks welcomed us. They didn't have a regular preacher, so when the Negroes learned that Bo was one, and that I was his son, they invited us to stay the night in their little falling-down church and have a meeting the next morning. They were poor hard-working folks with lots of little children, but there was also one big, fat Negro man who rode up to church in a buggy. He was dressed in fine clothes of many colors. He wore a gold colored shiny vest, and he smelled of flowers. He smiled a lot. I recall thinking "he smiles too much, I don't trust him." The service was lively, lots of singing and shouting. It felt good being there with Bo bringing happiness to those poor people. He was doing good work, and I was helping him by just being there with him. Anyway, that's what he told me.

Bo baptized seven people, young and old in the river, after the service, and later in the afternoon, he preached again. There was barely standing room. It amazed me how fast word spread about Bo's preaching. People seemed to come out of the woodwork! Inside that crowded church house, babies fretted and screamed.

The heat of the day mixed with the sweat of all those bodies was incredible and somewhat overwhelming. The meeting went on, but when Bo sang the first of his rousing songs, he marched all those people out the building and into the field under a big tree. Once again, time and nothing else seemed to matter while Bo preached the Word of the Lord. Amens, Hallelujahs, and Praise Gods echoed in the grove. It was cooler here. Babies fell asleep. The meeting went on, and Bo's "few words" ended with nightfall. His sermons spun a spell. They were different each one of them, but with the same purpose. Until seeing Bo preach, I'd had no idea that he knew how to read. He held The Bible and quoted it loud and clear. Much later, I learned that when he was a child, he'd put a great deal of it to memory. He couldn't read a word. No one would have ever known! His voice changed when he preached. It was loud and commanding; The Spirit spoke through him.

We usually didn't stay in one place for more than a few days, but after the service, the big, fat man asked us to stay another week. I'd been told by one of the boys that he was "one of those Reconstructionists". He pleaded with Bo to stay at his house. His house was two streets off the main street of town where the white folks lived, not where the other coloreds lived. Bo accepted his invitation immediately, but I wasn't so sure.

Bo's admonition to me was "Johnny, we go where de Lord done want us to go, and we goin to de Big Man's house." I went, but I was a mite troubled to be back among all those people who had treated us so badly on our arrival in town. The Big Man whose name was Joe gave us a little room behind the kitchen. His woman fed us three times a day. We hadn't eaten so well, since we finished the last of Mrs. Bea's sandwiches. Needless-to-say, I liked that. We had a bed to sleep on again, and a roof. That was pretty nice too.

During the day, Bo went visiting and sharing The Word with the colored women and children mostly. The men folk were out working in the fields or whatever work they had. Some of the ne'r de wells, as Bo called them, were home. You know what, I think Bo was happier when he found them at home, because it gave him a chance to share his own conversion story with them. He knew he'd probably not see them at church because of their bad habits, but this was an "extry chance the Lord done give me," and he took it. "Who knows, maybe it be a tiny seed to grow later." I hung around the house doing chores for the Big Man's woman. I didn't call him Joe. I didn't particularly want to get on close terms with him. I was wary. He was loud and boisterous. I just couldn't let myself trust him, no matter how good the food tasted or the bed felt. I tried to keep his woman happy though; I helped her out with chores. Nobody bothered me, but then I didn't venture too far away, except when I went with Bo visiting at night.

Come Friday morning, I overheard Bo telling the Big Man and his woman that we were going to spend the night at the church, so that he could pray and figure out what the Lord wanted him to sermonize on Saturday and Sunday. The woman packed us a big basket of food to take. She told us that she'd be coming to church on Sunday and she'd bring us more. I was happy to hear that news. We collected our belongings and went to the church. Bo told me Sunday would be our last meeting here. "Time fer us to move on." I was ready to go, and yet, I must admit I'd enjoyed the comforts! Still, that was what we were bound to do.

I fell asleep Friday night listening to Bo recite. I couldn't keep my eyes open any longer. Besides, I knew I'd hear it all and much, much more on Saturday. Next morning, we ate the biscuits and grape jelly we'd been given. Oh! Was that sweet! Bo prayed some more. I went outside. Children and mothers were already sitting waiting on the grass. I played chase and enjoyed the company of boys closer to my age than I was accustomed to. We climbed trees and had a pine cone fight, and in the afternoon, three other boys and myself went for a swim. When we returned, the meeting was just beginning. It was a beautiful day. Once more, we had the meeting outside. The singing commenced. The blue skies were filled with hallelujahs. I sang loudly with the others. I learned to love singing. I didn't worry if my voice cracked any more. I'd heard too many voices off key. Bo told me often "De Lord don't care if'n you cans carry a tune o' not. He jez want you to sing of His glory!" I did. I couldn't believe my eyes at how many people filled that grove. The Big Man was there with his woman and four, no five other folks. I even saw two of the men folk, the ne'r do wells, who came with their families. Bo was especially pleased to see them there. He introduced them to me with a wink. Their hands shook a bit, but they were there! There must have been well over a hundred people come to meeting. Out of those, twenty-seven came to the Lord. Bo was set to baptize them in the river early next morning. When we fell asleep on the church floor that night, we were feeling mighty good.

Late in the night, I heard shots fired and hooves pounding. I started to get up, but Bo pushed me back down to the floor. "You stays here boy, no matter what! No, on second thought, you hear me say 'I doin de Lord's bizness', you get you self out dat lil winder back by de pulpit, and you be kerful to hide yo'self good somewhere and don't come out til dey's gone. I mean it! Don't you come out no matter what you done hear!" I promised. I heard hollerin. Bo said a quick prayer as he walked to the door of the church and opened it slowly.

"Can I help you Sirs?" he asked politely.

'GET YO'R BLACK ASS OUT HERE BOY!" Two men leaped up on the steps and drug him off into the field. I heard scuffling and angry shouts. Peekin out the front window, I saw a group of people dressed in white cone-like hats and white robes. They were kickin Bo while he lay on the ground, cursing him awful. I wanted to run outside, but I'd promised Bo. I saw one of them put a rope round his neck.

"What you's gonna do? I ain't hurt no one. I DOIN DE LORD'S BIZNESS!' he shouted loudly. I scurried to the front of the church and squeezed myself out the tiny window, and I shamefully tell you now that I hid. Not because of what Bo had said, but because I was scared to death. That's the truth. I'd never been so scared in my life. I thought for sure I might mess my britches.

Peeking from my hiding spot under the bushes, I saw Bo hoisted on the back of one of the horses. Hollers came from the mob.

"YOU UPPITY NIGGER!

WHO DO YOU THINK YOU BE?

GONNA FRY YO'R ASS!

YOU'LL WISH YOU WAS DEAD LONG BEFORE YOU ARE!"

The noose hung loosely on his neck. He recited loudly.

"THE LORD IS MY SHEPHERD; I SHALL NOT WANT. HE MAKETH ME TO LIE DOWN IN GREEN PASTURES.

"WE GONNA MAKE YOU LAY DOWN IN THAT THERE PASTURE, PREACHER MAN!"

HE LEADETH ME BESIDE DE STILL WATERS. HE RESTORETH MY SOUL."

"WHAT MAKES YOU THINK AN OLE NIGGER MAN LIKE YOU GOT A SOUL!"

HE LEADETH ME IN DE PATHS OF RIGHTEOUSNESS FER HIS NAME'S SAKE, YEA, THOUGH I WALKS THROUGH DE VALLEY OF DE SHADOW O' DEATH, I WILL FEARS NO EVIL;;

'TAKE HIM DOWN FROM THERE. WE GONNA PUT THE FEAR INTO HIM. HE'LL WISH HE'D NEVER A-WALKED OUR STREETS. HURRY UP! PULL HIM ON DOWN!" yelled a man who seemed to be in charge. A bit softer now, Bo continued.

Fer thou art wid me; Thy rod and thy staff dey comfort me. Thou preparest a table before me in de presence o' mine enemies;

They drug him to the ground. They began to beat him and kick him. I was terrified. I could only look. "God," I whimpered, "God, if you is really here, Save him. Save him." Two of the mob lifted Bo to his feet and held him up. I saw blood whipping in streams from his face as the man-in-charge hit him first on one side of the face with a fist, and then, the other. Bo, between the blows, continued to recite, but he was no longer shouting.

Thou anointest my head wid oil;

"I DONE GOT YUR WOOLY HEAD ANOINTED, PREACHER! I'M A-WASHIN YOU IN THE BLOOD. YOU AIN'T NEVER GONNA RUN WITH NO WHITE BOY AGAIN! YOU AIN'T NEVER GONNA THINK YOU CAN WALK IN HERE A-THINKIN YOU CAN TAKE OVER!"

Surely goodness and mercy shall follow me all de days o' my life; And I will dwell in de house of de Lord fer ever."

The two men pitched Bo onto the saddle. They tied his hands behind his back. Another man put the noose back round his neck.

"MAKE SURE HE KNOWS WHAT'S HAPPENIN!" I watched as three of the hooded men set the little church on fire. Smoke billowed out the windows. A tall crude cross was being forced into the ground just in front of it; in front of Bo. It was set on fire as well. "THERE'S YOUR HOUSE! AND YOUR CROSS! BURN IN HELL!"

The horse's rump was smacked. It bolted from under Bo's helpless body. Men raced to their horses and rode away in a cloud of dust shoutin and hootin. They fired their guns in the air. Bo was swingin; his feet, jerkin.

I was out from under the bushes in a second! Tears streamin down my face, I ran to Bo, grabbin hold of his swingin legs, pushin them up. "Don't die Bo. Don't die". "Help, somebody help me!"

Help came scurrying like roaches in a sudden light. The rope holding Bo on the tree limb was cut. Strong hands lowered him to the ground. I was inconsolable. I threw myself over his body screamin. "BO! BO!"

I heard a slight cough; then, another, followed by a chokin raspy noise. I felt Bo's hand lay weakly on my head. "I's hear Johnny. I's here. God done heared you."

Men carried Bo to a nearby shack. An old darkie, who reminded me of Mammy, washed him and bound-up his wounds. I waited outside. I overheard the old woman tell Bo, "The Good Lord, He done got a lot more preachin fer you to be a-doin. You is hurt bad, but I done seen worse. You gonna be aw right Preacher."

I felt a hand squeezing my shoulder. "Come on now Johnny. We got to get Bo and you on de road. Ain't a minute to lose." I looked up through tears, and there was the Big Man. "I's got a buckboard fer you, and my best mule to take you way from here. You's got to go now! Them mens, they ain't gonna be happy when they finds out Bo ain't hangin dead. Come on now!" I stood on trembling legs. Joe and I went to get Bo. The watchful men folk carried Bo to the wagon. Inside was the mattress that me Bo and I had slept on at Joe's house. I recognized it right off. (Funny, ain't it, how in moments of great despair, you notice the simplest of things.) They laid Bo on it. All kinds of bags were stuffed along both sides of the bed. "Now, boy, you got to straight'n yo'self up. Stop that weepin like a woman! It up to you to get out of dis territory. Dis here's a good ole mule. He take you far. Be good to him. Don't you never come back dis way!" He pushed me up into the seat of the wagon. "Walk him much as you can once you done good outta here, but fer now, you run like de devil chasin yo'r tail!"

I run dat mule. We went like de devil was a-chasin us. He was. I'd seen him…and his helpers!

Chapter Nine
New Beginnings

That ole mule took us away on winged feet. Bo was tossed like a limp rag doll from one side of the wagon to the other, but when we finally slowed and stopped, he was alive. We were safe. God freed him to preach another day. He freed me to know that He is always with us to comfort us in times of our greatest despair, whether we have "knocked on His door or not". I kept that knowledge for myself. I knew it deep in the core of me without a doubt.

We stopped only to feed and water ole Wings, which was what I named him as we flew away from danger. At the time, the name of the mule wasn't an important issue for Joe to share. Besides, he was ours now, and Wings fit him. Slow as I later found him to plod, he carried us swiftly away to safety that terrible night. The first night we hid back in the pine trees. I didn't build a fire for fear those men would be lookin for us. Exhausted I squeezed onto the mattress by Bo and fell asleep. Next morning, I poked them bags around us and found grain for Wings and food for us. There were clothes there too. We had a bite of food and water and fed Wings. Bo was awake and talking just a little. Little specks of broken blood vessels dotted the already purple-blue landscape of his swollen face. He was a pitiful sight. Peeking at me through a small slit in his eye, he mouthed carefully "Don't worry. We be fine."

Sure, I thought, we sure are fine. We're both alive and moving farther away from that hellacious place all the time, but I didn't say it. I smiled weakly and reassured him that we'd put more miles between us and them today. The ride had to be hard on Bo. I could hear him grunting and groaning, but he never complained. Two days later, we came across a shanty town where colored folks lived. They took us in.

We stayed a few nights. The weather had turned icy. Bo was up and around, but he remained in a great deal of pain. There was no standing straight. He needed help to rise from sitting or lying. Bo told me when it was time for us to go again. We thanked those sweet people and were back on the road.

The weather was with us. The ice from before had melted, but it was still cold. So, we had to cover up more. I preferred that to fighting the heat and bugs. We kept to the edges of Dallas and Fort Worth, as we moved through Texas. I felt better about us starting a little fire now at night. My nerves were settling down. Digging through the remainder of the sacks, I found a skillet and a pot for boiling creek coffee. It was warm and soothing to the both of us. I could never get enough coffee, night or day. Neither could Bo. I made us up some corn mush. We managed. Thanks to Joe and thanks to his Missus.

We crossed out of Texas and went through wild country all the way to Kansas. Lots of cattle along the way, but not too many people. Where there were colored folks though, they wanted preaching, and Bo did what he did best. One day I was digging down to the last of our flour, and I was thinking that come the next town I would have to find some work to replenish our supplies. They'd lasted a long time, but I saw we didn't have much more. I dipped my cup into the flour and out came a small leather pouch. Inside were gold coins! Joe and The Lord done saved us again. Just goes to show, sometimes you think you can tell what a body's like just by lookin. You listen to the warnings going off and build up walls to protect yourself, and then you find out, you were judging that person by the words of others and not themselves. I was so wrong about Joe! He was indeed a Man of God, even if he did talk loud and wear shiny clothes! I'm not saying, don't listen to your warnings. I guess what I'm saying is watch and wait. It may be a "Joe" coming into your life!

Farms and folks, especially coloreds were few and far between in Kansas. What we found was that most of them collected in small groups alongside a township. Maybe they felt safer that way. There were still Indians roaming the countryside. Winters were cruel. But, there was food. Corn and beef were a plenty. Grains too. The Negroes were still serving others; however, I think that's what we're supposed to be doing. Not just Negroes, but everyone, serving others however we can.

We served, Bo and I. Bo served by preaching and teaching. I served Bo by taking care of our worldly needs. I took care of ole Wings. I took care of our wagon and our supplies, so that when the time came to leave one place and move to another, we were ready. The peoples, well, they took care of the both of us. I never want to forget all the kindnesses. They fed us. Some even clothed us. They gave us a warm place to sleep when it was cold outside. They shared their lives with us.

We developed a route through Kansas, and then on through Missouri. We made the circuit about once every six to eight months or so depending on the weather, depending on the roads, depending on Bo's and ole Wings stamina. Me, I was the driver. I didn't do much of anything in all of this. I got much more than I gave. Fair is fair.

I was seventeen. Time had passed so quickly. I felt a strange yearning for something more in my life. I didn't want to stop traveling with Bo necessarily, but I wanted to do something more. As providence would have it, Bo fell sick. He was real sick. We couldn't travel. He couldn't preach. I found me a job in a little general store in a small Missouri town. I chopped wood and sold it. I ran errands for people too. I made enough money for us to room and board with a young Negro family just outside of town. They had lots of children running round. The mother of these children was a sweet and very tired young woman with a great, giving heart. She took good care of Bo. He had pneumony and died within a month.

All I had left was his pocket knife, the one I'd given him so many Christmases ago. Nothing was holding me any longer. Days after Bo passed, I got down on my knees. "What is it You want me to do now? I know You're there. Answer me. Answer me. Please."

I didn't get an answer.

I hitched up ole Wings and told him to pick a direction. We wound up in Kansas City. To be honest, I didn't know if it was

Kansas City, Missouri or Kansas City, Kansas, and frankly, it didn't matter to me. It was a thriving town. Lots of people. I walked the streets, and no one bothered me. I was tall and lanky by now. My hair, dark brown and wavy. Not bad looking for a dumb colored boy! Ha. I'd have to write Mrs. Bea that! I found a job in the telegraph office. The man said I could run telegrams to folks, and if I wanted, he would train me to work the telegraph. Seemed like a good idea to me. I guess Mrs. Bea was right. Reading and writing does open doors.

Mr. Taft was a fair man and paid a fare wage. I lived well there. I met people that I would have never met any other way but delivering telegrams or sending them! They liked me. I had been kind of a shy boy-man, but the confidence that I was finding in myself as a "telegraph operator" helped me to speak up. I always liked people, but through my entire life, I had been taught to know my place, be seen and not heard, and sometimes not seen. Something was changing about me!

Are you curious? Did I tell Mr. Taft I was colored? Yes, I did, but he didn't care. He told me "Don't matter to me. Do your job. Take care of business, and we'll be fine." I did. As my confidence grew, something else did too. My stature grew. Before I blinked, three years passed. I was now well over six feet tall. My mind grew too. I was able to buy books and newspapers to read. I was strong as a mule; well not Wings, but a younger mule perhaps. I'd found out what it meant in a small town to be a nice looking feller. I made friends, some good, some not so good. The not so good ones took me drinking with them. We went other places too. Places that reminded me of unhappy times with Mam. I decided to choose friends that didn't take me down. I went back to church. The preacher couldn't hold a candle to Bo, but I enjoyed the singing.

One day I was sorting through messages in the office, when a family of colored folks came in to send a telegram. They were on their way to St. Louis, and they wanted to let their relative know when they would arrive. Love struck! With them was their daughter. Her name was Elizabeth, but they called her Bitty. I liked that. It fit her. She was tiny, not even close to five feet. Her Pa and I jawed a bit. I learned they'd come from Louisiana. Using that as an excuse, I asked if I could treat them to dinner. They agreed, and we spent a lovely evening together. To me it was. I couldn't keep my eyes off Bitty, and she wouldn't put her eyes on me! In the looks department, Bitty wasn't really pretty. Some might have even said she was ugly, but not me! I thought she was beautiful, and I was drawn to her from the moment I saw her. There was a calmness about her. "She was solid," as my Mammy would have said. Her Pa, well, wouldn't you know! He was a preacher.

They left early the next day. I saw them off at the station. I already had their address from the telegram I'd sent. I was smitten. I started writing a letter everyday to the family which of course, meant I was actually writing Bitty. A few weeks later, I gave my job over to another feller, and I went to St. Louis.

Don't you know that woman made me work for her? Her Ma and Pa liked me from the start, but Bitty didn't seem too sure. She didn't have much to say to me. I just kept on coming around. I went to church where her Pa preached. I sat with her and her Ma. She hardly ever looked at me. I shared meals with them. She was aloof, but one day I made a little joke, and I caught her covering her mouth with her hand to stifle a giggle. I saw that as encouragement. I guess it was, because her Pa married us in the fall.

I saw her comin down that aisle to me, and I was so full of feelings. I'm a blessed man. She was beautiful. She wore a white dress with dainty blue cornflowers stitched into the neck. Her waist was so tiny that I could put my hands around her and still have fingers to spare. She wasn't shy that day; nor, that night. She looked me straight in the eyes. She knew I loved her. To me, she was the most special woman in the world. No one was ever prouder of his bride than me!

I worked in the telegraph office in St. Louis when me and Bitty married. She was happy with that, but I wanted to do more for my family. I was always on the look-out for something that would bring us more money. We were doing all right though. We had all we needed, and a little bit more. Most of all, we had each other. We loved each other. Oh, I was looking forward to having a baby, but that didn't happen right away like we were hoping it would. Our first year together was sweet. We had us a little place not far from her Ma and Pa. It was just a one room cabin, but she and her Ma fixed it up nice. We had a little garden out back. Bitty even planted some flower seeds in front. It was a nice place to come home to in the evenings. Mostly just being there with Bitty made it nice.

Being that Bitty was an only child, she and her Ma were pretty close. Her Pa too, but different. The first year of marriage over, Bitty changed. She talked about wanting a baby all the time nearly. "Why cain't we have no baby? We sure is lovin enough. This just ain't right. That Susie, she done had one and has another one in the oven since we's been married. It ain't fair. It just ain't fair." She repeated this refrain almost daily for months on end. I thought I would scream if I heard it one more time!

"Bitty, you got to stop this frettin. Let nature take its course. We gonna have babies. We gonna have lots of babies. We're young. Now stop it Honey. Come on over here, and give me a kiss. Maybe if you just stop worrying so much, it'll happen." I wrapped my arms around her. She was such a tiny thing. I could see she was hurting, but I guess I didn't understand why she was so much. Her Ma wasn't a help in the matter. She knew Bitty's times, and she kept track every month. Her doing that seemed to make Bitty even crazier than she already was. I understood Ma wanted a grandbaby, as much as Bitty wanted a baby. I tried my best to be patient, but pretty soon, when she started that crazy talking, I'd just tune out. I'd leave and have a drink with my friends. I know that wasn't nice of me, but I got tired of it.

Months went by. Still no baby. Bitty stopped talking to me about it. I was relieved. I thought, well, she's gotten past her frettin. Now, she's just going to let things happen as they will. If only that had been the case.

Joy left our home. I don't know when it left, but it did. Bitty was gone most days when I came home from working. She spent all her time with her Ma. I put up with it for a while, but finally I lost my temper. I went to her folk's house. I went in the back of the house to the kitchen where she was. "Woman, what you doin here a'gin? I's tired of comin home and findin no supper, no wife. Get yo'self home now!" I don't think I'd ever raised my voice to her until that moment, and it couldn't have been at a worse time. Her Ma was in the parlor with some church women. I didn't know that within the hour everyone in the congregation would know our business. Bitty did. Her Ma did. Bitty came obediently home with me. She made my supper, never said a word. I felt like a jackass! I couldn't bring myself to tell her that I was sorry. I was the man. She was the wife. Her place was with me.

Next night I came home. No supper. No Bitty. I couldn't believe it! I went to her parents. She was there. "She ain't comin home wid you. John, you hurt her bad," Pa explained. "No, she don't want to see you. I'll ask her again, but I don't think she's gonna see you tonight." He left the door, and in a few moments, he returned. "Bitty's already asleep in her room. I'll talk to her tomorrow, and maybe she'll be ready to talk to you then." I left feeling devastated. How could this have gotten so out of control? What was she thinking?

Not only did Bitty not talk to me the next night, but she wouldn't even come to her Pa's church on Sunday. I had thought that maybe I could see her there, but it didn't happen. Instead, all the ladies gave me the evil eye, and I felt about two feet tall. I went back to her Pa. His advice was to just let things be for a while.

I saw her through the window of the Telegraph Office twice with her Ma. Then, I didn't see her. Weeks went by. I couldn't stand it anymore. Late one night, when I'd had a drink or two of whiskey with some of the boys, I pounded on her family's back door. Pa came to the door. "You get on outta here John. This ain't gonna help nothing." I tried to argue with him, but he shut the door in my face. Full of anger and the drink, I slammed my fist into the door, and shouted loudly, "Fine Bitty, you don't want me no more. I don't want you neither!"

It was a terrible time. I was so alone and lonely. I couldn't even go to church anymore. I was ashamed of myself, but other than my temper fits, it was her that done me wrong! Why couldn't she just face up to that and come on home! What was the matter with her anyway!

I lived alone. It was hard to believe my wife didn't want me anymore. Where had I gone wrong? What did it matter?

Eight months passed since Bitty left. I came in late one evening, and I found her Ma sitting at my table in the dark. "What's the matter? Has somethin happened to Bitty? Tell me!" I demanded.

"Sit down John. Sit down and settle down!" she countered. "Bitty ain't well John. The doctor say she's grievin herself to death. At first I thought she was just tryin to teach you a lesson, but then I saw her coilin up around herself. She didn't go out of the house. If someone came to visit, she went upstairs to her room. Not even her old girlfriends could coax her out when they came to call. I tried to talk to her. Pa told her she was to cleave to you, but she just acted like he hadn't said a word. Next thing, she was only eatin a little soup or a glass of milk all day long. I cain't remember now when she ate a proper meal. This last week I haven't been able to get anythin down her at all. She sleeps most of de time. She never wants to talk. I don't know what to do," she was crying hard. I reached out to her and held her hand. She allowed me to cradle her. I rocked her until she stopped cryin. "Do you still love her John?"

"I never stopped lovin her. You think she'll see me?" I asked hopefully.

"Pa and I don't think you should even ask. You just come on up to de house, and we'll open de door to her room. No matter what she might say or do, John, she needs you. See if she won't let you help her get over whatever this is."

We left together, my arm supporting her. It had to have been hard for her to come to me. I felt like my insides were turned outside.

"Bitty, Darlin, it's me. I'm here. I'm an idiot. Won't you please forgive me for being such a fool?" I spoke softly to her in her darkened room. "I should have come a long time ago, but my pride done got in the way. Bitty, I love you. I never stopped lovin you. Please come home to me." There was no answer. I walked closer to her bed. The covers were pulled up high over her face. I reached down and patted the covers. "It's me Bitty. Wake up." I pulled the quilt off her face and gasped aloud. My little "Bitty" was hardly there. Her face looked more like a skull from a graveyard that anything! I bit my hand. "Oh, Bitty, what have I done to you!" I fell to my knees beside her bed. She turned her body towards me flinching with pain as she did.

"What? Who's there?" came the weak voice.

"It's me Bitty. It's your husband. I'm so sorry. I love you Bitty. I'm so sorry for being such a fool. Will you ever be able to forgive me?" I begged desperately. Her tiny arms reached out to me. There was hardly any flesh left on them. I was afraid to touch her for fear that I would hurt her. I leaned my head on the pillow next to hers, kissed her gently, and let my tears fall unashamedly.

"It's aw right." She patted me. "It's aw right John." She whispered.

It wasn't all right, but it was going to be. I quit my job and let our little house go. With their blessing, I moved into my in-laws home to take full time care of my wife. I took care of everything for Bitty. I fed her the soups and soft foods that Ma made. I encouraged her. I even gave her a little beer to put some weight on her bones. Slowly, very slowly, she responded. It was almost a year by the time Bitty was able to come downstairs without being carried. The doctor told me, "Her heart ain't never gonna be the same, John. You gonna have to protect her and watch over her. No children ever for her. She cain't do it." That was the crushin blow. Bitty wasn't told. She was too fragile. It took all of us to help her to get well. It was a slow process.

Almost six months later into her recuperation, Bitty said to me, "John, you needs to get outta here and get yo'rself a job. You's makin me crazy!" She laughed as she said it. So did I. I couldn't get my telegraph job back, but I became a teacher at the colored school house. I liked it. Not a lot of pay, but chickens and vegetables came to school with the children on occasion destined for our house. Bitty came some days to bring me lunch (Mrs. Bea sandwiches when she could). Many of those days, she stayed outside to sew and watch the children play in the sunshine. It was nice to have her there. It was especially nice to see her beginning to be herself again. We stayed on with her folks. We were truly a family now. We'd gone through the fire and walked out of it all of us still together.

Bitty was expecting a baby. She was so happy when she told me and her Ma and Pa. "I waited til I was sure. Ain't y'all happy?" We were stunned, but as a group, we hugged her and told her how happy we were. Inside, we were wondering what in the world we were going to do? I thought I'd been so careful with her, but I guess I wasn't careful enough! Pa and Ma weren't mad at me, but they were upset. We each put on a happy face. It was God's Will.

It wasn't to be. Within two weeks, Bitty lost the baby. The doctor took it upon himself to tell her that she shouldn't have any more babies because of her heart. She was so sad. She stopped eating again. I let her be for three days, and then, I went to her.

"Bitty, I know yo'r sad as sad can be. I am too. There's nothing more I wanted than to have lots of babies with you. Thing is, I want you more than I want those babies."

"Really John, you do really?"

"I do. No one could ever take yo'r place. You a good woman. Yo'r my woman. You the only woman I want. If you sure you want children, there's lots of little children out there that need a mother just like you. How about we find us a few?"

She broke down. I couldn't tell if she was cryin for sad or happy. I never could when a woman cried. I guess I never would.

"I was so worried that if I couldn't has yo'r children that you'd up and leave me. That's why I left a'fore. I disappointed you." She was whispering now between sobs.

"Bitty, stop cryin. Don't cry. I don't ever want to lose you. If you don't want children, that will do fer me! If you do, we'll get us some. You get better now. Our little one just wasn't strong enough to come here, but we'll have others. They might not be our own flesh and blood, but they'll be just as loved." We held each other close.

It was four months later that God sent us a miracle. Early one morning as I arrived at the school house, I spied a basket on the steps. I figured it was someone paying me in vegetables or the like for teaching, but it wasn't pay! Wrapped in a rag inside the basket was a tiny newborn baby still wearin birthin blood. I ran all the way home with that basket bundle.

"Bitty! Bitty, where is you?" I hollered.

"I's here in de kitchen. What wrong?" Bitty leaned back from her bread making looking past the kitchen door frame.

"Come! See what God done brought us!" I sat the worn old basket on the parlor table. She came wiping her hands on her apron.

A little mewling sound issued from the basket. She put her hands on her hips and said, "John, you better not brung me no kittens!"

Grinning, I answered "Not kittens."

She peered into the basket. I thought she might faint. Awestruck, she looked up at me, "It's a baby. She paused, "Boy or girl?"

I laughed. "I don't have any idea, Woman! Does it matter?"

"Not at all" she said softly, as she lifted the tiny mewling infant towards her face. She kissed it. "Let's us jez see what the Lord done blessed us wid, Daddy." She unwound the rags from the naked baby.

Our first son arrived safely home to his mother. His name was a given. We named him Moses, because he came to us in a basket.

Chapter Ten
A Want Deep Inside

We were happy, truly happy. Ma and Pa were grandparents. Bitty and I were Mother and Daddy. Our love grew stronger one for the other just watching Moses grow. He was a happy little feller, but he didn't have nothing to be unhappy about, except for maybe cutting teeth. He barely ever cried, because one of us had him in our arms long before he could manage a healthy bellow. There was no leaving Ma and Pa's house now. We were there to stay, and I knew it. I was fine with the arrangement.

Six months passed so quickly. We were struggling by. I didn't make much money teaching, but I really didn't want to stop. I found I was good at it. I taught those children just like dear Mrs. Bea had taught me. We had fun. I learned more than they did just preparing to teach them. I had all ages in my little school house. I didn't tolerate the ones who caused trouble. I'd sit them down, and we'd have a little chat. The following is my conversation with a tough boy by the name of George.

"So, George, why are you coming to school if all you want to do is make the girls cry and fight the other boys?"

George defiantly said "They started it!"

"That's not what I asked you. I asked you why you are here in school."

"My momma done make me come. My pa, he don't care if I's here or not."

"So, George, if I send you home today, what have you learned in the time you've been coming to school?"

"I ain't learn'd nothin. Don't want to learn nothin!" was the instant angry response.

"I'm surprised that you'd say that with a name like George!"

"What's de matta wid my name?" He was ready to fight.

"Not a thing is wrong with your name. You have a fine name, an outstanding name. It's a name to be proud of. Do you have any idea that a very great and wise man was named George?"

Interested now, he quizzed me. "What you know 'bout dat George?"

I told him about George Washington...that he was a Statesman, a General, our First President and the Father of Our Country. He was interested now. I asked him to think about staying on in school just for a while, so that he could learn about the man that he was named for. "You could be that kind of man, but you'd have to learn a lot. I don't know if you'd even want to, but you could if you wanted."

"What other things cans you tell me 'bout him?"

"There's all kinds of stories I can tell you about George Washington. If you study hard and learn to read, you can read books about him yourself. You can learn all sorts of things from books. A very smart lady told me once when I didn't know how to read that if I'd learn, I could go anywhere. Reading and writing will open doors for you! I'm sure you can learn, George. You've got a very smart name, but you have to want to. I can't make you, and neither can your Momma. Learning has to be a want deep inside of you."

George stayed on. I loved it when it worked out that way, but it didn't always. Still, I did love teaching.

When we were brought a little girl of nearly two years by a member of Pa's congregation, I had to think about what I was doing with my life all over again. She was the apple of my eye. What a little sweetheart! Pretty as she could be, and she knew just how to wrap me around her little finger. I was her favorite. Most days it was me who braided her hair, not Bitty. She waited at the window for me to come home from school, and it warmed my heart when she'd squeal and run to me. I was her hero. However, being a hero, wasn't always easy. I was soon aware that as much as I enjoyed spending my evenings with Bea, little Moses, and Bitty that I had to bring more money to the household. Little Miss Bea, after all, would need some pretty dresses! Yes, we named her after my sweet Mrs. Bea. She was so pleased when I wrote her the news.

I took an extra evening job at the Telegraph Office where I'd worked when Bitty and I first married. It was just for part of the time, Friday and Saturday nights, so I could still teach. It wasn't all that busy at night, so I used the time to plan my classes and write letters, and I must admit, to catch a little sleep if I could. I'd rigged me up a little bell on the door just in case some one came while I was snoozing. That worked pretty well.

And that brings me to the night that I will never forget as long as I live. I nodded off, and in my sleep, I heard the ringing of a bell. I woke, but it wasn't the bell on the door. It was a big bell clanging. It was the fire bell. I jumped to my feet and ran outside. People were shouting. "Fire! Fire!" I could smell the oppressive odor of fast-burning wood. It took me back to memories of the past. I raced with the crowd to the scene of the fire. Folks were already passing buckets hand-to-hand. I joined the line. Looking around, I saw two other houses on fire. Wails and the cries from the burned filled the air. We made another line, and then, another.

"LAWSEY!" I shouted to no one in particular. WE CAIN'T STOP DIS!" The heat drove us back. The sparks floated upward carrying clouds of destruction to roofs nearby. It was when I looked up into the night sky full of sparks that I had a knowing…a heavy feelin in my chest! We were only two streets from my house, my family! I dropped the bucket and dashed home past clusters of houses already engulfed in flame. I was too late. Flames hungrily devoured our roof. Through the upstairs windows I could see curtains melting. Downstairs was almost as bad. Standing in their night clothes, I found Ma and Pa. Bitty was with them holding Moses tight. He was screaming with fright.

"WHERE'S BEA?" I yelled at the top of my lungs.

"She inside." Pa answered solemnly. "We cain't get her."

I didn't hesitate. I ran into the burning house calling her name as loudly as I could. The smoke was thick and pitch black. Within seconds, I was driven to my knees. I couldn't see in front of me. I could barely breathe, so I felt my way through the parlor. "If I can find the stairs, I can get her. God, help me get her." I prayed. I knew I could get her. I could! I crawled and groped my way. I felt my hand on the bottom step! Thank you God. Up I crawled, and as I neared the top, I reached out for the next step. Fire seared me. There was not another step. My hands were enveloped in the heat of the fire. The flames licked me. I could smell my flesh burning. Steps, where are the steps? "Bea! Bea! It's Daddy!" I screamed. The heat poured into my lungs. "Come to Daddy Bea!" What was left of the stairs collapsed with me on top of them.

Dazed I lay there. I heard Pa calling my name. I feebly called back to him. He pulled me from the wreckage and the starving flames.

In anguish, coughing and sputtering from the heavy smoke and heat, Pa whispered, "I did my best John. I tried to get her. Couldn't find a way up." Pa moaned. "She gone John. She gone to be wid God now."

Bitty hung on to Moses for dear life. Terrified, she looked at me lying on the ground with smoke rising from my charred hands and face. "I could only get one John. Only one! I don't know why I picked Moses first. What have I done?" Later, she would tell me that she'd tried to wake Bea. She called to her, but she didn't wake up. Unable to carry both children downstairs, she took Moses to Ma, and when she went back to get Bea, the flames were already between them. She was hysterical! It was a hysterical and painful period of our lives.

My hands were severely burned. My face was blistered. I had trouble breathing. But nothing hurt me as much as the loss of my sweet Little Miss Bea. For that, there was no salve, no healing.

It hurts me to tell this story, even today. I didn't know if I was angry or sad. I didn't know what I was. I couldn't understand for the life of me why this had to happen! Why did He have to take my Bea? Didn't make no sense! There was no way to stop imagining her alone in the flames calling for help, calling for her Daddy to save her! She would have been calling for me when those flames burned through her. I wasn't there. I was sleeping at work! How would I ever endure this! I was defeated inside and out! Thoughts of her screaming for me haunted me night and day. I pictured her on fire, helpless, calling. Days slipped into nights, and nights into weeks. In those agonizing days lying in bed with bandages wrapped around my hands and head, I had a vision. I saw Little Miss Bea. She was standing beside my bed pretty as a picture with her hair all braided and bowed. She looked as she had in life. She was smilin, and with her was Mam and Mammy each holdin a tiny hand. I felt so beaten, so sad. I was in so much pain. I dismissed it. Had to be the belladonna makin me see things. I dozed off, and there they were again. It happened another time, but this time, I heard Mammy say authoritatively in my head, "Boy, what do it take you's to understand? She here; she happy. She never felt no burnin. She be wait right here wid us fer her Daddy when yo'r time done come." I wept.

Pa shared the sick room with me. His burns weren't near as bad as mine, but his chest was worse. When he coughed, he spit up blood and gray-black stuff. He could barely talk above a whisper. Pa was never the same. What good was a preacher who couldn't preach!

A kind family took us in. Lots of families shared their place with folks that were burned out. It was the saddest time in my life. Ma and Bitty took care of us, and they did their best to help out with all the chores to keep an already crowded household running. We had no money, no jobs, no clothing, no nothing left. Most of all, we had no Bea.

Pa sat in a chair close to me. In his coarse whispers, he prayed over me. He asked the Lord to give me peace. He begged the Holy Ghost to comfort me. He pleaded with me to open my heart and let Jesus come in.

I couldn't. I was angry when he started his prayin over me! But I couldn't tell him to stop. He was grievin too. It seemed to help him to pray for me. I just tried to shut my mind off and not listen. I was, however, a prisoner there with him in a small room. As my burns healed, I couldn't help but hear the things he was saying in his fervent pleas. I knew from past experience that the Lord did give comfort. I'd had it. I believed that. What I was havin trouble with was why He took my innocent Bea. Why not me? I would have gone instead of her. I wouldn't have thought twice about it. That was when I realized something.

Jesus, He died for me, and he didn't think twice about it. God the Father done gave His baby boy to die for me. Who was I that I couldn't trust Him to take care of my Bea? He gave her to me to begin with! Maybe, just maybe, he needed her back. My life was different after that night. Pa was prayin over me. I reached out with my bandaged hand and touched his. He looked at me. "I believe Pa. I know Jesus done died fer me. Everythin gonna be aw right. I's saved Pa. I's gonna be wid Bea and my Mam and Mammy a'gin one day…Bo too. I's saved."

Barely a whisper, I heard Pa say, "Praise God! Praise His name." Together, we said "Amen."

Chapter Eleven
Do The Best You Can

Amen and Amen. I recovered quickly after that. Life went on. That's the way it was meant to be. I knew it in my heart. When my hands were healed enough, and I could get around again, I went looking for work. They had a new school teacher already. The Telegraph Office had hired a replacement for me. There were no jobs to be had. I didn't lose my faith. I'd found it, and I was hanging on as tight as I could. I spoke with old friends who told me that the railroad was hiring baggage boys. I went to the Depot and asked about work. "Not today, maybe next week." I went back next week, and again the next. I think I finally got the job, because I was always hanging around asking about it, and they got tired of me. Maybe so, but I had a job.

It wasn't easy pulling and shoving and hefting bags and heavy boxes, but I did it. My hands had lots of scars, and they were tight and caused me pain when I had to use them so much. Bitty took care of me as best she could. Me, I did what a man is supposed to do. I worked to take care of my family. Pa couldn't work no more. It was just me. I worked hard. I earned enough to move us into a little shack. We had to start all over. Everythin was gone. Pa couldn't hardly walk more than a few steps without having to rest. He was still coughin up blood and black stuff. I will say this, he never quit. He kept tryin to do whatever he could to help out. I'd find kindling that he chopped off the big pieces of wood when I'd come home. Bitty told me that he worked all day on that little pile. He'd chop and rest, rest and chop, but he did it. Moses, well he was Moses. He brought us joy. He brought laughter back to us with his antics. We healed.

It was a mighty cold winter. I thought we were goin to freeze to death. That shack was nothin but a draft with boards around it. Some days all we could do was cover back up, and stay in bed...except for me. I had to report to the Depot, but I was glad to go. They didn't honor the Sabbath, but I felt honored to have a job. I figured the Lord understood.

My boss man came to me one day and said, "Hey John, what would you think about moving your family to Kansas City? They need a good man up there. It would mean more money, and a little house comes with the job. You'd be a switchman. What do you think?"

"I think that sounds mighty fine, Sir."

They wanted me right away. Bitty wasn't mad at me for accepting the job, but she was none too happy that I didn't even mention it to her before I accepted. She got over it. Womenfolk! I declare they whine if you don't make enough money! They whine if you can, but you didn't get their permission to do it! The promise of a house helped. Hitch was, I had to leave instantly. I'd send for them when I'd made enough money to get us settled.

It took a month more or less. That was a long month for all of us. I've never been a very good bachelor.

I bought a few sticks of furniture to go in our new place. Two beds, a table and some leather-hide seated chairs. We were back in one big room, with a small afterthought of a room attached to the back of the house. It wasn't much, but it went with the job, and it didn't cost us anything. An oil lamp and a rocking chair later, we were ready. When they arrived, I'd placed a little jar full of the first spring flowers on the table to welcome the ladies to their new home. They were so pleased for that little touch. Moses was delighted to have new territory to explore. Pa seemed resigned. He was very quiet.

We settled in. We were grateful for our blessings. Little-by-little, we replenished our worldly goods. Pa was feebler, but he smiled more now. Bitty found him a buggy ride to church. He just couldn't walk and breathe at the same time any more. Ma rode with him. Bitty, Moses and me walked together when I could go with them, but if there was a train comin, they went alone. Time was healing us.

Moses turned three. What a little bundle of energy he was! No matter how we put things away or up high, he could get into them! Crawling bugs were his favorite playthings. Bitty wasn't happy about that, but the boy could find them anywhere. He slimmed down once he started walking, I mean running! Ha. The best thing was that he loved to strip his clothes off and run naked outside at every opportunity! Bitty had her hands full. When I was home, I tried to ride herd on him to give her a rest. He was a rough and tumble kind of boy. He was growing up right before our eyes and way too fast! Everytime I'd leave for the Depot, Moses (Neked as a jaybird or not) would wave goodbye to me, and yell to anyone who could hear him, "My Daddy "Railin"! Daddy "Railin"! It became the family phrase for where Daddy was when he was at work. He was a fun little feller.

My job required me to report to the Depot Agent at least once a week. The Agent and I liked each other immediately. Sometimes you know how you meet a person, and you feel like you've always known them? Well, that's how it was with me and James. We talked about all kinds of things. He had coffee going all the time. We played checkers if business was slow. When we could manage it, we ate lunch together. Bitty made Mrs. Bea sandwiches for me. She knew how much I loved them. Usually we could manage bread and butter, but sometimes she surprised me with a slice of ham. She was a good woman, my woman. Anyway, if I got lucky and had ham, I'd share with James. We were the best of friends. I hadn't had a good man friend since Bo.

When a job as a conductor came up, James mentioned it to me in passing. "Too bad we ain't colored, we could probably get that job!" He laughed. "It's a good paying job…pays more than you and me get put together."

"But I am colored!" I blurted out.

"YOU'RE WHAT?" James asked dumbfounded.

"I'm colored. I'm a Negro. I thought you knew."

He threw his sandwich on the ground and stalked away. We never spoke again about anything other than business.

I put in for the conductor job. I got it, but it took a while for them to replace me. I had plenty of time to think about how my friend behaved. Some folks just can't get past themselves. I prayed for him. I forgave him, and I asked the Lord to help him see different.

This conductor job was going to make a big difference to all of us. The best of it was I would have enough money to get us a real house with more than one and a half rooms. I could buy it on my own, and we wouldn't be worried about being put out ever. I wanted that for my family. Next, we wouldn't have to be pinching every penny til it squealed. The bad thing was that I would be gone for a week to ten days at a time, home for four, and then back on the road, or I should say tracks. It had to be. It was the only way to take care of my family. "You get, you give. Fair is fair." I heard Mam say. This time it felt a bit like I was going to have to be "giving away" an awful lot to "get" what we needed. I didn't like being away from my family, but I had to do what I had to do. I was the man.

New to the job, I tagged along with an older gentleman by the name of Edgar. He'd been conducting for almost five years. He knew everything. I do mean everything, and not just about the job, but about all the people who worked on the train or in the depots. He was never at a loss for words. He knew all the gossip. I tried to change the subject with him often, but he was unstoppable. Still, he was a helpful feller. I'd ridden on trains a few times, but it's a whole different story when you're conducting. A conductor makes sure people are seated on the train when they're supposed to be, and he puts them off when they don't have a ticket. Part of the job is making sure packages and freight are loaded correctly, tickets punched. And then, there are the children. God bless the children! The good and the bad! I enjoyed showing the good ones around. I prayed for the bad ones. Mostly I prayed that they would get off the train soon. Seriously, I enjoyed the children because they were so curious. They wanted to see the engine, the caboose, everything. I was teaching again. I loved my new job.

It had a few perks that I hadn't planned on. I hadn't even dreamed of. There was a woman, a colored woman, travelin with her three small children. They were all under six, but well-mannered, good little ones. She was sickly. I sat with her and helped with the babies when I could. I shared my food with them while she told me about herself.

"My man done run off and left me and the children as soon as he found out I's sick. I's takin my lil ones and goin to de orphanage dere in Kansas City, Kansas. I's a-dyin, the doctor say. I's got the tuberculosis. My auntie, she say I cans come dere to die, but she ain't got no room or way to takes care of my chilluns. She old and jez barely able to do fer herself. My po lil chillums, dey ain't gonna have no one."

Yes, I did. I took those kittens home to Bitty. Mary was five; Joey was three; Jane was barely a year old.

It was a good thing that Bitty and Ma were good with money, because we had a house full of blessings now that needed a lot more food and clothing. Those little ones had nothing but the clothes on their backs. Bitty and Ma scrubbed them, hugged them, and fed them continuously. Before long, we couldn't remember what it was like before they had come to us. It felt like they'd always been part of our family.

Mary was a pleasant child. She was definitely the mothering kind. She was very protective of Joey and Jane. It took her a spell to give up her role as mother, and let Bitty have it. The day did come, but not without a lot of loving coming before. Poor little thing had been taking care of them her whole life. She wasn't quite sure what she was supposed to do without taking care of them. To Bitty and Ma's credit, they eventually turned her back into a little girl, complete with her own doll to play with and mother. Even as young as she was, she wanted to do absolutely everything that Bitty did. She liked me, but since I'd taken her away from her mother, she wasn't too trusting of me. I couldn't blame her.

Joey was the outgoing one. He never met a stranger. He and Moses became fast friends. With Moses being the oldest boy and established in the house, he was the leader. Joey was happy to follow in his footsteps, even if they led to the highest shelf on the wall!

Jane, sweet Jane, what a darling little girl. She wasn't walking when she came to us. She was barely crawling, but it didn't make us no never-mind. We toted her everywhere. She didn't smile at first. She watched us through wide dark eyes questioning our every gesture, every word. She cooed, but she didn't talk. She was our baby girl. For the longest time, Mary was the only one who could get her to sleep, but Bitty and Ma worked on that. It seems, they discovered, that Jane had a fondness for snuggling and the rocking chair.

Bitty glowed. She was in love with her children. It made my heart happy to see her like that. Ma and Pa, well, they always wanted lots of grandchildren, and now they had them. I wondered if Ma didn't wish she lived somewhere else at times. Pa, he'd just sit outside smiling and watching them play. He kept a little pan and spoon with him (because he still could not speak above a whisper), and when Moses and Joey got into something they shouldn't, he'd whack it once. If they stopped, fine. If they didn't, he'd keep whacking it until Bitty or Ma would come out! The boys made a game of trying to hide his pan and spoon, nasty little buggars! After the first time they ran off with his alarm, he'd tied a string on his pan and then to his spoon, and tied that to his suspenders. He wasn't fast enough to catch them, but he was wily enough to keep them in line. Thank goodness he was there and smarter. Ma and Bitty just didn't seem to know half of what those boys were doing. Or maybe they did, and just ignored it. I was never quite sure.

Me, I was "Railin". It seemed like I was always gone, but I knew I wasn't. I knew it, because I found myself tireder after I left home to go back to work than I was when I came home. I think I tried to make up for lost time whenever I was home. I wanted more than anything to be a good father like Pa was.

Pa grew up wanting to be a preacher. Even when he was a slave, he preached to folks, so it was only natural that he continued to do that after he was free. He was a forgiving person. He was a patient and a tolerant man. He was full of love. I don't think I ever heard him criticize a single person, not even me when Bitty and I had our bad times. I wanted to be good like he was. Not only him, but I wanted to be like Bo too. Bo had bad times for sure, but he came around. He showed me what it was like to "overcome evil with good". He preached and sang from his heart. Come to think of it, they, Pa and Bo, were a lot alike. I wanted to be a good man.

But, it wasn't easy being good. Travelin all the time was hard on a body, especially a body like me. I loved my wife, but I couldn't be with her, if you know what I mean. I missed that part of our lives so much, but it didn't take away from the fact that I loved her dearly. It was a good thing that I didn't drink any more, or I would have fallen easily into terrible, evil ways. I missed Bitty.

Almost five years had come and gone, since our last three babies had come. We were a family, a big one, but I felt alone much of the time. Sometimes I felt alone, even when I was home with commotion going on around me. It seemed to me that Bitty hardly knew I was there anymore. Pa didn't talk much. It hurt him. Each time I went home, I could see he was worse. It was Pa that I would talk to and tell how I was feeling. He listened. He'd whisper painfully to me trying to shore me up. Sometimes it helped to know he understood; sometimes not. I felt like a visitor in my own house. I worked; I brought home the money; I played a little with the children, but even they were finding other entertainment when I was there. Everyone was older, especially me. I felt it. The children were all in school, except for Jane. Turned out Jane was, well, slow. She couldn't learn much at all. She smiled now though. She smiled all the time. If anything, she was our happiest young'un. She had the ability to melt my heart, even with stinky diapers. She was always gonna be our baby. Thing was, and I feel selfish saying this, but the truth is, all them children didn't leave any time for me with Bitty. The children were important to me. I loved them, but they weren't everything to me, Bitty was. I just wasn't that to her anymore. I felt the loneliness. I tried to fight the feelings, but I guess I was angry deep inside. I wanted to be near her, even just to hold her close. She was still in child-bearing time, so I couldn't do nothing else, but I needed her to at least want to be with me. Even I knew that I wasn't making much sense. I couldn't find the words to say anything to Bitty. She was happy tending children and making a home for all of us. And, she was tired all the time. There didn't seem to be anythin to do 'bout it no how!

I was a faithful husband. In body and spirit I was, but my mind was having troubles. I found myself drawn to women as I worked the train. I hadn't tried to do nothin I shouldn't, but I'd sure considered it lots. I felt ashamed afterwards, but at the time I just got carried away. I admit it. I flirted. Women seemed to like me. I was still a handsome man. My hair was still wavy; my skin clear; my stomach flat. They responded to me, and if anything, I've grown up a charmer. It felt pretty good to know that there were women out there who saw me, just me as a man, not a daddy.

One cold wintry day, I met Sophie. She was on her way to her brother's home where she was to be married to a friend of his. She was obviously upset when I stopped to punch her ticket, so I kidded around with her making her laugh. I made it a point to come back when I had a little break. She told me that she'd never met her intended. Her brother arranged the marriage because she was in her late twenties, and their mother had just died. Sophie was an educated woman, a nurse from back East. I enjoyed talking with her. She was a rather large white woman, but she was very nice. I felt sorry for her. I was attracted to her intelligent conversation. We spent every available moment talking. She told me about her life in the East, and how her father had no use for her. After her mother's death, he remarried, and forced her out of the house to eke out her own living. That's why her brother sent for her. I told her about my wife, my children, how we'd come to have them, and before I knew it, I was telling her things that I'd never told anyone about my feelings, not even Pa. I hadn't even admitted it to myself. I told her personal things about how I missed the loving with Bitty. She felt sorry for me too. We were both lost at that moment.

When we shared that first careful, tender kiss, suddenly a flame of passion welled up between us. It was like an explosion! I don't know what happened to me. All I could think of was having her right there, right then. She wanted me too. We disappeared into a half-loaded freight car, and there we made love. It became our place. The heat was unmistakable between us. Even with my Bitty, I never felt that kind of draw. Every moment we could, we were touchin, kissin, makin love. We stole away and stole each other from our emptiness. Four days later, we said goodbye to each other amidst tears. She went to her intended. I began the homeward-bound leg of my journey.

Happiness for having felt loved and wanted flooded over me in waves. Also, in waves came shame and guilt. What have I done? I've committed adultery. I've betrayed Bitty. I prayed, but I felt disconnected from God. What was I going to do? I worried that Bitty would take one look at me and know immediately what I'd done.

When I arrived home, she looked at me, but she didn't know. I could tell. A little peck on the cheek, a quick hug, and she went her way. She didn't know. I did. I was so quiet that poor Pa asked me what was wrong. I told him I was just tired. I lied. I took to bed saying I was sick. As I lay there, I thought about Sophie. I remembered everything about her, her touch, the passion, her tears of joy, mine. How could I be so deceitful? I'd look at Bitty and think of Sophie's touch, the way her fingers trailed over my body. What kind of man am I?" Time came for me to leave, and I was glad to go. Bitty packed me Mrs. Bea's sandwiches, gave me a peck. I left.

At least, I thought I left free and clear, but Guilt went with me. What a match was being played in my head! I found myself aching for Sophie. Would she come to the train depot? Would I ever see her again? I wanted to see her. No, I didn't. I wouldn't leave my wife and children. I had responsibilities. In my mind, I'd shout "What are you thinking?" Still, I couldn't help myself it seemed. Sophie was in my head.

Another trip completed and another. Still another. Bitty asked me, "John, you aw right? You's actin funny. Everythin aw right at work? You feelin sick?" I reassured her that I was fine, just tired. She seemed relieved. It wasn't fine. I was thinkin it would probably never be fine.

Months passed. I tried talking to Pa, but he was slipping away. Still, there was one night when his head seemed clear. The women were putting the children to bed. I asked Pa if he'd ever strayed from Ma. He shook his head "No". Did you ever think about it? He nodded "Yes". I guess that gave me courage. I emptied my heart to him. All of it. Every joy, every sadness, every bit of shame.

In the stillness, he motioned for me to come close. His lips close to my ear, he whispered, "One day you may tell her. She may forgive, may not, but you's got to ax fer fergiveness now from de Lord. You's a-sinkin. He's de only one can pull you back up and he'p you be de man you done want to be." I asked for forgiveness.

I returned to work with a somewhat lighter heart. I tried to stop lookin for Sophie. I tried my best. The Lord helped me, but sometimes I just couldn't help it, and then one day, there she was! She clutched a baby tightly against her chest. She bought her ticket and boarded the train. I deliberately went to another car. I didn't want to be there to greet her yet. I had to pray for composure. I moved through the cars as the train pulled away from the station. Punchin tickets I moved towards her smilin and talkin to folks. I saw her from the back. Her baby was cryin, as she struggled modestly to put him to breast. I bent to ask for her ticket, and when she looked up at me, I saw her face was covered with bruises. She was cryin, beggin me with her eyes for something. I wasn't sure exactly what. "I'll be back as soon as I can, Sophie. We'll talk."

Escaping to an empty car, I fell on my knees to pray for strength. Strength to not fall back into adultery. Strength to help Sophie in whatever way I could. Strength to be able to get through hearing what she had to say. More composed, I returned.

"What happened?"

"My husband beat me. He threw me out. My brother gave me the money to go back East. I don't know what I'm going to do!" She wailed.

Trying to calm her, I focused on her baby. "There, there, it cain't be all that bad. Let me see your little one. Boy or girl?"

"A boy. I named him Job." As she said this, she pulled the covers away from his face. I looked into the face of my son, my colored son. There was no mistaking his features. He was mine, fair, but colored, a coffee color, darker than a white person.

"Oh, Sophie!" I drew in a deep breath.

"At first, he was white like you, but then he began to get darker. My husband noticed. My brother noticed too. When others in town saw him, the truth was out. Everyone knew. That's when he beat me. I betrayed him. I deserved it. I left, and now," she sobbed, "Now, I don't know what I'm going to do."

I took her by the arm and guided her to a private place where we wouldn't be disturbed. There was no passion left in either of us. There was only suffering. We talked. She would stay in Kansas City. I'd give her money for room and board. She could take her time deciding what would be best for her and Job. She could rest and heal. No strings.

She left the train when I did. We walked to the boarding house. I helped her with her bags. I went home.

If it wasn't a mess before, it certainly was now. Pa was dying. He'd waited for me. I sat by his bed and held his withered hand, as he slipped peacefully away. We buried him. It was sad, but his time had come, and he was glad to go. No more pain for him. The last thing he said to me was "Be true to yo'r self, Son."

I thought about that a lot. I was back on the train. I was sad. "Oh Lord" I prayed, "Help me know the right thing to do."

I brought money to Sophie each time I returned. I took what I gave her from my tips, so Bitty wouldn't suspect anything. It was a sufficient amount to keep Sophie and Job for now. Sophie was losing weight, lots of it and fast. Job didn't seem to be hurt from her loss, but still, he was a small baby. When I came to see them after two months, Sophie was ready to talk.

"I've been thinking, John. What would you think about taking Job home with you for you and Bitty to raise. You wouldn't have to tell her anything. She might suspect, but there's no way she would know. He could be another baby given to you from someone on the train. I don't want to let him go, but what could I offer him? I don't see how I could even take care of him and work the long hours a nurse has to work. I never thought in a million years that I could give up my baby. I knew he was yours from the beginning, but I figured that he'd be fair, light, you know, white like you, and no one but me would know. I'd have my love baby." But here we are in this awful situation.

Frankly, I didn't know what to say, so I said something like "Let me think on it." I went home. All I did was think. We'd just lost Pa. Could I bring another baby here? We already had a house full, and then there was Jane who would always be a baby. Could I bring my baby here? Could I not? If I did, should I tell Bitty the truth? I prayed, but no answers came.

Another trip behind me, I went to see Sophie. I gave her my answer. I would take him home with me. She packed their belongings. As she handed Job to me with his clothes, we kissed for the last time with tears. I saw her off on the next train. I trudged home with a heavy heart and my son.

Chapter Twelve
Life Happens

Bitty took one look at Job. Then, she looked at me. I heard her say with a smiling voice "I's been a-wonderin how long it was a-gonna be a'fore you done brought me another stray kitten!" My heart broke as I watched her lookin him over from head to foot as she had all of our childrens. She introduced their new brother. What a lovin woman! How could I ever have strayed? I didn't know, but I knew for a fact that I never would again.

Job fit right into our family. He was a good baby. Like Moses, he didn't need to cry. There was someone ready to scoop him up if he scrunched up his little face. Now, Bitty never had any favorites with the children, until Job came. If she'd have ever admitted to it though, he would have been the one. She rocked and sang to him. It was obvious that he was a joy to her heart. He helped us all to get over our grief over Pa. At nights, she'd bring him to bed with us, and he'd snuggle between us. He smelled so sweet. .

Ma caught pneumonia, the old people's friend, the winter after Pa died. She never got better. I think she missed Pa so much that she didn't want to stay here without him. She was buried next to him in the frozen ground.

Life happened, while we weren't looking. The ups and downs of having a large family continued. I worked on the railroad. Because I was gone so much, Bitty carried most of the responsibility for the family while I was away. Something changed between us after Bitty was orphaned. She changed. It was as if she suddenly understood me. I don't know if I would be harsh enough to say that she grew up, but maybe being without her Ma and Pa there for support, she had. When I was home, she turned to me more. She made it a point to kiss me like she had when we were first married. We made time to be just with each other in the nights after the children were in bed. I was there in every way. She knew I was there. I felt it. She was my wife again. I felt her with me, and I began to be happy to come home. I looked forward to being there with her and the children.

On one of those especially close nights, we were holding each other. I reached out for her. She reached back. I wasn't able to stop myself. Neither of us wanted to stop. It was wonderful, but afterwards, I held her close, and with fear in my heart, I confessed everything. I told her how lonely I'd been for her. I spoke of my chance meeting with Sophie, and how in the heat of the moment, Job was conceived. She was still, so still. I asked her for her forgiveness. I begged her to forgive me. "I love you Bitty. You are my life. I never wanted to hurt you. I'm so sorry. Can you ever forgive me?"

She sighed and reached for me. "I figured it out the day you brought Job home. He's de spittin image of you. There ain't no way you could ever deny that boy. I forgive you. Way I think of it is like in de Bible when Sarah couldn't give her Abraham a son. I prayed fer you to find someone that you could have your own son wid. You a good man; you deserved to have your very own son. My prayers, they was answered with Job. In all my dreams, I never did think I'd ever be fortunate 'nuff to be able to share him wid you. That be an extry special blessin." Her arms tightened round my neck. We kissed and lingered together until dawn. How good God is that he gave me such a wife! Such a mother for my children! Our lives changed. We were honest with each other now. That honesty cemented us together. For me, her unconditional forgiveness and acceptance of Job changed me for life.

Weeks later we realized that Bitty was going to have a baby. From that night of unselfish love came our own little baby. We were concerned what might happen, but the time passed uneventfully. A month early, Bitty delivered. She was weak, but she and our baby girl lived. We named her Sarah Bea. She would remind us of the best of the best. Sarah Bea turned out to be a wonderfully bright child, but a stubborn one. Of all the children, she was the most determined to have her own way. We laughed about it, because we figured she was what we deserved. Nobody could pick Sarah Bea up fast enough to keep her from sounding off!

Mary turned fourteen. She was blossoming into a beautiful young lady. Moses was twelve and still leading eleven year old Joey around by the nose. Our sweet, always happy Jane was nine. Job was two and running everywhere. He was healthy and happy and into absolutely everything. Now, another toddler voice exclaimed each time I'd leave, "Daddy Railin."

Sarah Bea was two months old and nursing at the breast of her mother who never thought she would have that privilege. How happy Bitty was as she marveled at Sarah Bea greedily sucking! We were caught up in the wonder of it all.

I had seven children, six living. I was a proud man, a content man. Indeed, I was.

On one of my routine trips, I was checking the freight cars when I found two boys. They were older than my Moses. They'd been hiding in the car hitchin a ride to nowhere in particular. Filthy and hungry urchins, they were. I'd found people all along in the open freight cars, but these boys touched my heart. They told me their parents had died of the cholera. They had no family anywhere. I brought them home. And then, there were nine children in the quiver, eight living.

Bitty, as always, welcomed them with open arms, but she passed on the inspection. Instead she made me oversee them scrub themselves, and we were somewhat surprised to see that under all that dirt, they were two sixteen year old identical twin boys. Their names, they said, were James and John. 'They were helpful with the chores and took a lot of the hard work off Bitty when I was away on the railroad. They took their place in the loft with Moses and Joey. The girls and little Job slept in the room that had been Ma and Pa's. Sarah Bea slept with us. We were a cozy, big family.

Bitty cuddled close that first night after we put everyone to bed. She quietly suggested "John, I think you'd better not be a-bringin me no mo kittens. We done got a-plenty." Snickering with her, I agreed to do my best to resist the temptation.

I'd like to say that everything was wonderful with all those children, but they were people growing up into their own selves, and growing-up is hard in the best of circumstances. James and John were the oldest. The time they'd spent on their own had molded them in certain ways. Unfortunately, they'd learned all to well how to survive by stealing and the like. That didn't set well with us. We struggled and so did they, as we tried to teach them differently. It's just not easy when a child is already set. I guess I hadn't thought about that too much when I brought them home with me. Each trip home now became a battle of wills between me and them. I hated to think what Bitty endured while I was gone! Unfortunately, Moses and Joey were not happy with their positions either, since they were not the oldest boys in the family any more. It was obvious by their unruly behaviors that they were angry at having to share attention. The fighting began. The four boys fought constantly over any little thing at all. We talked to them. We preached to them. We gave them plenty of chores to wear the meanness out of them. We whipped them. We shamed them. Nothing worked. Then, one Sunday, John was saved, and things changed again. Instead of the fighting all the time, John spent more time downstairs helping out with the other children. He'd even sleep by the fire on the floor rather than going upstairs. He did his best to avoid any kind of conflict, especially with James. We pretended not to notice that there was less contention, but we were grateful for the blessed relief.

 James was furious that John was avoiding him. I think he thought that Bitty and I had turned John against him. To retaliate, he proceeded to buddy up with Moses and Joey. He was their best friend and big brother. He let them tag along with him everywhere he went. He taught them to steal and not get caught. I found out about the stealing when I returned from a trip. Bitty had them sitting at the table waiting for me. Seems she'd sent them to the store to get flour and sugar and a few other things. When they came home, she heard them upstairs talking way too quietly for boys. Her mother's instincts took over. She climbed the stairs to the loft to take a peek. There on the bed in the middle of them was candy, a can of peaches, and a book. Since they had no money, she knew they'd taken it. Enraged she screamed, "I ain't raisin' no thieves! Get yo'r selves down here right this minute!" She was hysterical. They weren't used to that from her.

"We didn't steal nothin'" James exclaimed. "Dat woman at de store, she done felt sorry fer us. She gave us dem things."

My tiny wife yanked those boys up, and each of them carrying their booty were marched down the road. She herded them in a fast march to the store. Seeing the store keeper, she inquired "My boys here say you felt sorry fer dem and gave 'em some things. Dat right?" As she suspected, it was not true. Bitty grabbed six foot James by the ear and drug him face-to-face with the lady. She made him and Moses and Joey give everythin' back, apologize, and promise not to ever take anything from her store again. It must have been quite a spectacle! There's Bitty with them boys who stand a head or two taller than her, and she's givin them what for! Secretly I laughed. I wished I'd been a fly on the wall to watch! But to the boys, I lowered the boom. I paddled their behinds, even James who was near as tall as me. I thought he was gonna fight me at first, but when he saw that this was the way it had to be, he gave up. That night the loft was still.

I thought that was a good sign. Bitty wasn't convinced. James was never the same after that night. To mine and Bitty's face, he was polite and helpful, but behind our backs, he grumbled and stirred up trouble with Moses and Joey. He was sneaky and did his best to turn them against us. Joey, thank the Lord, could not keep his mouth shut. He told Mary, and Mary told us what was going on. Seems they were causing damage to other folk's property and stealing from their homes. They stole whatever James told them to steal, but now James was selling it or giving what they stole away. He threatened to beat them up if they ever told. Moses thought it was great fun, as long as Bitty didn't find out, but Joey didn't like it. He was afraid of what would happen if they got caught. He should have been.

When I found out, I was livid. James and I went for a little walk. I told him that I couldn't have that kind of thing goin on in my house. "If you can't stop this, then you will have to leave." I tried to give him a choice, but thinkin back now, he probably couldn't stop himself. He was too full of anger and pain. Next mornin, he left. Watching him leave was difficult, but he'd given me no choice. It was worse I think than watchin someone you love die, because you know that if they die and they've tried to do good that you might see them again. With James, who knew what would happen. He didn't show any feelings at all. He said not one goodbye, not even to John. Some years later, I heard he joined the Calvary out West, but no one ever heard from him or saw him again.

John didn't seem to miss James all that much, especially once he found something else to do with his time. He courted a young lady from our church. John was seventeen, and I guess he thought he was old enough. Her parents weren't too favorably impressed by him. He could barely write his name, and he didn't have a real job, just odd jobs. John wanted a real job. He was a good boy, and he wanted his girl to marry him. He was an honest, considerate young man. I helped him get on with the railroad as a baggage boy. He was my first child to reach manhood. He married when he was not quite nineteen to his sweetheart.

Once James was gone, Moses and Joey settled down and studied hard. The one thing about them, for all their rambunctiousness, they applied themselves in school. Lessons were a very personal competition between the two of them. When the time came, they both went off to study in a colored college in Illinois. We were proud of them. Moses was seventeen; Joey, sixteen. Moses studied business, and Joey, our little talker, studied the law. Seemed fittin' somehow.

Mary turned nineteen the year the boys left. She was content to stay at home with us. She was a help and a comfort to her mother. Her Sissy Jane required a lot of care. Jane was stronger now, bigger, thirteen years old. Bitty couldn't handle her without Mary's help. Mary was a devout young woman. She had a sweet and kind way about her, but she isolated herself to the confines of our family and close friends. She would help anyone who needed help, but she preferred her family to anyone else. So, when a young traveling preacher came to our church, she ignored him. He didn't ignore her. She didn't give him the time of day. "I don't care if he likes me, I ain't leavin my family for no one!" Bitty confided this to one of her friends, who shared it with another friend, and before long, the young preacher knew what she'd said as well. Dejected, he left town. Mary didn't seem to notice. Two months later, he came back. Had she noticed? It was hard to tell with her, because she was such a private person. In many ways, she reminded me of Bitty and how she'd been when we first met. This time the preacher didn't give up. He knocked on my door asking permission from me to court her. He had decided that she was the one for him, and he declared "Whatever I have to do, I'll do it." I must admit, I liked this young man. He reminded me of someone. Mary pretended she didn't know he was there when he came to dinner. She ignored him when he spoke to her, but he wore her down. When our regular preacher had to leave town, this young man requested his position, and he was accepted by the congregation. It didn't pay much of anything, but preachers never did make a lot of money. Preacher Henry did a good job. He visited his families weekly which meant that he ate at least one meal a week with our family. Bitty wouldn't have had it any other way. Me neither. I was enjoying watching this.

Mary had very little to say to him at first. Bitty reported to me just how the romance was progressing with glee. "She say she don't want him here so much, but I sees she's a-fixin herself up real purty when we expects him." Next time I was home, she told me, "Preacher Henry come again last week. He brung some little treats for the babies and a fistful of wildflowers fer Mary and another one fer me. I saw her snitch one little flower from de jar when she thought I weren't lookin. She took it off to her room wid her. I think dat boy makin progress." We had a good laugh.

As I reflect, this was one of the happiest times of our lives. Job and Sarah Bea were growing like weeds. Jane smiled all the time. She reminded us of how wonderful the world is through the eyes of a child, and she would forever. Watching our Mary fall in love with her young man was a joy. By the fall, Bitty and I were grandparents to John and his wife's first baby girl. They named her Aida after my Mam, but they called her Aider. I was overcome with happiness. That Christmas, Preacher Henry and Mary took their vows. After a brief honeymoon, (in Wichita meeting his family), they returned to us. That's right, once more, we had a preacher in the house. Mary had her way. She didn't leave her family for no one. She just brought her a husband home to move right in with us. They took the loft, until we were sure that Job and Sarah Bea would be safe up there. Mary and Henry didn't seem to mind.

Chapter Thirteen
Mine Eyes Have Seen

I loved being a conductor. It was hard work, but I liked everything about it. It was a teacher and a caretaking kind of a job all rolled into one. I could be a father to young ones, a loving son to older folk, a preacher to those in need, a friend and guide to people who seemed lost and alone. What a fortunate feller I am, I thought as I looked at myself in the mirror. My uniform bespoke my position in life. My dark vest on top of my white shirt was spotless. A pocket watch with a gold chain dribbling from the small pocket of the vest announced to everyone that I am the man who knows when the train leaves. I am the man who calls "All Aboard!" I still stand tall and strong, even if I'm sporting a little round belly these days. My hair has thinned, but my cap covers the baldness. I guess I look older, but I don't feel old. How is it possible that I'll be 48 years old tomorrow. Where did the time go? I remember picking up coal from the side of the tracks when I was a switchman just to keep us warm in that little shack. I'm still young, and I still like to go "Railin." As Job now announces!

I feel young. I recall Bo telling me that he looked old, but he wasn't. Funny how it all comes back around if a body lives long enough. Bitty makes me feel young. I love her more now than the day we married. We've been through the fire, and then some. We've had some hard times and some wonderful times. We know each other. I don't think too many couples can say that and mean it. I was thinking such thoughts as I prepared to leave to catch the night train for my next trip out.

Bitty came into the room to give me my lunch bucket. She'd made my Mrs. Bea sandwiches and a bit of soup to take with me. There was still a nip of winter lingering in the air. I grabbed her to me and planted a big kiss on her sweet lips. "You ole horse!" she laughed. "Maybe I should git you another sandwich or two, if dat's what I gets!" I pinched her behind, and she went squealing like a little girl out of the room.

Job sidled up to me asking me for the tenth time, "Daddy, can't I just use Grandpa Bo's pocket knife while you're away. I'll be careful. I promise. I won't cut myself or nothin." This time, I gave in.

"You take real good care of this" I told him. "It can't be replaced. It's all I have left of Grandpa Bo. One day, it will be yours, but not for a while. It's still mine, and I'm loaning it to you. Lots of good memories connected with that knife." He promised, and bolted from the room to show Henry and Mary. He was excited. He's a good little feller, and so handsome too. I laughed. Of course, he's handsome.

Still chuckling, I came out of the room with my bag. Jane hugged me, until I had to sit her down. "Give me a kiss. You be a good girl for yo'r mother and Mary, and when I come home, I might bring you a little surprise." She loved surprises. I'd bring her something.

Sarah Bea jumped off the chair onto my back! "Bring me somethin too. I want a surprise." Flipping her sideways, I lifted her high above my head.

"Give me my kiss, and I'll think about a surprise for you." I kissed her, and she ran outside to play saying at the top of her lungs and to no one in particular, "Daddy's "Railin", and he gonna bring me a surprise!" I couldn't help chuckling.

Bitty walked to the door with me. "I put your birthday surprise in yo'r bucket." she whispered. "You be a good boy. Where's my kiss?" She gave me a "Come home soon" kind of kiss. Down the road I went smiling. I turned; she was still standing in the doorway watching me. I waved and blew her a kiss.

It was a normal day. I helped passengers board. I made sure luggage was loaded where it was supposed to be, and people were in the right cars. I rousted well-wishers off the train, so that we could leave on time. Everything was in order. I stood on the steps of the car leaning out and called "All Aboard!" in my loudest voice. The train lurched forward. Tickets were punched. Children put to sleep. I'd take them on their tours in the morning. God bless the children, they keep me young. Even after all these years, the rocking of the train soothed me. I know who I am in this world. I serve, and I am good at it. Mam and Mammy were right. I am smart. I was born knowing when to be seen and not seen. I'm a helper. That's me, and in a few minutes, it will be my birthday.

Feeling a bit melancholy, I took my lunch bucket and went to the space outside between the cars. It's loud out there, but it's private. I need something warm to drink, but the coffee's all gone now. I thought I heard something mingled with the clacking of the wheels on the tracks. I did. Someone was singing.

"Mine eyes have seen the Glory of the Coming of the Lord"

Now, where did that come from? It's been a long time, since I heard that song. That's Bo's song.

The platform quivered. I feel a gut-wrenching jerk! I hear the squeal of metal on metal! Sparks fly! Screams of terror assault the cold air! Gripping the handholds between the cars, I feel myself pitched upwards. My feet dangle above my head. Cars collide in a crazy dance! Midway between the roof of one car and the whirling wheels of another I somersault into a pile of twisted metal and arrows of flames. The fireworks carry me up to freedom.

LaVergne, TN USA
09 February 2011
215951LV00001B/3/P